Waypoints

Clyde to Orkney

Waypoints

SEASCAPES AND STORIES OF SCOTLAND'S WEST COAST

Ian Stephen

ADLARD COLES NAUTICAL

B L O O M S B U R Y

LONDON · OXFORD · NEW YORK · NEW DELHI · SYDNEY

ADLARD COLES
Bloomsbury Publishing Plc
50 Bedford Square, London, WC1B 3DP, UK

BLOOMSBURY, ADLARD COLES and the Adlard Coles logo are trademarks of
Bloomsbury Publishing Plc

First published in Great Britain 2017
This edition published 2018

A catalogue record for this book is available from the British Library

Library of Congress Cataloguing-in-Publication data has been applied for

ISBN: PB: 978-1-4729-3964-7; ePDF: 978-1-4729-3961-6;
ePub: 978-1-4729-3962-3

2 4 6 8 10 9 7 5 3 1

Typeset in Sabon by Deanta Global Publishing Services, Chennai, India
Printed and bound in Great Britain by CPI Group (UK) Ltd, Croydon CR0 4YY

To find out more about our authors and books visit www.bloomsbury.com.
and sign up for our newsletters

Contents

The stories

Introduction

YOU COULD NO LONGER CROSS STORNOWAY harbour on the decks of moored black boats but the older people always talked about being able to do that. You grew up with the names of surviving vessels, in decorated scripts. *Lilac* and *Daffodil* were drifters – their black cotton nets were held up by tarred lines, punctuated with floats of pale, round cork. Then came the trawlers. *Girl Norma*, *Braes of Garry*, *Ivy Rose* and *Golden Sheaf* shed long nets on to the pier, to be mended with hard orange line from yellow plastic netting needles.

I was always driven to go out in small boats, sea-angling. Sailing came later. Usually we remained in sight of land, so you knew your position from recognising points. You built up a knowledge of the names of features. Out from the harbour, in small boats, the landmarks could alter. Headlands remained but a conspicuous building might change. You might have to remember that the grey roof was now red. An aerial could be felled. You were told the transits and you repeated them, when you were taken out to pull up haddock and whiting, ling or cod.

I was taught to locate a position over the seabed by observing points on land and holding them in line, or allowing a gap to open. The beacon on the lighthouse. Arnish light just open on Lamb Island. A gap at the Chicken. People talked about 'the hard ground' and 'the roundabout' and the more distant marks with the summit of Muirneag, north Lewis, in line with the visible geo at Dibidail. A few of my pals took a berth on a local trawler or creel-fishing boat. Some of them went on to master the sextant and work through their tickets to go from being a cadet to a mate in the Merchant Navy. I didn't join a local boat, didn't go to a tech college to study the practical arts of the fishing industry, didn't apply for a cadetship. Instead I studied education and literature. In no time at all I had been 'away' to studies, in the sea city of Aberdeen, and back again. I had learned the basics of sailing by buying the most simple project craft, as a student. It was the smallest of Wharram catamarans, adapted from a timeless Polynesian design. I learned mainly by making mistakes. There was a fair element of luck in my survival.

After graduating with a qualification to teach English in Scottish secondary schools, I did shifts as an auxiliary coastguard in between writing short stories and poems. I also learned to take photographs, mostly by taking a very large number on process-paid Kodachrome that came back to me in yellow boxes of slides. First, the slivers of positive film were cased in card, then they were returned in plastic mounts. The words and the images were all elements of a need to keep a record of my own ways through water, or over land.

Much of my work took as its subject the topography, the built structures or the people of the islands where I was born and raised. Even the words or images composed in response to travels somehow related to home, by comparisons. Poems fell into groups and amounted to collections that I hoped were more than the sum of individual parts. Stories chimed off each other to explore themes. In the space of a few years, several books were published. An exhibition gathered together poems and photographic images. I gained a sense of being part of a wider community of writers, artists and publishers, extending way beyond native shores.

For about four years, my coastguard shifts were balanced with walking, sailing, fishing and making and writing in response to all of these. Then I fell in love and priorities changed. I met Barbara, a woman from Germany who was already enamoured with the Scottish landscape and the country's folk culture. She rolled up her sleeves and helped paint a boat or cut peats. I made a return visit to Hamburg. There were complications but she decided to take a year's leave from a teaching post and see how she fared, living in the Outer Hebrides.

Before long we were expecting a baby. I knew that my own part-time pay, occasional fees for published work and the fish we caught were never going to be enough to provide for a family. I applied for a local vacancy as an English teacher and also put myself forward to become a full-time coastguard officer. I did not even receive an interview for the teaching job but sailed into the coastguard service. Most of my colleagues were ex-Merchant or Royal Navy and the majority had been navigating since not long after they were out of nappies. I had to get a firm grasp of coastal navigation, working towards qualifying exams.

It was then I realised that many of the marks and names of features I'd grown up with were not on any official chart. I remembered seeing fishing-skippers producing from a back pocket their own hand-drawn charts. Biro marks on squared paper and a psalm of names in English and Gaelic and slang. I was taught that navigation is not an exact science. You always had to be sceptical about a given position, estimating the element of error. Was it gained by electronic means or was it only a dead reckoning – a guesstimate of where you were, gleaned from a measure of distance along a charted line? The line you have travelled will always waver, influenced by wind and tide as well as your own steering.

Now we can look at what we think is our actual line, plotted, second by second, on an electronic chart. You could be looking at your way through sea, mapped for you on your mobile phone. But there is still an element of delay, of error. The possibility of loss of power and loss of signal. So I suggest that there is always an element of sensing your way through water, whether or not headlands, reefs and high points of land are visible.

There is a significant shift from sailing an open vessel to sailing a boat with a lid. Once you have a deck, there is the possibility of berths. Your boat can then be your home for a night or two or maybe for longer periods. This means that you can go further. You have to find a way through waters you have not experienced before. You study pilot-books and charts but you also listen to other sailors' stories. 'That reef's not exactly where the chart puts it.' Or, 'Go straight through the middle. You'll get in there fine, any state of tide.' Sometimes an old chart, in fathoms, with its detailed engravings, can reveal information that is only broadly summarised in a new metric edition.

Conversation and watch-keeping have always gone together. Stories can lessen the hours of a watch as well as the miles of a journey. When I ran a coastguard watch I would gain some sense of ports I'd never visited from my watchmates' accounts of voyaging. I began to pass on things I'd heard from my mentors to my own trainees – the snags that could be dangerous, the possible misunderstandings. Then we seemed to come under so much pressure to account for our time on watch that we didn't have much time left to really <u>be</u> on watch.

Now and again, though, you signed off feeling that you might have helped organise a rescue. So, why did I think it was a good idea to resign from the coastguard after 15 years' service? I'd been able to continue writing poems and telling stories but I was driven to widen my personal experience of sailing and navigation.

Storytelling is just like navigating. You plot your way through a narrative by determining the waypoints. There is a planned port of departure and another place you're hoping to reach. In between these there are usually some significant markers. There might be a visible feature in an otherwise empty sea, like Whale Rock, out on its own, between the west coast of Harris and St Kilda. Or there might be an area off a headland, let's say on Île d'Ouessant, Brittany, where the tide will either cast you back to where you've come from or help you in to where you're going. Thus it is essential to arrive at that turning point within a given period of time.

Once you have listed these waypoints, you sense your way from one to the next, knowing that the weather will never be exactly as forecast. If you're not sailing alone, the dynamics of the relationships aboard – the conversations – will also be a factor.

This book moves from one voyage to another, in a range of different vessels. It is a history of my own love affairs, all of them with boats. Many of these were legally joined to other men or women at the time and some were even shared between different skippers. I will sketch the companions for those trips, the way Christine Morrison has sketched the vessel itself. Space is precious on a small craft, just as it is in a story. I don't think I'll be able to flesh out the folk aboard. My intention is to select snippets from the startling images of geography that are filed in my own mind now. All the navigable routes on the west coast of Scotland and on to Orkney abound with stories. I can picture their settings as I retell them.

As far as possible, the accompanying poems were made at the time of the journeys. Often these were excerpts from a log, whether on paper or as messages sent ashore. They were scattered through logbooks, journals, text messages on mobile phones and previous publications. They are perhaps a counterpoint to the more specific entries you make in the ship's log. As a trainee coastguard, I had to learn to apply clear marks on a chart to an accepted standard that other watch-keepers could follow. When you retell a story you use your own voice, but you have to be true to a storyline that might have been established over centuries. On the other hand, poetry seems to have become a way of saying what I could not express any other way. Each poem finds its own shape. I am grateful to other writers who have helped me to trust this sense that sometimes I must explore the form the words might take as well as find the words in the first place.

Robert Macfarlane has described two short voyages we enjoyed together in *The Old Ways* (Hamish Hamilton, 2012). He also discussed the fact that the skipper (me) happened to be a poet by his first trade: 'Poetry represents to him, not a form of suggestive vagueness but a medium which permits him to speak in ways otherwise unavailable.' In this book, I chose to use short verses, a bit like another way of drawing, as transitions, signalling a shift from a factual account into a story. But sometimes the poems simply seemed to me the best way of sharing something perceived along the way. They happened outwith the plan.

The poet and writer Tom Lowenstein provided a detailed reader's report, which helped me to trust the sense that this use of language is an essential part of the work and not merely a decoration. Tom redirected me to the Japanese poet Basho. This reading helped me trust that all the different elements will cohere to make one work. And of course no poet, writer or artist is on a lonely trail. When I first began to share poems, the Norwegian Olav Hauge (in Robin Fulton's translations) proved to me that the slopes of one well-known fjord could be a wide world. More recently, I encountered the work of the Canadian poet Rhea Tregebov, during a poet's residence in a vast country. The layers of culture, family and the personal seemed to me to coalesce perfectly in an understated but memorable way. I had already read novels by Anne Michaels and had met her on the Isle of Jura but it was in Canada I learned that she has at least an equal reputation as a poet. On returning home, I found that her direct poetry is available in the UK, from Bloomsbury.

Nearer home, I also feel an affinity with a line of Scottish poets who have taken the sea as a main subject. This is not a new trend. *Birlinn Chlann-Raghnaill* (Birlinn of Clanranald) by Alasdair MacMhaighstir Alasdair (Alexander MacDonald) is available in many translations, including a recent version by Alan Riach (Kettilonia, Newtyle, 2015). The level of detail could inform a shipwright to recreate the vessel's rig and gear. WS Graham's *The Night Fishing* is a more expressionist response to drifting for 'the silver darlings'. Andrew Greig's *Found At Sea* (Birlinn, Edinburgh, 2013) details a small Odyssey, by sailing dinghy, in Scapa Flow. Angus Martin's selected poems, *A Night of Islands* (Shoestring Press, Nottingham, 2016), is the work of a poet who can walk with the ghosts of past sailors.

As it is no longer so common to introduce stories with pertinent verse, I have had to think about why these lines seemed to me a part of the fabric of this book. A beach-launched boat cannot carry any unnecessary timbers or tackle. Several readers have suggested that these pared-down responses in verse can contribute something which is more difficult to share in more expansive prose. I hope they do serve this purpose but each reader will be their own judge of that.

Back to the work of Hauge. I never met him, though I did once visit the deep fjords of that section of the long coastline of western Norway he describes. I did, however, meet Ingvar Ambjoernsen, a Norwegian writer who was writing Scandinavian noire, translated into German, long before that genre became a huge industry. He told me his story of visiting the great poet, at his home. My memory of the conversation is that Hauge asked how long it took to write a crime novel. 'About a year.' Then the visitor asked how long it took to write one poem. There was a long pause for thought. 'About ten years.' This is a poet who was a craftsman, like the Orcadian, George Mackay Brown. By contrast, contemporary Scottish poets Iain Crichton Smith and Norman MacCaig both described a process whereby they write a poem in an expressive way and it works or it doesn't. MacCaig's famous answer to the same question of how long it takes was: 'About two cigarettes.'

In my own case, the writing process is a bit of both. Above all, I hope that all the elements in this book, whether traveller's narrative, a poem or a story retold, are concerned with the attempt to be truthful. These poems began as a spontaneous response but most of them have been altered, just a bit, over time. In that way, they may form a bridge into stories that have been honed over a far greater expanse of years.

Back in my own home town and port, Stornoway is seen as an outlying curiosity to some and a vantage point to others. Its strategic setting, to the mariner, opens up many possible routes for small craft, in fair weather. Historically, it was a key place in international trade and a potential NATO base during the height of the Cold War. In recent years, the Stornoway Port Authority has recognised the sway from commercial to leisure activity, investing heavily in yacht pontoons of a very high standard. Already, demand has exceeded supply.

The Viking origins of the name indicate a natural haven, but the port must also be seen as one point in the chain of harbours and anchorages that make the west coast of Scotland such rich cruising territory. My own voyages from the port have taken me to Brittany. I have twice crossed from Scandinavia to arrive 'back home'. There were other trips where I was never so far from home shores but during which I have felt the exhilaration that comes from sensing that gear and self are being tested by the adventure, maybe close to their limits. These brought back the acute awareness of each moment of the journey, the way my first, naïve excursions in *Broad Bay* and *Semblance* did. Yet I realised that the areas from the Clyde to Orkney provided a huge scope for any one book. I hope to relive other voyages and the stories they brought me to in a future volume. This one has a focus on Scotland's west coast.

There is an inevitable criss-cross of lines, from different voyages. But the experience, in different weathers, varied craft, alone or with companions, was never the same. The observed geography never looked the same. The stories, retold, will never be exactly as they sounded, last time they were heard.

I am grateful to the other sailors who have invited me to join them, the skippers who have looked after me and the crews who have put their trust in me. Thanks also to the designers and builders of the varied craft celebrated here.

Broad Bay

I SAW HER CERTIFICATE OF REGISTRY after I bought her, the first vessel I had owned since my first boat – a tiny plywood catamaran – fell into decay. *Broad Bay* was not always known by that name. Her history as a small fishing vessel was revealed in inked scripts by different hands.

She was built in Deerness, Orkney in 1912, and first registered in Kirkwall. She has been in Harris and Lewis since the 1940s. She worked from bays on the east side of Harris. Under skylines scattered with grey stones, said to glint with garnet. Then she was sold to owners who worked her in the Lochs district of Lewis. Islands and promontories in that area tend to be capped with cropped green turf or dense heather and bracken. From there, she went to take part in the longlining for haddock from the sand and shingle shores of Loch a Tuath – the wide bight to the north of the long promontory known as the Eye Peninsula. It stretches out north-east of the Approaches to Stornoway, sided by conglomerate rock, to culminate in the cliffs of Tiumpan Head, marked by a major lighthouse.

There were arable crofts close to the alkaline shores but most of the riches were in the sea. Stocks lasted into the early 1970s. I can still see these gasping fish, pulsing in a bronze-grey, heavy in the belly from feeding on pout and shrimp and sand eels. You drifted over a mixed ground of sand and stone. They came, usually three at a time, to our baits of orange mussel or silver herring-strip. They usually ranged from a pound or so in weight to 2–3lb, but there were occasional 'jumbos' of 4–5lb. You could easily lift 9–10lb of prime whitefish in one haul. You pulled them on your soft line, hand over hand, from 7 or 8 fathoms of water. A fathom is 6 feet – a bit short of 2 metres. I still think of the depths of fishing-marks and reefs in fathoms. Maybe that's a bit like the way my mother would lapse into her native Gaelic to come out with a phrase that was simply, to her, the most natural for the subject.

'Small lines' of 90 hooks or so were set from *Broad Bay*. She carried a mast that could easily fit inside her own length, which would be lowered into the boat to reduce windage when you were fishing and would be lowered again when she was brought in to the beach. The wooden spar that supports the top edge of the sail is called a yard. This is slightly longer than the mast in the North Lewis rig

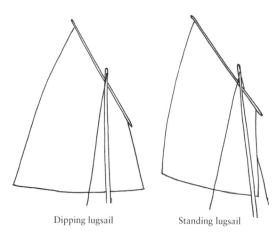

Dipping lugsail   Standing lugsail

Lugsail rigs

but it still must fit inside the vessel. The feature gives the sail a unique shape – similar to a lateen sail on an Arab dhow rather than a more standard Scottish lugsail.

There is a reason why every part of the gear on a vernacular vessel developed the way it did. This sail shape gives you power to cut through surf, essential in a boat launched from an exposed shore, and it does not generate too much heeling force because the main area of the sail is carried low and spread along the length of the vessel. The action of 'tacking' the boat – turning towards the wind until it catches the boat on a different side – requires a coordinated crew. There is a sequence of actions and this must be in time, like music. If the crew do not have eye contact, the efforts of the individuals at the bow, midships and stern will work against each other.

The person at the bow must release a hook that secures the 'tack' or front corner of the sail. However, if this is done too soon, the vessel will not have sufficient power to cut through the waves to take the wind on the opposite side. If the hook is released too late, the sail will be forced against the mast and the pressure could be dangerous, in strong wind.

Forget the idea of instructions in strange nautical language being shouted out all the time. A smooth boat is usually a quiet boat. A few words are indeed required but so is consideration for your neighbour in the crew. The lifting and pulling is shared. You can't do this work on your own.

Due to the difficulties encountered while tacking and the necessity for another crew member, I redrew the rig of the old *Broad Bay* and had a new sail made. This was of a type called a standing lugsail, which essentially means you don't have to shift most of the gear when you 'tack' the boat. The mast had now to be fixed in place with three tense wires. These were fastened to strong points at the bow and on either side. I sourced metalwork and bolted these through gunnels and planks, with backing plates of timber to distribute the loads. She could then be sailed single-handed. The vessel could be my companion as well as my transport.

I had a voyage in mind – sailing the route suggested by a Gaelic song, *Ailean Duinn*, which has a haunting melody and heart-tearing words of loss. It takes you on a physical journey out from the harbour of Stornoway. It also takes you below the surface of these waters.

I had only just bent on that new sail to a shorter yard, which was easier to handle. The cloth was a synthetic material but with the look and feel of tanned-cotton sailcloth. This was to be my first passage as skipper in exposed waters and I wanted to make it alone. I knew the principles of coastal navigation but had to become more familiar with the issues of taking to open sea in open boats before I could consider taking more responsibility. As a coastguard, I had been helping to organise the rescue of others, so I was acutely aware of the risks of swamping or capsizing, as well as hypothermia. Trainee coastguards are always shown a video that documents the effects of this condition as it develops. In it, an Olympic swimmer is monitored as he is subjected to the water temperatures you are likely to find in the North Minch, summer or winter. He becomes disorientated and the lulling of other senses prevents him from realising that he has lost his stroke.

Stornoway to Lochmaddy

THIS WAS MY PROVISIONAL PASSAGE PLAN, subject to weather: steer *Broad Bay* from Stornoway to Lochmaddy, staying overnight at

Stornoway to Lochmaddy: provisional passage plan

anchor by the Shiant Islands. I had first visited these turf-topped columns of basalt as an auxiliary coastguard when we were taken out on a fishing boat to a cliff-rescue exercise with a ram as the casualty. We did these animal rescues when off duty and were able to use official equipment because it was likely the shepherds would otherwise put themselves into danger by using lengths of hairy string if we did not. We usually took home a bottle of whisky for the Christmas party.

There is one rounded green island, eastwards and separate and known by different names. They say that *Eilean Mhuire*, or Mary's island, is an uncomfortable reminder of the form of religion brought by voyaging monks, long before the Reformation. To the west of this outlying landmass lies a lagoon, noisy with seabirds. Dense flights are layered, from sea to sky, from bright-beaked puffins to the blacks and whites of barnacle geese. The dark cliffs that plummet from green grazings meet a liquid mottling of white and blue-brown. The swirls are like the sweets we used to call 'boilings', sold by the quarter, to last you through a complex sermon. Continuing westwards, we meet one island with two names. There are high stackings of rock and reeds and heather and turf, joined by a narrow isthmus that is constantly moving.

Eilean Tigh is the part with the house, now a bothy from a storybook, with a roof of red-painted tin. Garbh Eilean reaches from its joined-on neighbour, towards the coastline of Lewis and Harris. And no, I don't think I can explain why we can't be content with one name for each island except that, in this case, they will be separate when the tide floods.

A line of jagged summits, with water just about navigable for a small craft in between each one, takes your eye even further westwards, towards the undulating line of mainland Lewis. Follow that coastline south and it takes a sudden jump up. Your eye can then take in the line of the North Harris hills, the Clisham horseshoe, if the cloud is high enough.

In this part of the Minch the lines of the sea can be as interesting as those of the land. Tides can be strong enough to keep the trawlers tied up, when the range between high water and low water is towards the maximum in this area – more than 5 metres. Races and overfalls are marked on the chart as pretty waves. They do not always occur, but they often do. In a small vessel that does not sail so much faster than the tide can run, you need to time your passage to have it in your favour. But you can't even consider this route if a fresh or strong breeze is against the four- or five-hour flow of all that weight of sea. After that, there will be an hour or so of slack before it all begins to run back in the opposite direction.

The day of my planned departure, the inshore waters forecast predicted a dry and bright breeze from the north-west. If that held, it would provide power to cover the 18 miles to the Shiants, on one ebbing tide. There would be no fear of the chop and wallow that must follow the turn of that tide. I would need only four or five hours of settled breeze, fresh but not strong. It looked good.

Before clearing the pier, I tied in one of the three reefs to reduce the area of cloth. This sail had a choice of three fixing eyes, at both the front and the back edges. As the wind strength grows you pull down some of the sail and use higher fixing points, front and back. This reduces the sail area. You will see lines of cords on a sail of this type, which are used to gather up the folds of cloth left at the bottom of the sail when you reef down. The cords are tied with a slip reef knot, which won't jam when the pressure comes on.

Next, I tested the hand-held VHF radio by calling on channel 16 then passing my plan to Stornoway Coastguard, on the frequency they used for working radio traffic. In an emergency, you remain on channel 16 so all can hear.

Broad Bay was looking as if she was cared for. It's no easy thing, balancing work and family responsibilities with finding the huge number of hours you need to keep an old wooden boat alive. Some years, the maintenance involved the whole family. Sometimes it was a way of a father finding some personal time with either of his children, one at a time, while his wife did other activities with the other. My elder son had helped clench copper nails and my younger was careful with the paint. *Broad Bay* was Baltic blue with a white whalemouth and gunnels of Admiralty grey. Her spars were oiled.

I'm quite short and slightly built but folk often say I'm strong for my size. As I'm sketching all the crews, I have to step out from myself now and describe the single occupant of this vessel, as he was then. At that time I still had a shock of curls. There might have been some grey in the ginger.

Once *Broad Bay* sailed herself clear of the flukey winds that circulate round buildings and headlands of the harbour approaches, I found that the steady breeze was coming from the north-east. I hoped it would shift soon and settle in the north-west, as forecast, but the direction remained constant. This wind would now be blowing over a longer stretch of sea. The strength of 10–15 knots would be enough to induce significant waves once we lost the shelter of the extending peninsula.

Training and my experience have taught me that a passage plan has to be reviewed in any change of circumstances. I still trusted that the wind would indeed be from the north-west once we were out of the distortions caused by geography. But the wind continued to blow from the north-east, across that open stretch of sea. It freshened, driving the boat faster. If there had been anyone else aboard, I would probably have made for the shelter of one of the many secure anchorages on that indented coast of Lewis. I had a sleeping bag and camping stove aboard so was not bound to put in for shelter to any place where there was a bothy or hostel. There is often a point when a key decision has to be made. Sometimes there's no turning back, against strong tide or strengthening wind.

You never see your own boat when she is sailing well but you sense it all right. *Broad Bay* looks every inch a sea-boat, though she is only 18 feet long from sternpost to stempost. Her stern swells out, very like the lemon shape of fishing boats in Ian Hamilton Finlay's witty visual metaphors. I'd encountered the simple cards, prints and booklets by this very individual Scottish artist in a small gallery round the corner from King's College Library in Old Aberdeen.

Back on a real boat, with generations of repairs since it was first built in 1912, I was conscious that this was neither an idealised vessel nor a page in a book. There were no decks to shed any waves that might break over the small craft. The silent outboard motor was cocked clear of the water to reduce drag. There was no liferaft but I was towing a rubber dinghy that would stay afloat even if she were fully swamped. There was the satisfying sound of water lapping on the clinker planks of *Broad Bay*. A slapping and clapping.

The rhythm told me that the vessel was making best speed through the water. Unless it can plane on the surface, a vessel has a maximum speed, based mainly on the length from bow to stern where she meets the water. Once she reaches this, she will not go faster, even if you apply more power by sail or motor.

The sea miles fell away. I had a flask of hot coffee, a simple gas burner in a metal bucket and enough water, tea and food to be at sea for a week rather than overnight. I had a protective polythene camping bag to keep off the rain, although the northerly airstream promised dry weather.

Five miles out, there still wasn't any west in it. The strong breeze was now causing steeper waves. I reckoned it was over 15 knots. That does not sound like much on land, but it was more than I wanted then. I considered reducing sail further but realised I needed the power to ride from one wave to the next. I did not want to get caught, wallowing between seas. The breeze went up another notch. It was now around the maximum for this area of sail.

At about that point, the speed increased as she rode above the higher seas. She was surfing free of the physics of her waterline length. The drag of the dinghy was slowing her, just keeping her from accelerating out of control. Exhilaration overpowered my anxiety. Elation is as intoxicating as whisky. We had now sailed beyond the point at which the sensible option of altering course for the shelter of any sea loch was still available. Considerable seas were rolling in and I did not want to take them on the beam. They could roll us far enough to take in water over the side. Nor could I reduce sail easily, without risking loss of control. It was now too late for that to be an easy action to take. I could not risk leaving the tiller or even lash it in place for a minute or two.

The best thing to do was to maintain the present course and keep the same amount of sail. Considerable strains were being applied to the whole structure – the original timbers and planks and the ones replaced. The last repairs were better than my first attempts. She was creaking, now. Rigging, ropes and spars were all substantial but my concern was for the shell of the hull, made up from different generations of materials. The unmistakable outline of the Shiants was now before us. The shapes of Eilean Mhuire and Garbh Eilean were not yet distinct, separate, but I could make out that jagged graph of outlying reefs extending westwards. The skyline is just as it is depicted in silhouettes in old pilot books.

The wind was probably now close to 20 knots. The waves started roaring, behind us. I looked back once or twice then decided it was better to look ahead and concentrate on the steering. In the blur of islands, you look for the gap opening up between indistinct shapes. When we were up on the crests I thought I was seeing the narrow gap we were aiming for. The course was good, according to the compass fixed on a thwart. It was then the waves became still more steep. This was the effect of shallowing depth. Someone aboard said 'Oh, oh,' out loud. That must have been me.

I thought then, it would have been terrible to have either of my sons aboard and worse to have both of them, even though an extra pair of hands would have helped. Even with iron ballast, the camping gear and a decent-sized anchor, the boat was light. The seas were beginning to break. That's when a fearsome amount of energy is dispensed. If the tide had been against these waves, conditions would have been impossible – for bigger vessels than this one. Even with the tide in alliance, the incoming waves would sometimes release their energy as they were compressed by the uneven, but still shallowing, underwater geography.

We were now carrying too much sailcloth but I couldn't do anything to address that. I remember thinking that the odds were better than 50/50. If she did swamp or break, I was wearing a lifejacket and had a hand-held VHF radio close to me. Again, I thought of sending ashore a message with my position, just in case. But I knew I had to concentrate fully on the steering. If I let her head turn towards the wind and we took one of these seas beam on (hitting her side rather than closer to the bow or stern), we'd capsize.

I had placed fishing buoys as fenders but tied below the level of the thwarts so they would probably provide buoyancy to keep afloat, even with the weight of gear. However, this had not been tested by a controlled swamping. I was glad of the Avon dinghy, following like a collie.

Broad Bay rose on every individual wave that caught up with us. Our repairs could have been tidier but they seemed to be strong enough. I knew then why so many passers-by stopped to admire the shape of this boat when she was beached for that work. It was the way her planks are kept out wide, almost to her sternpost, then take a sudden tilt and turn into that post. Thus her buoyant beam is carried almost to her end. You might think this a buxom way to finish a shape. Rather, it is a complex curvature that seems easy and natural. This shape was not only rising to the challenge of powerful water – the vessel seemed to be revelling in the conditions. She was meeting the circumstances that she had been built to take.

It took more than one craftsman and more than one lifetime for this shape to evolve. In that respect, the vessel was like the song we were sailing through. There are passages ascribed to the tragic Anna Campbell but the song that carries her story was developed over many generations.

There was a deep sigh when we were through the gap and in the lee of Eilean Mhuire. That must have been from me, too. The seas levelled out at once, but we would have to round the outlying tip of Eilean Tigh to find shelter off the western side of the gravel isthmus. We made an easy slow-time turn downwind (a gybe) to head for the more sheltered anchorage. That would also put me in a good position to continue southwards, when wind and tide allowed. The outboard would have been useful at that point. It would have driven us up close to the lee side of the stony spit that joins Garbh Eilean with Eilean Tigh. The motor was fussy, however, and I had no appetite for fiddling with the carburettor or throttle cable. Instead, I sailed a zigzag course upwind in a series of stitches – another visual metaphor used often by Finlay.

I noted recognisable points in line (transits) that would let me know if the boat's position altered significantly. I slung the hook. The heavier anchor, bought for this trip, plummeted to the kelp. I paid out chain and rope. She settled and I checked my transits. They were constant. We were secure, for now. I could gaze at the shapes of the falling hills on both sides of that shingle bank. This is a loud place. Bird calls from different species were criss-crossing, like the visible flight paths, at different levels. I could take my hand off the tiller now, flex my fingers and think of brewing tea.

In the shelter, there was time to think. I'd made the right decision by sailing on the information and forecast known at the time. I'd made the wrong one by failing to alter course for Lochs Erisort or Mariveg at the first signs of the wind staying in the north-east. After passing these refuges, I'd probably done the best thing by sailing on to reach the lee of the islands before the tide turned. *Broad Bay* had carried enough sail to drive us out of trouble. But we'd been close to our limits, the vessel and her rider.

Even if it's choppy outside, it's often glass calm in the sheltered places. You frequently see the rocky shoreline twice. The line that separates the reflection from the image above the surface is like a horizon. Visibility was good and I could make out the shape of Eilean

Glas lighthouse rising from the island of Scalpay. The landmarks, viewed from this anchorage, brought my mind back to the story within the song that was behind my desire to sail this route.

There are several different versions of the song *Ailean Duinn* from the east side of Lewis to the Southern Isles. In the Uists, it was a waulking song, one for the women as they beat the tweed, stretched out around a long table. The song takes the route we've just sailed.

While the burner was hissing blue under the kettle and the dense flights of a dozen species of seabird were whirring and calling above us, I told myself the story. I heard it first from Norman Malcolm Macdonald. He wrote what he told me was a Japanese Noh play, in Gaelic, from Anna Campbell's lament for her lost lover. There must have been tension in my telling. The words will not be the same when I tell it now and I will have the chance of revising and shaping the written version. But I'll do my best to bring you the spirit of a timeless story. By way of preparation for this, which is a responsibility as well as a pleasure, I'll share a short poem in the hope that this will also help to share observations of a fast-changing short stretch of sea.

Learning to read
then distrust
charted rates for
The Sound of Shiants.

Listings fold
to implicit sense
of rules of this road,
not that wide.

The only guidance is belief
in a history of observations.
Phases when the sun and moon
fall out of line

and when they make up again
on their nearly predictable course.
That's when they really pull
to make water swell.

Brown Alan (Ailean Duinn)

There are all these stories about the daughter of one merchant
promised to the son of another. How the feelings of the young were
disregarded, to further the ambitions of the old. Aye, but this is not
one of them. This is the story of the meeting of Alan Morrison from
Stornoway and Anna Campbell from Scalpay.

Alan, lean and brown haired, was indeed the son of a prosperous
Stornoway merchant. He had mastered the sextant as well as the
compass and taken his father's slim black ship of oak as far as
the Isle of Man and on to Spain. The family prospered. Anna was
blessed with the black hair and deep brown eyes they say were a
mark left on Scalpay by the Spanish Armada. Her family were not
chiefs or lairds. Her father was the tacksman who rented much
of Scalpay to raise cattle on that island. She was learned, and
composed lines of rhythmical language that rang like any harp
could. The two had met and found there was no shortage of things
to discuss – debate as well as courtesies – and most would say that
the handsome couple belonged together.

In the Hebrides, the tradition is the *reitach* – a meeting of
families to seal a contract of marriage. They say these gatherings
needed at least as much whisky and wine as the wedding itself.
Alan's family travelled southwards by horse from the town. They
rested at the house of a relation and then were ferried over to
Scalpay. Alan and his brother were to sail down. They did not
bother to take the ship for this small distance. Each took the helm
of a simple skiff with a tan sail, a crew of a few friends on each.

They say that Anna became restless before anyone else on Scalpay sensed that the wind was rising. She could see the straw wavering in the thatches. She walked out to the point, looking out over the mouth of Loch Seaforth towards the Shiant Islands. The seas were rising fast as the wind increased. Soon it was howling and the waves were charging at the shore. At last she caught sight of a scrap of brown sailcloth above the white caps. She could not see the second one yet but she ran to the harbour to join those who were catching the warps of the first skiff.

Alan's brother could hardly look at her. They had lost sight of the sail of the leading boat. She had just dropped into the troughs of very steep seas. His own crew was bailing and praying and they were fighting to keep her going over the waves. They came through the overfalls but there was no further sign of Alan's boat. There was no chance of fighting back against that tide.

Hour after hour, Anna and members of both families and their friends and most of the able-bodied folk of Scalpay walked these shores. Nothing was sighted and nothing was found. Anna composed the most bitter and painful song for a lost one. She sang of the teeth and the claws that were tearing into the body that should have been lying by her. The lament survives in many versions, mostly sung to the same melody. So far I have not been able to attribute this translation:

Dreadful indeed is my separation.
Tonight, again, I can have no thought of merriment.
Brown-haired Alan, I would share your sojourn.

Tonight my thoughts are not on happy things
But on the fury of the elements and the fierce hurricane.

The crew were driven out from the land.
Alan, my heart was set on the finest
Though I heard your vessel was overcome.

I heard she was overcome
That black narrow shapely boat of oak.

Alan my dearest, object of all my thoughts
I gave you my esteem and then my love, from youth.

Tonight my story is one of deep misfortune
Not because of the drowning of beasts
Not because of cattle, choking in a bog

But because it's your own shirt that's soaked
Because the sea is in your lungs
And there are creatures tearing you apart.

Though I had folds and pens of the best of stock
That would not mean much to me tonight
I would not wish for any other partner
I would wish to join you on the hill.

Brown-haired Alan, I heard that you were lost
I heard that you had been drowned
And I regret I am not beside you
On whatever skerry you are washed ashore

Or wherever the tide leaves you on the wrack
My earnest prayer, Lord on the throne
That I should not be buried, in cloth on this earth
In a hole in the ground or in a secret place

But in the spot where you are, Alan.

The strain was too much for her and she passed away. There is no depth of soil for a burial on Scalpay. Her body was placed in its own small ship – a casket made from the boatbuilder's best oak. That was placed aboard a Scalpay vessel and her own brother was trusted with the charge of bringing it by sea to the churchyard at Rodel. That is a half-day's sail, on fair tide, to the south once you're clear of East Loch Tarbert.

When they had gained open water, the wind rose again. Things became desperate. Heavy gear was jettisoned to keep the vessel buoyant. Anna's brother judged that the living had to come before the dead – a skipper's duty. His sister's casket was cast to the mercy of the sea.

The flood tide sets north-north-east from that place. That drift will take you to the Shiant Islands. Alan was lost in the Sound of Shiants, close to that huddle of islands, where the tides scour round. He would have been caught in that cycle, waiting. Anna would have progressed north then gone back a bit on the ebb. But the flood, there, is stronger than the ebb. I did promise you that Alan and Anna would meet.

Between Eilean Tigh and Garbh Eilean there is that isthmus of shifting boulders – a thin neck of gravel, as the pilot book says. That's where they met, the bodies washed up together. I can't say if they were buried together. I can say that the whole area of the Shiant Islands, the waters, the land and the air, are abundant with life.

I slept sound, on the boards, under the sail. Waking early, to a clear day, I looked over the gunnel to see small ripples on the water. The breeze was light, as forecast. Best catch it, while it lasted. After a brew-up, the anchor was soon hauled and I raised all sail to head southwards, with the barber-shop pole of Eilean Glas lighthouse clear to starboard. The bands of white and red were now distinct.

A mackerel line went out when I lost both breeze and tide, well abeam Scalpay. A local boat, out hauling creels, came close. A lone fisherman called over for a yarn. 'Where did you spring from, this early in an open boat? It was a bit breezy last night.'

When I told him I'd sailed from SY, he asked where I'd spent the night. When I told him I dropped the hook west side of the Shiants, he gave a wee whistle and then said, 'That must have been peaceful, once you got in there.'

When he heard my outboard was running a bit rough, he said he'd be heading in to North Harbour himself shortly. He'd look out for me in case I needed a pull. If it was running smooth, or the breeze came back, I could work the evening tide all the way to Rodel or even further.

She ran fine and I took his advice after frying up a few fillets for myself. I also grabbed the chance of an hour or two of sleep, stretched out on the warm boards. The breeze held and I went for the more distant option. *Broad Bay* covered the 20 or so miles to Lochmaddy under sail and I picked up a mooring before the hotel closed. The local guy who manages the arts centre had a rum up in front of me before my pint was in my hand.

Lochmaddy to Stornoway

I HAD A GOOD WEEK IN LOCHMADDY but then it blew up a bit – just not the right wind for taking the boat home. A sheltered mooring off 'the wee pier' was pointed out to me and I went home, by buses and ferry, to jobs and family till it looked a bit more promising.

My young son Ben, maybe eight or nine years old, came with me on the return trip to Lochmaddy by public transport. We could have slept in a friend's bungalow within sight of our boat but Ben wanted to be a full crew member, sleeping under the sail as I'd done, on the way down. He was already tall for his years and well filled-out. He had wavy ginger hair worked into a short pigtail at the back. He took everything in. We had to be careful about reading material and films. Any violence or injustice, even something most would think of as mild, could give him nightmares.

We had read *Swallows and Amazons* more than once. That was fine. So we paddled out to the mooring and made ourselves comfortable. We rolled out our yellow mats on the floorboards and arranged the soft tan sail so it could work as a tent. Soon my son was clutching his mug of cocoa and I was reading him a chapter of Arthur Ransome's *Great Northern?* That is an exciting story, with a strongly built yacht as one of its characters. It is set in the same part of the world we were about to navigate, the complex coastline between North Uist and Stornoway.

We sailed, early, with a red flying jib out ahead of our bow on a short sprit of spruce. I'd adapted this from an old mainsail that had come, as a spare, with a Mirror dinghy project. I'd taken time over the hand-stitching and knew it to be strong. This recycled old sail was now helping *Broad Bay* out towards the Little Minch. There are several possible routes between the high reefs known to us as 'The Maddies'. I will quote my master-mariner friend's more full description. Angus M Macleod has taken many coasters and yachts into the nooks and crannies of Scotland's west coast. He combines that experience with the local knowledge accessible to a native Gaelic speaker.

'There are three Maddies, more correctly they are *Madaidh*, Gaelic for fox. The northernmost one, almost slap bang in the middle of the entrance, is Madaidh Beag, or "wee fox". The channel north and south of it is passable by large craft as there is a minimum depth of 12 metres. Madadh Mor, "big fox", and Madadh Gruamach, "miserable fox", are well clear and to the south of the navigable channels.'

So it's not just me who considers the possibility that inanimate chunks of gneiss or granite or basalt or even pudding-like, pebble-studded conglomerate masses have their own personalities.

Our mainsail, the tan standing lug, was out on our starboard side as we approached the wee fox but we allowed the red foresail to 'back' or work against the other one. This is one simple means of 'hoving-to'. You will have heard the phrase, which means that you choose to take the power off the vessel so she will not drive onwards. Our soft brown lines, on simple wooden frames, were cast over with their lead weights and wormy lures.

It was Ben who felt the tug. 'The bottom?' I asked, but I could see the excitement in his eyes even though he managed to sound low key. Lythe, or pollack, live and hunt among the kelp. When hooked, they make a strong dive for the tough dense strands. But this one came to the surface. This is the fish with the pouting lip, as if it's sulking. I used to tell my lads to stop looking like a lythe and they usually laughed at that. The species takes on the colour of the tangle it inhabits. This one was gold and verdigris, shining in rain. The lateral line is dotted rather than solid and takes a steep dive close to the pectoral fin. In contrast, the whiteish line on the darker-backed coalfish or saithe is solid and straight.

We had our supper in the bag but I had my doubts about sailing on. The wind was still pretty much against us. 'Can we not do that tacking thing?' Ben asked. I said we could but there would be quite a few tacks to make. Ben shrugged. I knew he wanted to prove himself, crewing as his big brother would. The worst option, if we failed to make enough progress to reach the tidal harbour at Rodel, was to turn back once we'd run out of tide. We made long stitches and shared out the tasks each time we made a turn. The tacks could not have been too bad because we made the entrance to Loch Rodel in the late afternoon.

We had nothing to prove and I let the prop of the outboard lower to the water. She spluttered and started and stopped. This was a recent addition to the boat and serviced for the trip. 'Archimedes law, I suppose,' said Ben. I must have told him about the law of outboard motors, how they run perfectly when you test them but not when you need them.

With the breeze funnelling down the loch, it's a long way in, tacking against the wind till the hint of an entrance opens up. The gusts were too strong for us to row against them. Before the proper channel there is an apparent entrance that the pilot book says you must never attempt in any circumstances. But the tide was fairly high and we were only drawing a couple of feet. 'Just go forwards, Ben.

Watch out for rocks. Never mind about saying port and starboard, just point.'

We were going in nicely on the red jib and Ben was concentrating. He began to point, first to one side then the other. 'There's a rock there. And there. In fact, Dad, there are rocks everywhere.'

There was a scraping sound as the keelstrap rode up on stone. 'I told you there were rocks everywhere.' Thankfully we'd renewed that protective metal band recently. We were in full view of the lounge window in the hotel but no one had spotted us. I jumped out, wading to my knees, and pushed us back out the way we'd come. Ben looked down, inside the boat, for any sign of water coming in at the lower planks. It looked like we'd got away with it. This time we tacked the full way up till the proper entrance opened up and we were able to sail her alongside the stone jetty.

Ben was tired out. 'Do you think, Dad, we could permit ourselves the luxury of a night ashore, in the tent?'

We rowed out a short distance, to anchor the boat where she would not dry out with the tide. Then we paddled ashore in the dinghy and pitched the tent, together. Sleeping bags laid out and ready, we walked the short distance to the cottage of a friend, with Ben carrying the bag with his fish.

Edi Thompson had been diagnosed with Parkinson's. He was also deaf. He had worked in the library of the Royal Scottish Academy of Music and Drama but he'd settled in Harris because he loved its rocks. Until recently he had climbed the hill behind his cottage as a daily act of meditation as well as exercise.

There is a lot of rock to the acre in Harris. He made stoneware and porcelain objects that were sometimes designed to be functional and sometimes not. They always referred to either the shapes or the colours found in the landscape he observed. Tonight he had baked red peppers for friends who had not arrived. Yes, he did eat fish.

After we ate, on plates he had made, Edi told us he was on new medication, which seemed to give him about one good hour a day.

This was it. The shakes were manageable. Would we mind if he played piano?

I think it was Brahms but don't trust my memory. There's nothing in my log of events on the boat or off it. But I do know that the music was beautiful and Ben fell asleep in my arms. Edi found a blanket for him and drove us back to our tent, before the last of his good hour was up.

We had a visitor at the pier in the morning. A retired coastguard, who happened to be my mentor in navigation, pulled up and dropped off a 4 horsepower Suzuki. 'I never thought I'd buy anything Japanese, the rest of my life.' That was Ivor Horton's way of saying hello. He had retained his north-of-England accent even though he had been enticed to remain on the island by the woman from Harris who had been his wife for many years. I'd given him a call the night before. He took our outboard to deliver back to the repairer.

Ivor, of lean and lanky build, had been in Hiroshima not long after the bombing but he also knew several survivors of the Japanese POW camps. I'd helped him sail the small yacht, bought for his retirement, from Portree to Rodel. He'd instructed me to do the chartwork and had me work out hourly fixes from compass bearings. He also checked I could make the step from working out tidal calculation on a chart table that didn't move, to logging them on a boat about to cross the Little Minch.

Neither of us was very keen on the idea of being rescued by lifeboat volunteers or our colleagues in the coastguard service. Now he asked me what I'd worked out for the best departure time and where I might reach. He gave a nod, which I knew wished us a good passage. He also asked if I'd caught the morning forecast. I knew it would freshen by evening and tomorrow looked like no-go. I planned to anchor *Broad Bay* in Loch Seaforth or leave her in Scalpay. 'You should make Loch Seaforth.'

We nearly did. With two reefs in, sailing hard off Eilean Glas light, it was time to make a decision. We might pick up a vacant fish-farm mooring in a bay off Loch Seaforth, if we carried on that bit further north. But we couldn't be sure of that. We had a good-sized anchor but I did not want to leave our boat unattended in this area where the winds increase as they gust down the high slopes of North Harris. You could be in Norway.

We had the tent, sleeping bags, camping stove and food. Ben had done well but I did not want this to be an ordeal for him. We could phone Barbara and ask her to pick us up. We lost a bit of the ground we'd gained as we took her into the choppy tidal water under the new bridge to the north harbour, Scalpay. Soon she was secure.

Safe harbours are rare enough in the Outer Hebrides but Scalpay is blessed with a south haven as well as this one to the north. Perhaps that is why it prospered and the surviving community was able to lobby for a fixed bridge to replace the small ferries. These had provided an intermittent link with mainland Harris for most of the 20th century.

We'd had two days good but hard sailing, working our way home. The Scalpay fishermen are known to care for their own vessels and those of visitors. *Broad Bay* would be safe here. While we waited for Barbara, we chewed the fat with fishermen and admired the colours and the lettering on the local boats. Most had an arrow-tipped yellow 'cove-line', purely for decoration, like that on a classic yacht. I remembered the black herring drifters from this island port and the sheen on the yacht-varnished ring-netters that replaced them.

There are only 27 nautical miles between North Harbour and our own haven of Stornoway. There is also a good push of tide if you time your departure well. This was a leg we could leave for Ben's elder brother, Sean. The wee man had earned a night in his own bed. I was also happy to rejoin the whole family for some days. Yet, as a sailor or as a poet, part of my mind was still concerned with seawater.

I have always been wary of sweeping general statements and summaries. I found some notes, sketches, all drafts of a poem begun many years before. This is the shape it took. I'm going to trust my feeling that these words might ease a way into one of the best-known Lewis stories. And yet, the dialogue at the heart of this tale is not recorded, in detail, in any audio or published version I've found. Maybe that's a reminder that you can't always rely on a formula, whether sailing or composing verse. The tone of the dialogue surely has to be a response to the mood of the place you're in, at the telling.

> And when tides turn
> to confront
> wind-driven current
> or the airflow luffs
> to change tack –
> this opposition
> rips inconstantly.
>
> Buoyage sways.
> Random frayings
> bleach in the salt.
>
> Blue plastic strands,
> out in the streams,
> are confusing
> until you cease
> ordering them about.

The Blue Men of the Stream

One of the first lessons drummed into you when studying navigation is the difference between a vessel *underway* and a vessel *making way*. These are definitely not the same thing. A vessel is underway when it is not made fast to the land or the ground. Thus you can be underway but with no means of propulsion of any kind. That was one definition Ivor Horton had me repeat till it became second nature. There's a reason that it's important. It's a way of thinking. It's about security.

It wasn't Ivor who told me about the blue men but it was probably another of my mentors, maybe Shondan or Dohmnall Caley or Jock Stewart or Willie Matheson or another of the kind folk who showed patience to bolshy teenagers when they took us to sea in small boats.

You might think you're making way through the Sound of Shiants but you're not. The jabble is high. The spray is coming over the boat. She's doing her best, still driving on, but she's going nowhere. You get a sight of Kebock Head and it's still off the same part of the boat it was five minutes before. That's when you know the blue men have got a hold of your vessel.

You might spot a bony hand, a thin arm, over the gunnel but that's about all you will see. Sooner or later you'll hear them. They give you a chance. One by one, they throw out a challenge. One of the crew has to reply to it. It's a test and every single member of the crew has to take a turn.

This time there were three souls aboard. It often is three when it comes to stories. The youngest is leaning over, waiting for the question he knows is going to come. You have to tune in to a thin voice, hear it above the chop of wind against tide, the gusts playing the rigging wires. It's a bit like turning the dial on a green enamelled radio transceiver. Analogue days. The big set.

At last, the young fellow deciphers the challenge. 'What is the richest thing in the world?'

The others can't help him. The lad behaves as he's been trained to behave. Stays calm, even if he's not really, under his own surface. His elders get twitchy but at last he answers, 'You can take any amount of water from the sea. Somewhere in the world the rains will fall. It will always fill up again. It will never be any the poorer. That's why the sea is the richest thing there is.'

That must have been acceptable because a second question was offered to the next man in line. 'What is the poorest?'

This fellow was quicker off the mark. 'Fire is the poorest. The best of oak joinery, a sail made of silk – they'll all become ashes. Fire consumes everything and is never any better off. Fire is the poorest.'

The final question was for the skipper himself. 'Any vessel, any place in the world's oceans, what is the trickiest course to steer?'

The skipper wasn't that much to look at but the other lads respected him for a reason. There was no hesitation. 'Honesty is the trickiest course,' he said. 'And I think you fellows were human once so if you've anything honest left in you, you'll release our vessel now.'

They did. The blue men slid back to their own territory. The waters slackened off and the boat began to make way again.

Broad Bay remained in commission as a family boat for another couple of years, but then there came a time when she seemed to be beyond repair and she was given to a local maritime society. There was some discussion about exhibiting her as part of a display of local history. Instead, joint funding was found to have her completely rebuilt.

A Stornoway building of historical importance – the old sail loft – was being renovated to be transformed into housing and, as part of that project, resources were allocated to recording and celebrating local maritime history. It was proposed that contributing to the renovation of two small vessels, also of local historical importance, would do more to achieve this aim than the commissioning of more conventional public sculptures.

As *Broad Bay* was worked in the Loch Erisort area for some years, the Erisort Trust also contributed. Iain Louis MacLeod, a local joiner who had developed a taste for what he called 'the peculiar form of insanity which is boatbuilding' was commissioned. He dismantled the hull. The remains were still sufficiently intact to provide templates for entirely new planking, in Scots-grown larch. Members of the Maritime Society contributed by sourcing windfall oak and larch with the curved grain necessary to make sawn frames. These were milled at the local sawmill in one of the few island woodlands. The Trust that runs this publicly owned estate also contributed clear Douglas fir for the yard. The curved timbers were installed at three points of the boat, where the strains from the rig are at their strongest.

Another boatbuilder, John MacAulay from Harris, wandered into the shed out of curiosity and was press-ganged in to assist with installing intermediate frames of steam-bent oak. The team of volunteers primed, painted, oiled and varnished.

The existing mast was swapped for a reclaimed spar of pitch-pine, better suited to take the strains generated by a North Lewis dipping lugsail. One of the last sails to be made on Lewis was used as a model for a new one.

Broad Bay has proven to be the ideal training boat for the larger North Lewis dipping lug craft.

Her renovation could not have been achieved without the vision of Mia Scott. At the time, she directed The Highland Buildings Preservation Trust but her fascination with architecture does not exclude her passions for vernacular culture. That can take the form of a fiddle tune or the shape of a boat. Both hold particular meaning for local people and resonate everywhere.

Broad Bay is moored within sight of the restored sail loft and remains in active use. Sailing skills are passed on, like stories.

Semblance

EVEN THOUGH I GREW UP ON AN ISLAND, that did not stop me hankering to set foot on other, outlying islands. When the tides swelled high, they also fell low. Then you could risk walking out to green places that had seemed impossible to reach. I read a lot when I was young and could also enter other territories that way. I was not sure if I was exploring the 'real' world or a landscape in a story.

Sometimes we cut it fine when we crossed to outcrops of rock that would be cut off by a rising tide. A couple of times our small gang had to wade back, carrying shorts and shoes. It was like being in *Kidnapped*. David Balfour thought the natives were cruel when they rowed past him, 'stranded' on the tidal island of Erraid. He did not realise he just had to wait for the sea to fall then walk the breadth of the white sands to reach the shore of Mull. The author, Robert Louis Stevenson, knew that geography well. He stayed on Erraid with his engineer father to observe the granite being quarried for the great offshore lighthouses of Skerryvore and Dubh Artach.

Ralph, Jack and Peterkin, however, could not walk ashore from the coral island on which they were stranded, though they did have a sure sense of their own moral superiority on their side, thanks to their creator, RM Ballantyne. That writer never did set foot on a like landmass, jutting up from the South Pacific. He borrowed and mixed in other, more informed, narratives. Even now it's difficult enough to distinguish between accounts of charted islands and imagined ones.

There are plenty of stories of islands that are sometime there and sometimes not. There was a bronze one that could appear from a wine-dark Aegean Sea. That one drifted. There was one which might be found out to the west of Ireland. It would be nearly impossible to leave the charms of that place. Even if you succeeded, you would turn to dust if a foot were ever to hit on the mainland again. Growing up in Stornoway, you heard plenty of stories of islands out in the ocean. You could not separate the tales of the islands of the bird-men – people who were more at home on cliffs than on the sea – from those in myths. My next-door neighbour was born on St Kilda, 40 sea miles west of our island group. Not one person lived out there, since 1930, but others in our street had relatives who steamed out, 40 miles north of Lewis, each year to Sula Sgeir.

These hunters still brought home their salted gannets. We all had a taste of one my mother boiled outside our house on a camping primus. It was stronger than kippers and I found these salty enough. But I wanted to know how the men lived for the weeks they would be abandoned out on bare rock in the Atlantic, until the Ness boat came back for them and their catch.

Even then, I could see that the most beautiful islands of all were difficult to reach. You caught glimpses of them, lying out from the

'Long Island' of Lewis and Harris, in the chain of the Outer Hebrides. We could drive to the long sands across from them, in my father's Austin A-40. This was a forerunner of the hatchback family car and I got to ride in the boot, with its vinyl cover removed.

We looked out from the stone jetty on the Valtos peninsula to Pabbay Mor. It seemed to be very fertile. A couple of wide, tarry boats were usually there, drawn up high above the tideline. These would take sheep as well as people back and fore. A cow might swim

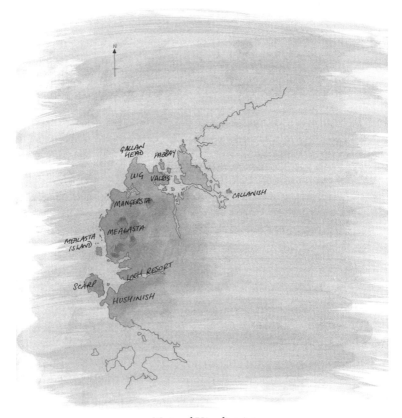

Map of Uig district

behind a boat, towed on its tether across the Sound. There were rumours of lagoons but we did not know anyone who could lend us a rowing boat. None of us were very strong swimmers and my father was jittery at the thought of getting in any boat. The *Loch Seaforth* took you to the proper mainland at Kyle of Lochalsh. She was all right on a good night. I remember my father looking very nervous when the car he'd bought new was swung in nets from a derrick. My mother was always in a good mood because someone else was doing the cooking in the ship's cafeteria.

When we drove once to the very end of the Uig road, you saw another group of broad boats. Out there was the island of Mealasta, which had been abandoned for some years, though the shepherds still crossed to it to do their seasonal tasks. The island of Scarp, visible a few miles to the south, still had its houses and its school, though the post office was on mainland Harris. These village boats all had their purposes, mainly for transporting people and animals to and fro but also in setting creels or nets or lines for subsistence fishing.

It's not that island people didn't enjoy being in and around boats when I was young. But they were there for definite reasons. Although I grew up in a harbour town, very few of my pals or relatives had the use of a leisure craft to take you across to the places you could not otherwise reach.

When I joined the coastguard service I received proper training in the ways of tides, weather, seamanship, cliff and shore rescue techniques and the handling of power-driven craft. I gained the confidence to take *Broad Bay* further out from Stornoway. We could have invested in a road-trailer to take her over to explore the west side of the island but I was anxious about the stress to the old boat associated with launching and recovering. Some of my colleagues wanted to club together to buy an inflatable with a powerful outboard for the very purpose of visiting outlying islands. I was reluctant, not just because I had been warned about the pitfalls of sharing a boat and the issues of its maintenance but because already

I had gained a sense that the relationship with the craft was part of the experience.

Barbara, now my wife, had done more dinghy sailing than I had. We were given a Mirror dinghy that needed a bit of work but came complete with a sturdy trailer. Our VW van had a towbar already fitted by a coastguard mate, so we could tow our sailing craft to suitable launching places. I compiled a list of island slipways on a coastguard watch and examined many of them at low water, when you found holes and slime and other hazards, which narrowed down the possibilities. But the slip by Valtos pier remained on the list and so did the one at the very end of the road in south-west Lewis. No track has ever joined the Uig district to the township at the end of the snaking road that bounces round the hairpin bends through the grey and bare rocks of North Harris.

Despite this, the communities kept in touch because transport was easier by sea than by road, until recently. Now, in the late 20th century, we had to launch our own boat to reach these abandoned islands. Its light plywood skin, joined with fibreglassed tape to its sides, was designed to make watertight buoyancy chambers. If these leaked, the dinghy was not safe. A housing for a 'daggerboard' that would resist sideways drift was also reinforced with tape around the boat's bottom centreline. These are notorious for leaking.

Mirror dinghies were so called because they were made popular, sold in kit form, by that newspaper. No specialist skills were needed but you had to be careful with the new chemistry of mixing resin. This would result in a rigid glass-fibre join, assisted by measured drops of catalyst. Sailing clubs often used them as trainer boats. More than 70,000 were built. They could become competitive, with ball-bearing blocks and bright, light, low-stretch cordage to tune crisp, red sails. Vestiges of spinnaker gear could be found on this one. However, we wanted to make a solid cruising dinghy that could survive beaching on rough sand and the inevitable bumps on the trailer. Our elder son, Sean, became involved in the gluing and screwing of reinforcing slats of timber and solid new fittings.

One spar slid up and down the short wooden mast to extend it so that its red mainsail was carried higher. This is called a gunter-rig. The Mirror also carries a matching red jib, up front. Another piece of clear-grained and varnished fir stretched the terylene mainsail back over the transom. That's the blunt back-end of the boat, as if it has been cut short. But the bow is like that too. This type of shape was nothing new. It is known as a 'pram' and is widespread because of its ease of build but is especially common in Scandinavia.

Meanwhile, our van had been welded and patched by the expert across the river. We were shocked to find it had also been repainted. 'What's the damage for that?' I asked and braced myself. The repairer said he had to do something about the patchwork of steel our van had become. His bill was not too bad. She shone but the finish was 'Charlie Morrison's paint' – or yacht enamel, named after the town's ships' chandler. This finish was applied by roller in thin coats of International Orange until it made a smooth skin protecting the repaired metal. So Sean and myself took a tin of the same shade to our dinghy, also now back in one piece. We also had some contrasting yacht enamel left over from detailing on *Broad Bay*. I wondered if the colour 'Snow White' was simply the most pure shade or if there was an allusion to the story. Ben, a very sensitive child, would have been horrified by the versions of that story that didn't find themselves worked into the Walt Disney film, in which the wicked queen is torn apart by stallions driving in different directions.

I got carried away with the motif of mirror-image reflections. An artist friend called it a 'Russian Suprematist' Mirror. But we did not name our craft in homage to Rodchenko, though I did think of that. It was simply *Semblance* but I turned my cardboard stencil on one side so it was reversed. Our dinghy looked the business, matching the VW colours, out behind the van.

We arrived at Valtos pier too late to launch that evening. As we were raising the roof of the van to allow the boys' hammocks the space to stretch, a smiling fellow I recognised from coastguard patrols greeted us with a fry of fish for our supper. He suggested we might go for the smaller island of Vuia Mor to camp the next day, as the owner of Pabbay Mor was in residence. The 'fellow from away' had developed a dug-out bothy with a green felted roof for his family's holiday home. He wasn't too keen on people landing on 'his' beach. Our local friend saw our exchange of glances and knew we would be landing on the beach as planned, just the same.

'Well, you wouldn't be the first to insist on your right to roam,' my colleague said. 'There was a bit of an altercation here on the pier the other day. The owner asked a regular visitor if he wouldn't mind not landing on his island this week. The other fellow said yes he would mind and he would land the way he always did, when he took his grandchildren sailing, as he did most years. Then the owner started muttering about contacting his Edinburgh lawyer. Which firm would that be? What is that to you? Our firm just happens to be Edinburgh-based too and I just happen to be a lawyer by trade myself. And he wasn't kidding.'

Barbara found herself commiserating with me, at the number of trips it took to sail the family and camping gear and provisions across the narrow sound. I had to zigzag back against the breeze with the empty craft each trip. Then she saw my grin. This was a man who had been cooped up in a stuffy Ops Room on 12-hour shifts. 'I'll just get into Siddhartha mode,' I might have said. In fact, I'd once been tempted to apply for a ferryman's job shortly after reading the Hesse fable.

You could say that I really learned to sail by going back and fore over a short distance, whatever the wind shifts. That dinghy, donated to us by another family, was all we could afford to maintain at the time. We all wanted to resist the idea that it took a powerful and thirsty engine to make these crossings safe. We could lift our Mirror above the high-water mark without the worries a heavier craft would bring – leaving it at anchor or stressing about the possibility of an expensive engine being drowned.

I came across some old slides that catch something of the experience the customised Mirror, *Semblance*, brought us to. Sean and Barbara are seated on the rocks. They are both doing nothing other than looking out to sea. This time, the enclosed lagoon on the west side is greyish rather than its usual turquoise. I can recall the eery echoing of crested shags nesting within a huge natural arch. In another slide a very young Ben is looking downwards to his feet, swamped by cottongrass. He is sensing the orchid-rich pasture that lies in the glen between our landing place and the grey lagoon.

This is still rich grazing and the raised ribs on the slopes, mainland and island, reveal that much of the terrain was cultivated to feed a significant population. The stretches of sands are at the white end of the yellow spectrum. Unless you're close enough to see the pink thrift, the rocks are mainly in a paler range of greys. More heron than raven. The higher islands and the pronounced headlands make West Loch Roag a refuge from the turmoil of the open Atlantic. You can still get a surge of power that will gather fleets of lobster pots and mangle them into pretty scrap along the shores.

For several years our family returned, from time to time, making that crossing in our sailing tardis of orange and white. Once there was a group of four students from a college in North Carolina. Students took at least one 'practical' subject as well as any academic course. So Kate, for example, took English literature as a major with a minor in plumbing. Our friend, the folklorist Margaret Bennett, was a guest lecturer at their college. She had brokered this visit. The students paid for their keep in chores. Our peats were never tidier. Our reputation in the village was never higher than when one fellow convinced a neighbour he was being charged for the privilege of cutting them. The Mirror was hard-worked, that trip, sailing folk across, two at a time, with myself at the helm. It never seemed strained.

Our lads played with any kids who happened to be on the island beach. None of them seemed to bother much about different languages or different accents. One time an older boy said to Sean, 'You know that my father owns this whole island?' And I remember Sean gently pointing out that we also had an equal right to land there, camp and leave nothing behind us when we left.

The crossing is short and we only ever made the trip in settled weather. The question I now have to ask myself is why I think of the crossings in that dinghy to islands a few cables out as voyages that left all the family and our companions changed, afterwards. At that time I would have been paid to put some hours on the powerful outboards of the under-used coastguard inflatable craft but I chose to launch our own dinghy instead. The stubby-looking craft would come alive. She would lean towards the wind, board down and hold her track. She would skite in spray, downwind, board up. The droplets would be caught in an intense light. Yet all of this would only happen if you perceived where the wind was coming from and tuned the sheets according to your angle to that breeze. *Semblance* would take family and visitors over the yellow shallows and past a russet kelp line to where the sea swirled deep like squid ink.

The other part of my answer lies in much older narratives. My mother once told me that one strand of her family background could be traced to the MacAulays who once prospered on the fertile peninsula of Valtos*. She grew angry when people said the Highland Clearances had not affected Lewis because that family had been cleared to the stonier ground that lies to the north of East Loch Roag. There are well-researched accounts of such evictions.**

My mother died quite young so Sean and Ben never had the chance to hear her stories or appreciate the speed of her wit. The lads have been recognised in the town as coming from her family, just from the look of them, with their wavy ginger hair and a good crop of freckles. Her own father died too young for me to really get to know

---

* Part of the family crofting history is told in a book written by one of my mother's brothers: *Around the Peat-Fire*, Calum Smith, Birlinn, Edinburgh, 2010.

** www.ceuig.co.uk/the-clearance-of-vuia-mor/

him. His gifts as a storyteller and principled orator have become a Lewis legend. He would have known all the lore of clan disputes. By good fortune, these oral legends have been valued by those who could transcribe them. One Donald Morrison, born 1787 in the Uig area of Lewis, became a cooper by trade. He increased his own stock of stories from under the clouds of black twist tobacco that hung over the herring town of Stornoway. One volume of his collection was lost but another two were published in the 1970s. This is one he wrote out in English.* I'm retelling it here, in the same way as my mother retold stories. By way of introduction, I've reframed a few lines in celebration of *Semblance*, the Mirror that skimmed us over water. I'd forgotten that she was once red.

The skin of the Mirror
blisters through sheen.
Laminates buckle.

Red leaves
flake to the deck
of the neighbour's shed
– lost gloss.

When material falls
there is residue
that finds its own
new content

and on the decks
or paving
or planking
or on our grasses

* The same story is told in a very detailed form, as the very first tale in the collection published as: *The Morrison Manuscript: Traditions of the Western Isles*. Author, Donald Morrison. Editor, Norman Macdonald. Stornoway Public Library, 1975.

detritus

becomes

a new thing.

Sons and their Fathers

Like many disputes, it all started over livestock. The MacAulay stronghold was on the fertile Valtos peninsula on the west side of the Isle of Lewis and they kept a good head of cattle. But one Norman Macleod, a brother of the clan chief, lived across from there on the island of Pabbay Mor. This family was also known to keep beasts of high quality.

The Macleods would ferry their stock back and fore across the narrow Sound. One day, a cow belonging to the mainland MacAulays strayed into the Macleod herd, just as the beasts were being boarded for the crossing. The MacAulay cowherd came looking for the cow that had gone astray. He recognised the animal at once. But old Norman Macleod was there himself and he did not seem to notice that one of the beasts they'd boarded was not their own. The herder ran for the MacAulay lads and several of them arrived at the shore, just as their neighbour's boat was about to depart for the island.

One of the young MacAulays waded out, put a hand over the gunnel and placed the other firmly on one horn of their own beast. Old Norman put his hand on the other. The MacAulay lad gave his horn a tug. The older man fell face first into the vessel and came up with two of his teeth loose in his mouth. He was taken home to Pabbay along with their stock, less the beast that was reclaimed. Seeing the blood, his wife wanted the full story. Her husband just grunted and took to bed with a dram, but his wife was not one to let matters go.

She waited until their five sons returned from a seal hunt out at the Flannan Isles, then threw their father's teeth on the table. They were being accused of being cattle thieves, she said. Old Norman Macleod knew nothing of this till he heard the clamour, over the water, in the still night air. His sons were attacking the MacAulays across on the peninsula. The aim was to kill every last one of the males in the family. Men and boys were slain as they slept, all but two.

One survivor was a son, born out of wedlock but still kept among the family. The Macleod brothers got a hold of this infant and cast him over a wall. His leg was badly broken. He lived but could never be much of a threat to anyone. The other had been fostered out to a childless relation at Mealasta, down the coast, so he escaped the fate of his brothers. That was John Roy MacAulay and we'll hear more of him.

When Norman Macleod found out what his sons had done he shook his head in shame. There would be no end to this feud now. The MacAulays had their kinsmen in other districts. They would be bound to seek revenge. He knew at once he was likely to lose all his own sons in the reprisals that would follow. His own brother, the clan chief, closed his eyes when he heard of the murders committed in the clan's name.

'What can we do, to put an end to this feud?' Norman asked.

'I can think of only one thing that could help,' replied the Macleod chief. 'We must bring that orphan MacAulay lad into our protection. If anything happens to him, there will be centuries of bloodshed.'

The orphan John Roy MacAulay was still with his foster father, a man known as Dark Finlay. Norman Macleod and his brother the chief set out to talk to this man, taking their ponies down the rough track to the settlement of Mealasta, nestled between the shoreline and the hills. The island of the same name lies about half a mile out to sea in the direction of Scarp.

They could never make amends for the massacre but they could offer to give every advantage to young John Roy. Finlay and his wife could hardly bear to give up their foster-son, but they could see that he would receive an education they could never provide. This might also be the only way to break the spiral of revenge.

They gave their permission, on condition that John Roy would be protected and that he would be brought back to their home at the Yuletide and New Year.

Norman Macleod did look after the boy, taken into his family. He taught him how to fish and how to sail and how to hunt. The clear waters out from these sandy shores abound with dabs and haddock. Heavy red deer make their strangely delicate runs on the high ground up from Valtos peninsula. He treated John Roy, in every way, with a tenderness you might think you'd find only for those of your own blood.

However, this treatment instilled jealousy in the same fellows who had taken up arms to avenge what their mother saw as a slight on the family. And the mother did not have her husband's feelings for the young MacAulay lad who was now under their roof. Norman seemed to have more time for the youngster than he'd ever had for their own sons.

The young lad was growing, both in stature and confidence. Norman wanted his sons to befriend their adopted brother. 'Take him with you, to the hill. He won't hold you back and he's good company. But remember our family's promise to make sure he comes to no harm.'

At last, one November, the Macleod brothers did take the growing lad out with them, heading beyond Kinlochresort, a deep inlet a few miles to the south of the pathway end at Mealasta village. Beyond that there is only a faint track, over the high ground. The Macleod family had the use of a shieling out there, with a stock of peats, cut in the spring and gathered in the summer. This was known as Kenneth's bothy. There was the promise of snow but the hunters would stay out, overnight, snug. They would pass John Roy's former home, at Mealasta, on the way.

Dark Finlay missed John Roy every day, but he consoled himself with the knowledge that the boy would get a good start in life. He would also play his part in trying to heal that terrible rift.

However, that very night, when young John Roy had passed by on the coastal path with the Macleod brothers, Dark Finlay could find no rest. He woke up in a sweat. He was listening to the blast of the north wind. He woke with the dream of his foster-son, in danger. He could see the lad, out in the cold, exposed to the falling snow. His wife said it was nothing but natural anxiety.

He woke a second time. Again, he was persuaded to lay his head back down. When he woke for the third time, the foster-father could see the very place, Kenneth's bothy, out beyond Kinlochresort. He saw the poorly clad boy, shivering, out in the open. This time he dressed and prepared to walk out into the night. He paused only to ask his wife to fetch some fresh milk from the cow. She heated it further and placed it in a small bag of hide. Finlay wrapped that in sheepskin, to keep it warm.

Even in the flurries of snow, Dark Finlay recognised the marker stones – simply a few boulders and slabs, leaning against each other. They were enough to suggest a route over the bare hill. He was still agile but he knew he was up against ruthless men. The snow was lying, at the final stretch. Finlay walked backwards from that point on so the prints he left would appear to be heading northwards.

At last he came to the very spot he had seen three times in his dreams. He listened and heard weak moans. He found his foster-son dressed only in a long shirt and tied to a rock. The Macleod brothers had left John Roy to die in the cold. No doubt they would make up some story of being separated in the snowfall and planned to return with the lifeless body.

Instead, Finlay put some drops of warm milk to the lips of the boy. He wrapped him well and put John Roy on his shoulders, where his own body heat would get through to the shivering soul. He knew that the Macleod sons would soon be back.

That squat but wiry man retraced his own footsteps, but this time he walked forwards with his precious cargo, placing his feet in the tracks he had already made. That way the trail would suggest that John Roy had made his own escape. The tracks would fade when they descended again, to the heather.

First, they found shelter in a cave with two entrances and a warning stone that would clatter if anyone came close. When he had to fetch provisions, he left John Roy with a trusted man. The two took turns to keep watch.

The warning stone clattered. The companion was grabbed by the Macleod brothers, but then John Roy showed himself. He held the captors at the point of his arrows until his kinsman was released. This time they had escaped by their wits, but everyone knew it was only a matter of time before the surviving young MacAulay was taken.

Dark Finlay met with Norman Macleod, who was devastated by the actions of his sons. It was decided that the fast-growing boy must leave Lewis for a time. He'd be safer under the protection of the MacLeans at Lochbuie, down in the Isle of Mull. He was to remain on that island for seven years.

The old chief disowned his own nephews and said he would not intervene if the returning MacAulay were to seek justice. MacLean of Lochbuie also backed the young man's claim. Old Norman Macleod became withdrawn. He must have blamed himself for the pride that started a cycle of revenge that now seemed impossible to stop. He must have been estranged from his wife, who had played her own part. He has no other active role in the story but you have to imagine him bearing witness to it all. Waiting.

John Roy sailed first for Harris in one of MacLean's birlinns. Then he crossed that same track to Mealasta to visit Dark Finlay, who had once rescued him. His wiry foster-father hugged him close but knew he could not be held back. John Roy had trained his body by running over the high ridges of Mull. He knew how to soak his sharpening stone first in water then drip more drops on it as the blade passed back and fore, always at the same angle. Sword, dirk and arrows all had edges and tips. Before he left the home of the man who had carried him through the snow, he whetted each edge once more.

First he went to the region close to the sanctuary at Baile na Cille, across the Uig sands. Young Norman, one of those Macleod brothers, had stayed close to the tumbling stone for all of the seven years. He expected vengeance at any time. He knew that no man would use his blade within the bounds of a sanctified space. But just how close to it could you remain all that time?

'Who is that tall man, crossing the sands?' he said, to his servant. Who could say, at that distance? But the nervous man who had once left John Roy for dead in the blizzard was now the fugitive. 'I'd know him,' he said. 'There's a way he has of putting his hand to keep his bonnet on his head when he's crossing the burn.' And that was exactly the movement he observed as the tall man strode closer.

Norman the younger made a run for the sanctuary. It was no great distance but his feet were taken from under him before he reached it. This was John Roy's first strike. It showed that he had been well taught in the art of swordsmanship on the island of Mull.

Next he overtook two of the remaining brothers, who were ashore at Valtos to court two girls. They could not have known that a very different promise was to be met. John Roy sent his arrows first, to separate them. Then he strode the ground with an impossible burst of speed and took first one then the other, hitting close with the short blade. Since that day, the sites of his revenge are known as William's plain and Alan's strand.

There were only two others to find. John Roy sought out his crippled half-brother, the one who was injured on the night of the murders that had led to this. That fellow had grown wily and soon pointed out the last two brothers who had taken part in that massacre. Neither was any match for the man who had once been left to die in the hail. John Roy then crossed to the island of Pabbay Mor. He knew that old Norman's wife was the main force behind the tragedy. He made sure the old man would be cared for, then he looked Norman's wife in the eye. She could live but only if she took herself back to her native Skye.

Now there was just one last surviving son of that same Norman Macleod. He had been fostered over in the east side of Lewis, a favour to a childless relation. That young man had taken no part in the killing of the MacAulays at Reef, but none could be left if the vengeance was to be completed. After all, John Roy had been the sole able-bodied survivor in his own family and he had lived to play his role.

One foster-son pursued another. The chase went through thick heather and bracken as far as the shore across from the town of Stornoway. Even in his exhaustion, the last Macleod brother took to the water. He attempted the swim across the harbour to reach the safety of the castle that stood there then. He did not get far. His enemy still had three arrows left. One to find the range. One to wound. One to kill.

The old Macleod chief kept his word. John Roy was granted an Uig farm, free of rent, for the rest of his life. He married the daughter of MacLean of Lochbuie and they had a son. It would be good if we could say that peace followed on from then, down the generations. But I think you all know that there were conflicts still to come. That very son of John Roy was to become a hero to some and an outcast to others.

Mealasta Island

MEALASTA ISLAND DID NOT SEEM MUCH further from the shore than Pabbay Mor but I knew to be cautious about approaching this crossing in a Mirror dinghy. As a coastguard, you have the benefit of observing many instances of things going wrong at sea. You could also learn from the stories of your watchmates, as long as you felt they were worth listening to. Our area of responsibility reached about halfway across towards St John's, Newfoundland. Ocean planning charts showed magenta wind roses. These indicated prevailing winds that were mainly south-westerly. Every year you could expect a high instance of gales. Storms would rise to the Beaufort hurricane strength of force 12, at some point, most winters. The depth contours in standard Admiralty charts show the banks west of the Outer Hebrides. There is a metric equivalent of the 'hundred fathom line'. Inside this, moving towards our islands, the depth shallows further. You will see a colour shading that indicates another depth contour, closer to land. Waves that have been building for hundreds of sea miles meet that line.

Even in summer, I knew that you could not afford to get caught by strong winds in this area. All that weight of water has no longer enough depth to hold it, so the long waves shorten in length and grow steep. At some stage, they will break. Then an impossible amount of energy will be released from the potential power of moving brine. Surfers have discovered this and now court Atlantic depressions. Wet-suit technology has allowed them to deal with the factor of cold but there are still conditions when no sane person will enter the sea. More than one Hebridean seaman has told me that the steepest waves he has seen were not in the Southern Ocean but close to his own home shore on a dirty night.

Tidal information is scant here. The currents are not as unpredictable as the Sound of Harris, which confounds even the *West Coast of Scotland Pilot*. But there is simply not enough documented information. You can't just open a sheaf of summaries and note the extent and time of the major currrents, the way you can for the waters round Rathlin Island in the North Channel or Stroma and Swona in Pentland Firth. That said, Mealasta Island is less than half an hour's crossing in a dinghy, given fair breeze. It might take an hour to tack against it.

I judged it safe for our Mirror, in light wind and neap tides, if we were not overloaded. I would make no commitment in advance and pick our day. As it happened, this fell when we had promised to show two keen visitors parts of our island chain they might not otherwise reach. We were a family of four, with a London-based jazz singer and her pal in tow. Neither had done much sailing but both were eager to make the crossing. We would not stay overnight so there was not much equipment to carry. We had food and flasks of hot drinks and some dry clothes. I judged three persons to be the maximum number for the Mirror, so that meant three crossings.

We had a dress rehearsal with the visitors close to the slipway so they grew used to moving their weight when the boat had to tack through the wind. Then I made the first landing. Sean and Ben both bounced from the dinghy into the smooth swell, just off the most innocent-seeming yellow-white slope of sand. They were up over their waists, but this lightened the craft. I pulled up the daggerboard at the last minute and we were all safe ashore. That was trickier than expected. It is deep right up close, unlike the shallow and sheltered landing places we were used to. I knew the lads would take delight in wading in to help the others ashore. They were both strong swimmers but I still insisted on buoyancy aids in the dinghy.

We three had our moments of wonder before I had to return, leaving my sons stranded. *Semblance* squatted on the beach and made a loud feature against the green sea. The island of Scarp rose high from the blue a few miles to the south. The ridges of North Harris, eastwards across a mile or so of sea, seemed immense though we had all been to the summit of Clisham, the highest, at just under 3,000 feet. Sea eagles were a rare sight then but it was almost routine to catch the high patrol of a golden eagle up over the Harris coast. Sometimes it would be signalled by ravens trying to harass the great bird from their own airspace.

I took Barbara and the bags of food and clothing on the next trip. I was gaining experience of the crossing with those who could sail and who knew the craft. The two young women came next. They were already handy in the tight space. I warned everyone about the landing but I think we all got wet just the same. The steady breeze would dry us off. For me, the day was largely taken up with my ferryman's duties. I savoured the vista, each solo return. I shared in a group sense of wonder, once the Mirror was safe, up the tideline. We had some hours to explore. We could all imagine the lives of those who had piled up sufficient soil and seaweed to grow their barley in this place that seemed to us anything but domestic.

Then came the roar of the RIB. It was a Sunday afternoon. The island's estates did not take part in either stalking or angling on the Sunday. Partly it is a show of respect for tradition and partly it is a conservation measure. I had no idea that Mealasta Island was under the jurisdiction of a privately owned estate. These paying guests had come, with the estate manager, simulating a family picnic. They proved louder than all the horses of their single outboard motor. Though they seemed to go discreetly to the next bay, where a mooring was ready for the inflatable craft, their beach games shouted across. I think we were all snobbish because we had earned our right to be there by going quietly with the wind, though I did have a small outboard on the transom in case of rig failure.

It was time to begin the return, which would again involve three short trips. The wind had freshened a bit so we took a roll or two of the red sail round the boom. Then she was comfortable, though the launching and boarding were still tricky. *Semblance* had just worked clear of the outlying reefs off the mainland slipway, out for the last pick-up from the island, when I heard the estate boat coming close. Our two friends were aboard. They came alongside the Mirror before the inflatable dropped them at the slip. I said nothing as the manager told me it was a bit irresponsible, taking people out there in a small dinghy. 'There are big tides here, you know.'

I never said that that was why we had timed the trip for neaps and our landings at the day's slack-water periods. I looked to their single outboard, with no auxiliary. I knew first-hand that it was impossible to control, far less propel, these inflatables with the paddles supplied but I did not say any of that either. The Mirror's oars are very simple. They look crude but they are effective. The women looked to my silence and thanked the man who had brought them from that beach and shortened their return. He made one more effort.

'At least I've saved you a trip.'

'Aye, thanks.'

The jazz singer said it once I was back ashore at the slip. 'We shouldn't have accepted, should we?'

'He thought he was doing us a favour,' I said. 'Anyway, we're all back safe.'

More than 25 years have passed since the day we crossed to that island. Sean now manages an outdoor-education centre in Harris. He teaches sailing and leads coastal and mountain courses. Ben is a professional drummer. He travels all over Europe to play in a gypsy-punk band but loves to come 'home' and walk the coasts abeam the islands we always mean to go back to. Their mother, Barbara, who is no longer my wife, has had her own small craft, of sweet lines, built in Scottish larch by a friend. Much of Harris and much of the Uig and west-coast areas of our Long Island are in community ownership after legal buy-outs. At least one was a hostile takeover from an unwilling landowner. This was made legal by the Scottish Parliament's legislation, applicable if a majority of the population hold crofting tenure.

We're nowhere near a Utopia. There are drug problems as well as religious conflicts, as in most places. Our harbours have shifted from being mainly havens for fishing craft to providing marina berths for visiting yachts. But the decline in our population has slowed. Community housing has been built under these imposing hills. In the interim there have been two 'take it or leave it' offers from multinational companies. One would have made us the largest superquarry in the world and the other, the largest single wind farm. Both were eventually declined, once the balance sheet of probable jobs gained was set against probable jobs lost to the tourism industry. Smaller-scale wind farms and research into other renewable energies have provided some work and even a trickle of funds to put back into community-owned development. Tweed is being made again in a snazzy range of shades. It's back in fashion, but who knows for how long.

There is a story rooted in the very island we were able to land on. The tone of it has something of the challenge and drama of living in that less-sheltered place. First, I have some lines. I've spliced together some phrases, jotted down around the time of our island-going with some from a much later return to the mainland area, with Ben.

How yellow, gold and even white are
all necessary but not sufficient
to indicate the sweating beach
on Mealasta island.

How green, even male mallard green,
even shag green under the crest
are not enough to say the colour
of the suck of the seep in the geo
on the track between the two road-ends.

Some of the illuminations
came on for us
in the last gasp
of a short day.
Mealasval sulked.
Suinaval shone.

The Girl who Dreamed the Song

There are narrow but fertile strips of land on the shorelines of the Uig district. The green on Mealasta Island also shines out, above a pale yellow beach, visible from across the Sound. That's yet another of our islands that once supported a population of its own.

They did well for grazing and for runs of salmon and sea trout migrating past them in season. When the high swell, usually running there, damped down to allow passage for their boat, they took their share of a sea harvest. They salted the split sides of cod or ling and dried them on the rocks so they could sell them. They ate the white-bellied flatfish that did not cure so well. They also took a proportion of shag and cormorant from the rocks.

These people just about lived aboard their boats. They were not like the *Hiortach* (St Kildans) further out in the ocean, who would only take to a boat out of necessity. Like their neighbours, the *Scalpeach*, the Mealasta folk would think nothing of sailing or rowing 20 miles to call in and see a neighbour or trade some provisions. Both communities used stout boats built by an Uig man. They had a wide beam on them, which would help them deal with the huge swell most of the time.

There is a story of one of the last in a family of these builders. They say he could build a boat, a substantial one, in a fortnight. Everything had to be ready for him – the timber, the nails, the helpers, the fire for steam and the pit for sawing. He gave out his directions. When they assured him all was ready he would come and just go at it. At the end of the fortnight there would be a boat ready for them to coat with pitch, to protect it. And the vessel he built would look after the men who sailed or rowed it.

The boatbuilder had a keen eye for a shape and the skill in the hands to bring it to life, without drawings or patterns. The shell of the boat might be there in two weeks but in another way it had taken many generations to find its shape. Some also say that a boat is not the only thing he left. They claim there was a whole line of strong lads and powerful girls, from Valtos to Hushinish.

The Mealasta boat would probably have been 20 feet or more. You'd think they couldn't haul a vessel like that up ashore – but they did. They were not as heavy as they looked. The building was economical in design, to save weight and work as well as precious timber.

Which brings us back to the reason the Mealasta men were taking to the sea this time. Families were growing. There was no shortage of stone which could be selected to build a new home with low stout walls. There was plenty of turf to roof it but you need timbers to span the walls. As in most isolated places, the jobs of the day were agreed collectively. One time, the gathering decided to take their best boat across to the east side of Harris, then cross from there to Gairloch. There was a link – a neighbour had married a daughter of one of the mainland MacKenzies.

The islanders were to have the run of the MacKenzie forests. They could take all they could carry safely in their own boat. It's no small thing to take an open vessel down abeam Scarp and Taransay, on through the Sound of Harris to enter the Minches. But that's what they did. And that was just the beginning of their voyage, steering for the great, glinting heights of Torridon.

I don't doubt but there was good hospitality across the other side. People loved to meet and get the news of family in other places. How was so and so doing? And that daughter of theirs, had no one snapped her up yet? There's more to catch than fish, boys. And so on. One story would lead to another after the work was done. But then it was time to set off back across the Minch with that precious cargo all carefully stowed so the boat was still seaworthy.

There were no forecasts to speak of then, only a whole range of sayings and they didn't always agree. That boat left with a favourable wind but it freshened to a near-gale. It's the snow squalls with a bit of the north in them you've to watch. That can bring lethal gusts. And when the snow flurries come, you can't make out a thing. On top of that, the boat was well laden. If a sea broke at the stern, the water was in. They would have aimed for the shortest crossing of the North Minch, maybe in the lee of the Shiants.

These fellows were famous for their skills and confidence in boats, under sail or under oars. The lads must have pulled together, worked the tack and the halyard so they were as one. That seamanship would bring them into the shelter of one of the inlets across from the Shiant Islands. There were no roads to the small settlements there. The boat of the Mealasta men was seen, and the people who saw them also saw that they were carrying a cargo of good, long logs.

Now we return to the west side of Lewis and the waiting women and children on Mealasta Island. They would have sniffed the changing breeze, felt the flurries of sleet. Heard the whistling gale. They would have prayed for their men. And they would have had no means of knowing how they were faring. With each passing day they would have grown more anxious. Then the days became weeks. People cling to hope, the way you might clutch at fronds of bladderwrack if you lost your footing and fell into deep water. One night, one of the waiting women had a dream that was so vivid she woke with its contents in a song.

The melody and the language came together. She sang it, first to herself, then she sang it again, to the other women. The song is in the voice of the man she was promised to. They still sing it in Uig. Her man came to her to let her know for sure he would not be stepping ashore at the steep beach of Mealasta Island. Their boat had taken the lads and their cargo through the gale. Their skipper had taken them by foaming reefs close to a small island and they had found anchorage. That was where they were struck. There were other men in need of timber to build their roofs. Thirsty and weakened by hours of fighting steep seas, the Mealasta men were easy prey. The timber was taken but the vessel, which would tell its own story, was burned.

How far could you trust the words that came to a grieving young woman in her dream? Some still clung to hope even after a message arrived from across the Minch. The Mealasta boat had certainly departed from the anchorage at Badachro, near Gairloch harbour. There were no other sightings, no more messages from the mainland nor across the Minch.

There must come a stage when it's a mercy to know the truth for sure. Even if the news is terrible then life can slowly begin to progress again. It was one year after the boat's departure when the girl who dreamed the song was with others from Uig at Beinn na Dròbh. This was the big market gathering outside the town of Stornoway. They came to it from all over the island. This was probably the only time when people from the far-flung corners would meet, unless they travelled to religious communions.

My mother would tell me about the market – it went on right into her own day. She would have one penny to spend. She could never decide between gingerbread and lemonade. She couldn't have both.

The girl who dreamed the song came to the Dròbh with a few of the others. Fellow islanders probably wanted to make sure that something at least was done to lift the spirits of those whose men had vanished without a trace. That girl was in a queue at the gingerbread stall. Her eye fell on the back of the man in front of her. She saw patterns she knew well enough. She knew them because her own hands had knitted them. It was a seaman's *gansey* made to fit snug. It had patterns in it that were a bit different from anyone else's. Her heart hammered against her bones when she saw it.

When the man that wore it as his own turned round she saw he was a stranger. Her scream was heard above all the sounds of the drovers' market.

The un-named Uig storyteller who passed on this tale reports that the teller was not aware of the conclusion. I've asked my friend, Maggie Smith, who has followed up versions of the song and story in the Uig area but she doesn't know either. Maybe there was enough evidence then for the law to take its course. That is a part of the purpose of the individual patterns in a *gansey* – to identify the drowned. But the man it was made for had not drowned. Maybe a confession or further evidence would not have made much difference. The Uig men would have seen justice done, even if it wasn't done by law.

But Maggie told me something else. She said that in one part of Uig, quite possibly Mealasta Island, there was the boat of the women. There had been a terrible loss – of a boat and its crew and it might even have been the very boat in the story – but there was also a smaller vessel that belonged to the village. There were not enough able-bodied men left to sail her and a community in that place could not survive without a boat, so she became the boat of the women. And, Maggie says, they were well respected all throughout the district.

Semblance became Sean's responsibility. She was left on her trailer but water would get in under the cover and not drain away. She needed bailing from time to time. Water is heavy. I was probably too hard on Sean when this did not happen and the hull was holed again, by pressure from the metalwork. Working 12-hour coastguard shifts, time off was precious and I had no appetite for further repairs. Another family took charge, made good use of her for a while and passed her on. Sadly, she was later wrecked, ashore, in a storm in the Uig district.

Sean put a great deal of work into projects around our house and I found him another Mirror as fair payment. This one was in sound condition and just needed a lick of paint. This time, the stencilled intervention on the hull was his own idea.

'Can you show me how to do that stencilling on the underside, Da?'

'Sure I can. What's the text?'

'PTO,' he said. 'In big letters.' I worked out the lettering on computer and printed it out on card. I put a new blade in a scalpel and Sean cut the script. His first attempt left the letters smudged but I showed him how to make sure the paint was applied sparingly with the stubby stencil brush.

There is a slide of him doing capsize drills with the request showing, sharp white on a blue ground. Two pals also had Mirrors and the three were out in the harbour every chance. They looked after each other and learned together.

An Sulaire

THERE IS A FAMILY OF VESSELS OF NORSE origins distributed throughout the Northern and Western Isles of Scotland and the mainland coasts. The technology of building boats by overlaying shaped planks is called clinker boatbuilding. This has remained unchanged since Viking times because it works. A keel is laid, usually in oak, and the planks, which are often a lighter but durable timber such as larch, are laid, one by one, to make the shape of the boat. Frames, for strengthening, are added later.

The size and shape of the vessel will vary according to its purpose as well as the purse of those who commission it. In the 19th century there was an expansion of boatbuilding in Shetland and in Lewis to supply larger vessels for an offshore fishery. The *sixern* and the *sgoth Niseach* were built to about 33 feet long, to enable them to work up to 40 miles offshore.

The Shetland boats were combination rowing and sailing vessels and equipped with a Norse square-sail. The North Lewis boats were beamier and higher in freeboard – the area of planking above the waterline. This made them harder work to row but probably better craft for open-ocean sailing. They carried the large, single, dipping lug sail on a long yard, as already described, but of course in proportion to the scale of the craft. The full-sized *sgoth* was labour-intensive, requiring good crew coordination to 'dip' the sail to the other side of the mast when changing direction. Vessels such as these would have had six strong fishermen and a keen lad aboard.

Surviving photographs and oral history document fleets of the large class of *sgoth Niseach* in the harbour at Port of Ness and on the shorelines of other North Lewis townships, such as Tolsta. The lines are very similar to those of the Stroma yoles, built to work in similar conditions – the currents and steep seas of Pentland Firth. These are close cousins in the international family of vessels, developed from Norse craft for varying purposes and varying conditions. Orkney and Lewis vessels have substantial beam to allow them to carry loads, whether stock, peats or the catch. This also resists heeling, so they can carry sails of sufficient power to cut through high seas. The rounded sterns were a matter of the builder's pride but the shape also provides buoyancy well aft so she will rise and surf on a following sea.

Because they were shore-launched boats, they could not be too deep. Stability was given by that beamy shape and by the addition of ballast, to make her float a little deeper in the water. Additional weight, deep in the body of the hull, can help resist the forces that will cause her to lean over or drift sideways. That ballast would originally have been round boulders, carefully placed. I've heard one man describe the selection and arrangement of stones as building a garden in the bilges of the boat. The stones could not be allowed to shift when she got a pounding.

Miles of 'greatlines' were set, off North Lewis, to take quality cod and ling. Ballast was jettisoned as the weight of fish increased. Bringing the vessel back to a shore of pounding surf or into a poorly protected harbour was often no easy thing. Back ashore, the catch was salted and dried on the rocks, for export. For some, this dangerous fishery was bondage – a means of paying rent to the landlord who supplied the vessel and gear. To others, it was adventure and enterprise – a chance to earn real currency from your own skills and labour.

By the 1970s there were no surviving examples of the larger *sgoth Niseach*. There were photographs, some wreckage, a model, drawings and memories. There was also a man who wanted to construct an example of the craft his father used to build. And there was a younger man who wanted to make a film that would document the complete process of how a growing tree could become the recreation of a historic vessel. First, John Murdo Macleod worked with a team of helpers to return the last surviving *sgoth Niseach*, one of a smaller class, to her original lines and rig. This was the 27-foot *Jubilee*, built by his father in 1935. The restoration was a vital project in its own right. It was also a first step towards building a new 33-foot *sgoth*.

Jubilee survived because she was motorised and kept in use as a working fishing boat. It's the east wind that kills boats, left to crack and dry away from the sea. Fresh water, from rainfall, will also cause rot, if left to lie in undrained parts. Saltwater and mud won't harm the vessel much, though these will destroy any machinery that has been installed.

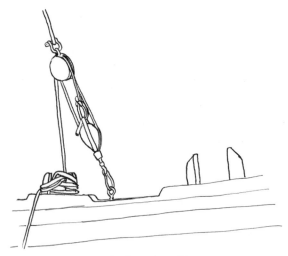

Block and tackle

The original *sgoth Niseach* had no machinery. The gear was very simple. Blocks and tackle were used to lift the heavy spar that carried the large sail up the mast. The same tackle supported that mast and was shifted aft to lower it when the boat was launched and recovered.

First, the spar (or 'yard') was brought down, under control, and set to one side of the craft, to leave a clear space for lowering the mast. That heavier spar was lowered out forward, on the tackle. It was then hauled back into the body of the vessel. All the gear had to fit within the length of the boat.

The Shetland *sixern* used a tackle on the sheet – the rope that controls the sail. This makes it easier to adjust but it is one more thing that can jam. The Lewis boats used only a single rope, carried through a hole in the top plank at the aft end of the boat. That could be taken round a strong point of timber (belayed) in such a way that it would slip and ease the pressure in a gust.

In my last year of working for the coastguard service, 1994–1995, I was one of the many visitors who would call by the shed where

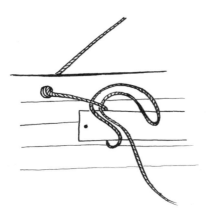

Belayed sheet

John Murdo Macleod was building the boat that would carry his father's knowledge onwards. My friend Sam Maynard had left his job as staff photographer on the *Stornoway Gazette* to make films, which were also shapes he carried in his own head. He saw the passing of the boatbuilder's skills to his assistant as a vital part of the project. Sadly, this has not yet resulted in another similar vessel being built, but we do now have a new working example of the large *sgoth Niseach* as well as *Jubilee*. We also have *An Sgoth*, a beautiful and accurate documentary film, shot by Sam, telling the whole story 'from tree to sea'.*

An Sulaire (The Gannet) was fastened with copper and bronze rather than iron. She carried lead ingots rather than stones, to concentrate the ballast. Like the original boats, she had a basic hand pump, which could remove water taken on board through the hollow, aft thwart of the vessel. This was fairly effective but hard work. Her sail and cordage was synthetic rather than of hemp or sisal. Apart from these modern improvements, she was a demanding open boat with heavy oars as secondary propulsion. Then, she had no navigation

---

* *an Sgoth, from tree to sea*, Sam Maynard, BBC2/MacTV (available from *Falmadair*).

lights or fixed battery for a radio. She did not carry a liferaft and had no additional buoyancy fitted. I knew from my experience of open boats that she was likely to sink if she was ever filled with sea when fully ballasted and also carried the combined weight of a full crew and all their gear.

She was finished in clear oil, inside and out, apart from her antifouling below the waterline in 'trawler red'. There was a whalemouth of white paint on the waterline at her bow. Her top strake was painted in the black-and-white checkerboard effect unique to the boats that had worked out of Port of Ness. Her fishing numbers had been applied by the local expert, in the local manner. She was a vessel to be proud of. But her shape was discussed more than her finish. Her stern was ample and well-rounded, like that of *Jubilee*. Her bow was different, carrying more of her fullness forwards. Some thought she was not as bonny as *Jubilee*, with her sharper bow. I viewed *an Sulaire* from different angles. There would be times when her crew was grateful for every bit of that interior fullness. It would help her bow rise to big water.

Isle of Lewis to Isle of Mull

As a committee member of the trust established to keep the new *sgoth Niseach* in commission, I argued for the installation of some minimum safety equipment but I was not ready to be considered as a skipper. In 15 years of coastguard service I had seen many things go wrong in the changeable waters of the Outer Hebrides. And there was a break in the chain of passing on the range of skills needed to navigate these powerful open boats with some degree of safety. The launch of *an Sulaire*, her larch planking glistening in Norwegian oil, made us all proud. Between the demands of shiftwork and fatherhood, I had only contributed a few hours of sanding and painting. It is difficult to describe what the re-creation of a unique type of craft means to an islander. On the day of her first launching, people who would never sail her turned out to watch her glide by.

My admiration always included an element of fear. It takes physical strength and coordinated actions to hoist the long yard that stretches her huge tan sail. Even in light wind it takes more than one strong person to 'trim' her thick sheet, in and out, to shape the curve of that cloth. It was therefore just as well that three or four souls were gallus enough to take charge. That Scots word is the only one I know to convey the mixture of qualities required: 'self-confident, daring, cheeky, stylish, impressive...'* among them. A measure of prudence, in with all that, would not go amiss.

My elder son, Sean, and myself joined the crew on a delivery trip, aiming to take *an Sulaire* to Lochmaddy. This was the first leg of an intended voyage to the islands of Tiree, Iona and Mull. Sean was in his early teens.

This was only a couple of seasons after her launch. New crews and skippers were learning the art of handling such a vessel. By this time, she was fitted with a tricolour navigation light, so she could tackle longer passages. There had been debates on whether to install an auxiliary engine, inboard or outboard, but nothing had been agreed. The fully charged battery could also power a GPS. This piece of electronic magic was still fairly new and they tended to devour internal batteries. We also had a hand-held VHF radio, a compass and laminated charts, along with enough lifejackets for all, a man-overboard buoy and not much else.

The forecast was very light wind, drizzle, then a freshening northerly later. Much later. I couldn't see why we were leaving on a boat without any motor propulsion when there was little chance of breeze for many hours. Then I realised that our skipper had assembled his team and was not keen on letting them go again in case he lost them to the pub or the football. Sean and I brought our sleeping bags and polythene bivvy-sacks, flasks of soup and coffee and a box

---

* *The Concise Scots Dictionary*, Mairi Robinson, Aberdeen University Press, 1985 (many new editions eg Polygon, Edinburgh University Press and online versions).

of grub. Father and son would be able to keep warm between our spells of rowing. Without an engine to keep the speed up in light or contrary winds, you can't really know how long a trip will take.

There were one or two folk who had sailed in this craft before but others in our crew did not know what to expect. There was enough food for all but some were not prepared for camping, or the possibility of an overnight passage. Rowing means different things to different people. I had watched cigar-shaped skiffs skim across the Don, in Aberdeen. Their oars are hollow-shafted, of clear light spruce. They end in curved blades for maximum efficiency. They pivot on a fixed point at the gunnel so no energy is lost in unwanted movement. Seats slide back and fore so the rowers' legs are working as much as the shoulders. A *sgoth Niseach* is at the other end of the rowing spectrum. The long 'sweeps' are solid timber, as knot-free as possible but built with a tolerance for strength, as materials are not always ideal. They have square shafts where they pass over the gunnels. These sections fit between simple 'thole pins' of oak. There is little to go wrong – spare pins are carried. Our skipper demonstrated floating the oar into position to save handling its full weight. Once the oar is balanced in its place, its weight is manageable. You take long pulls to build up momentum, rather than short stabs. Once several tons of boat and crew have overcome the inertia, the momentum does carry you. Until, that is, you hit steep waves or unfair tide, or both.

Prepared or not, all of us were close to our limits of physical endurance by the time we'd rowed the dozen sea miles to Kebock Head. The lined features of grey cliffs could just be distinguished out of a dense, clinging damp. A simple white structure sat on a concrete base. Now we could be sure we were abeam the small light on Gob na Milaid, which is the northerly marker for the Sound of Shiants.

Then the breeze stirred. Most were for sailing on through the night, hoping to arrive at Lochmaddy in the morning. We could now show a light as we passed through the shipping lane. But the skipper had his heart set on camping on the Shiants and that's what we attempted to do. I suppose I was unofficial mate but I was used to accepting a chain of command. I didn't attempt to argue but acted as the go-between, to keep the crew in the picture. Visibility was still poor and we were now sailing blind, on the compass, at a good pace.

We caught the updated forecast on the VHF. The mainly northerly wind was forecast to freshen later. I suggested we steal in between Garbh Eilean and the outlying reefs to seek shelter to the west of Mol Mor. That is the same shingle bank I'd seen, from both sides, in my earlier lone voyage in *Broad Bay*. The chart showed plenty of depth. There was just enough visibility in the swirling mist to make out the geometric columns of basalt on Garbh Eilean and the quirky fins of the outlying group of reefs known as the Gailtachean. We could pull her the short distance under oars, looking out for lobster-pot markers that could foul our rudder.

However, our skipper seemed to have the lagoon firmly fixed in his mind and wanted to go by sail rather than by oar, so we reached on further, taking the wind on our port side. The mist was lifting but the daylight was fading. At last we arrived at that same gap I'd navigated in *Broad Bay*. There are two possible areas for anchoring in the lagoon, in good conditions. Both are uncomfortable if the wind is from the north and unsafe if it blows strong from the north-east. We failed to find a hold. Conditions were gusty, now. Once, I felt our keel hit gravel.

Sean had joined me on the bench and the two of us had been pulling for some time. We were used to working together at that time in our lives. I was still quite fit but I knew I'd reached my own limit for pulling the heavy oar. One strong person to each of the four oars is the bare minimum. Ideally, you want additional rowers so all get a short rest, in rotation. When these were working craft, the crews would be honed to the tasks by doing them day after day in a range of conditions.

This is a situation where the narrower and lower Shetland *sixern* would have a great advantage. But we were in the high-sided *sgoth Niseach*. Right now we had to get out of this place and we all knew it. I called for someone to relieve me on the oar. Then I took my place, ready to help hoist some sail to power us off this lee shore.

The skipper called for the hoist and we worked our way clear. Soon we gained some shelter from the high cliffs that were now but a dim shape. The skipper judged that it was better to hold off here rather than make an attempt to work further round to the more sheltered west side. I think he sensed that several of his crew were close to their limits. It was a dreich night, in the shadow of Eilean Tigh. We trailed long warps to slow our drift instead of sailing on. People are made anxious by different things. Some fear night sailing and encounters with blurred lights that never seem as clear as they do in navigation manuals. I fear lee shores and being close to land in areas where tidal streams are strong and complex.

The boat settled down. One of our number attached some wiring to crocodile clips so we had power to our little GPS. You could hardly make out the drop of the cliffs now. The numbers of latitude and longitude came up on the tiny screen. I was able to plot our fix on the water-resistant Imray chart. We would be able to make regular checks to make sure our drift was not taking us close in to dangers. Perhaps I'd been over-anxious because my young son was with me. Sean probably sensed the tension lifting from me. I felt his head rest on my oilskin legs. He was warm enough and at ease.

I was glad we were showing a light. We were underway, sailing on the mast, even though we had no cloth hoisted. Vessels of different sizes will sometimes duck out of the Minch to take shelter for a while under the high ground of the Shiants. Most of our team fell to rest on the bottom boards. They were tired out, so their damp layers did not bother them too much. Maybe we were all gaining a real sense of the working conditions faced by past generations of island fishermen. One poor soul hung over the high bow for most of the night. He would retch at regular intervals and groan quietly to himself. Most people find the motion makes you feel more nauseous when you are wallowing rather than driving on.

At dawn the skipper talked of taking turns to go ashore at the green archipelago. Everyone else was for sailing on while we had favourable breeze. This time he sensed the mood. Our warps were recovered and coiled. Our sail was hoisted, with a couple of reefs in. We had the ebb tide in our favour and the breeze on our quarter (just off our stern.) I think it was not only me who fell back in love with the demanding *an Sulaire*. On this point of sail and in these seas she was a very suitable craft. Even our casualty began to respond. We made a good passage to Lochmaddy, on one tack the whole way. We picked up a mooring not long after noon. Our skipper produced the customary half-bottle for an arrival dram but most of the crew were packing their gear. They could still catch a bus that would connect to a ferry that would link to another bus to take them home that night.

I think back to that night whenever I hear anyone become nostalgic about the purity of working under sail and oars alone. There were several similar situations in the first few years of sailing *an Sulaire*, under different skippers. An outboard motor, ready on its bracket, would have been enough to enable us to nose back out of that choppy lagoon. As long as it was working. The main issue is thinking ahead to imagine how a safe place can become hostile with a shift in the wind direction or strength. Very few places are ideal in every wind direction. You need sufficient strength and experience in your crew but I think you have to take a long-term view by building up that experience before expeditions. It's only fair to make sure that people know what might be entailed.

Most of all, I've come to believe that informed consultation is usually a very good thing on a boat, the same way as it is on a coastguard watch. But then of course one person has to take responsibility. And at that time I was not prepared to do that, on a powerful *sgoth Niseach*. We all still had a lot to learn and I am grateful to the gallus characters who succeeded in making several daring expeditions without major incident.

Sean was happy to stay and help me tidy up the boat while our skipper went ashore to meet the Uist folk, handing on the responsibility for *an Sulaire*. Their passage to Tiree and on to Iona has become a legend. Certainly these vessels are capable of a surprising turn of speed, in a following sea with the wind aft of the beam. Her full bow shape does indeed help lift her over the waves, out in open water. The shape of her stern helps her surge on.

A week or two later I sighted *an Sulaire* again in the Sound of Iona. The skipper for this leg was one Kenny Morrison. He had found enough local fishermen who wanted a busman's holiday piloting *an Sulaire* through the shallow waters that lie between the green lines of Iona marble and the pink granite of the Ross of Mull. I knew Kenny from our early years in Stornoway to be a strong swimmer and a graceful diver. Only a handful of us would willingly enter the cold and oily waters of Stornoway harbour. One branch of his family was from a village with a history of daring into the North Minch on fleets of *sgoth Niseach*.

The boats are all decayed or lost but their names are often passed down to later craft: *Fear Not, Brothers' Delight, Peace and Plenty*. Kenny has a winning smile and all aboard could sense how much this assemblage of timber and fasteners meant to him. He is of medium height but strongly built. This was his holiday, as a volunteer, free of his office job.

An Sulaire was moored in 'The Bull Hole' and we talked over the week's plans while enjoying a pint. I would crew, in between conducting workshops with the primary school pupils of Iona, Mull and Ardnamurchan. I'd worked my notice in the coastguard service, resigning from a permanent and pensionable post to take on the uncertainties of life as a jobbing artist. The income would always be unreliable but, already, my choice was taking me to landscapes and meetings that I could not otherwise experience. I have been fortunate to be able to return to the west side of Mull and the island of Iona several times to work in terrain that continues to fascinate artists and archaeologists, geologists and historians. Even in dull weather the light shifts fast and hurls itself at the varied rocks. The palette offers the blacker group of greys and the blue side of greens. In the flora, the yellows are often primary. The reds are on the pink side. No wonder many of the Scottish colourist group of painters returned again and again.

In one turn of the head, you can take in the evidence of pastoral cultivation and the most challenging Atlantic geography. The slopes rise fast, right up to the Monro-classed scree of Mull's highest peak. It is of course called Ben More – big hill.

Each day, I'd do workshops on stories and visual art, and the folklorist, singer and storyteller Margaret Bennett would share songs and tales in Gaelic. Then we'd swap the groups so all the pupils and their teachers were taken for a sail. The forecast was favourable and it looked like the Mull Arts Centre, *an Tobar*, had found enough interested folk to crew the boat on its intended route. The plan was to work our way round to the Sound of Mull and on to Tobermory in a series of hops. Without the back-up of an engine, you need both a strong crew and a sprinkle of luck.

Margaret had attended secondary school on Lewis. She is internationally known for her work in collecting songs, tunes, customs and stories in Gaelic-speaking pockets of Canada. Surviving examples of vernacular culture were found there when scholars thought these songs or stories were extinct. It must be like the moment the coelacanth (a rare order of fish) was found in a deep-sea trawl. Or when a Viking ceremonial ship was discovered, preserved in deep mud, revealing the skills of shipwrights and blacksmiths gone before. Margaret has long silver hair, well groomed. She is a classic beauty and blessed with daring wit. She suffered from polio and still limps but Kenny judged it safe to help her on board, with care.

There was warm sun and light breeze. Pupils who had just been for a short sail, along with their teacher and helpers, joined me on the shore. My eye fell on the huge sea-rounded slabs and boulders, dried to matt black. Now the pupils responded to their experience

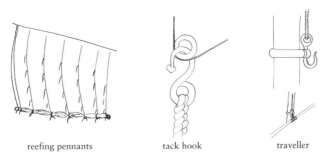

reefing pennants   tack hook   traveller

Rigging details

of the *sgoth* by drawing with chalk on black and pink rocks. They caught the details of our Lewis craft, the lines of 'reefing pennants' that shorten sail; the 'tack hooks' that hold the lower front eye down to the bow; the leathered 'traveller' that holds the sail and spar close to the mast.

These fluent drawings were spilling over the shore as the sounds of Margaret's workshop in song came over the water. I photographed the chalked images. They would be erased on the next tide. The song was developing and would also be gone from the air very soon. I knew this to be one of the moments of peace you savour as a sailor, the ones that erase the memories of shivering and the noise of breaking seas on a lee shore.

For Margaret, the continuation of a shape such as that of the structure that comprises *an Sulaire* is an exact parallel to the way a song, formed over generations, has a continuing life. This sense of culture is not at all solemn. Margaret's energetic mind will compare the versions of a story as told in Ireland and these islands. She will speak of discovering the form of a tune, lost at home but still alive in Cape Breton or Quebec. She has the voice of an adventurer as well as a scholar.

I've seen her look down at the variegated greens of silverweed clutching to thin acidic soil between rocks and heard her make sure that everyone in the walking company knows that this was starvation food. Like the limpets that took almost as much energy to eat as they provided.

One of our willing crew, a man returned to retirement on Mull after working as a shepherd on the Falkland Islands, delivered fresh crab sandwiches. There was a quick conference. Now we had our supper and the breeze and the crew to take the boat on an evening passage round from Iona to the bay at Carsaig. This time we could not take the pupils or Margaret but I think we had one or two of the parents along.

We went from the most gentle pottering to a driving reach, clear of the Sound. We had a strong team with local knowledge of the area. I had circled the Torran rocks on our chart. These are the reefs that wrecked the imagined vessel that carried Stevenson's David Balfour. When the intense light of the evening glances on the spray thrown high by their sharp shapes, the effect is hypnotic. But these rocks have claimed actual craft of skin, wood and steel.

You set a course from the chart to include a safety margin, to keep clear of such hazards. Then you correct it for magnetic variation and for the boat's own influence on the compass but it might not be possible to sail directly down that course if the direction of the wind is against you. Tonight, we had a reach – we were blessed with a wind on the side of the vessel.

We'd need to look out for the cat's paws that were bound to strike from the high ground of Malcolm's Point and green Ardalanish. You underestimate wind when the sun shines. There's something about the noise of beating cloth and the unease in the helmsman's eye that tells you you're carrying too much sail. The banter was good but this is an area where you have to remain vigilant. I'd heard how there used to be a constant commentary on the waters ahead, passed along the *sgoth*, bow to stern.

As bowman, I could see the turbulence ahead and signalled that to Kenny. I used sign language to say that we had to shorten sail sooner rather than later. You don't want to shout. That tends to roughen the edges of a task that should be easy as a dance.

Now that I sometimes take on responsibility for *an Sulaire* and similar craft, I usually rehearse the crew in the action of reefing the sails before we do anything else. But we were all still learning the nuances of the boat, then. It could have been sweeter but the job was done. We proceeded at much the same speed, with two or three reefs (out of a possible six) tied, to reduce the sail area. She no longer heeled. The man at the helm no longer had to swing his weight on the tiller. We were no slower.

The big 'fisherman' pattern anchor went over in a bay of mixed ground. There was a buzz of talk. A message was sent to the coastguard. 'Arrived safely.' We had taken our chance in an exposed stretch of water in an open vessel, working the opportunity of a fresh breeze, off the land, to advantage. You wouldn't leave a boat unattended for long in this anchorage. Kenny would camp by his charge. I'd get a lift back to Fionnphort to be ready for school in the morning.

Clansmen do fight scenes.
Priests disembark.
Iona is busy tonight.

Our bow's a chisel –
the hiss is our own breath
as we leave serifs astern.

Pink rock goes black
– the basalt fault.
We round a corner.

A brutal disruption
of a lifetime's fetch
on bitter skerries.

A skullcap of green
on Ardalinish Point –
we get the nod.

Helm till the lug shakes.
We'll have the sail down
when a fisherman bites the bay.

In the Tailor's House

There is an inevitable irony in sharing a folk tale. You have to put it into your own natural voice to keep it alive but you have to lose yourself in the telling. In navigational terms, you are like a vessel restricted in its ability to manoeuvre. The question of how much scope (another nautical term) there is for variations seems to me similar to the issue of grace notes in great Gaelic songs or Scots ballads.

Margaret's son Martyn Bennett made radical mixes and arrangements of traditional Scottish songs and stories. He settled on Mull and recorded his music in a studio that is part of the *an Tobar* arts centre. At first, this included his expert playing, on fiddle and pipes. Latterly, in his short but full life, he did not have the strength for that but continued sampling, mixing and composing. I believe that the long, strange Scottish traveller's story, told in full, on his final album *Grit** is reproduced with complete integrity. The samples of song also retain the rhythm and voice of the originals. Introduction of dance beats or rave refrains make startling juxtapositions but their rhythms are truly matched to those in the sung or spoken voices. Most of these singers and storytellers are no longer with us but their voices can be accessed. Martyn has brought them to an audience they could never have otherwise reached.

He was a charismatic figure, with his mother's good looks under a heap of dreadlocks. He was the first musician to choose bagpipes as his main instrument at the Royal Scottish Academy of Music and Drama. He was not a saint. In a documentary film about the making of *Grit*, he described destroying the beautifully made pipes and fiddle sought out

---

* Grit, Real World Records, 2003 (realworldrecords.com/release/28/grit/ vinyl edition, 2017).

for him by his mother. 'These pipes survived the First World War but they didn't survive my own battle.'

I'd suggest that the seminal recordings used as a basis for the work are treated with respect, even though Martyn Bennett's approach was always innovative. I'd contrast that with versions of stories that tidy them up, but without sensitivity. Or those that omit what may be uncomfortable.

At the time we were navigating *an Sulaire* round Mull, Martyn was still able to play his instruments and they were still intact. The passage to Carsaig, sailing by Erraid and the Torran Rocks, takes us into the trackline of a story collected by another folklorist, a contemporary of Margaret. I was told it by Mairi MacArthur, from Iona. She recorded it from a retired mariner and I'm retelling it in the first person, the way it was told to her.

We were all in the tailor's house. The tailor's house in Fionnphort. That's always where the ceilidh was. There would be a light on because he had to see his stitches. The Tilley lamp gave off a good heat. The stove was blasting away, burning peat like there was no tomorrow. The kettle was hissing away.

It was freezing hard outside. The snow was lying – an unusual thing on Mull. We were all snug, yarning away as usual. But then a shadow goes across the lamp and a blast of cold air comes through the house. The door's open and there's a man standing there.

He's very tall. Dark beard and a very pale face. The glint of brass buttons. It's a seaman's jacket. And he's dripping wet.

'Will you do something for me?' he asks.

'We'll talk about that when you're in by the stove. Come on in and get a heat, man.'

'No, I won't come in but can you help me?'

We all try to persuade him in but he stays at the door and he says, 'Will you go down in the morning to the white sands. The white sands of Erraid. You'll find me there. And just so you're sure it's me, you'll find a bandage that was on my thumb. It will be about this much,' – and he holds out a hand about 3 feet from his white face – 'this much from my head.'

Of course we all say aye, we'll do what we can but he's to come in. He's gone. The tailor sends a young fellow out to bring him back but the lad returns without the gentleman in the seaman's jacket.

'I couldn't find him.'

'What do you mean you couldn't find him? Could you no follow the footprints?'

'There's no footprints.'

So someone gets up then to get a cloth and wipe up all that water that was dripping on to the floor by the door. The floor is dry.

Now the ceilidh is well and truly finished. No one is in a mood for teasing or laughing any more. And we know we've to get up and catch that tide in the morning. So everyone's away home to get some rest if they can.

In the morning we gather down at the ebb. The tide's out a long way and we spread out in a line. It's not long before we see it. There's a long dark shape on the white sand. Sure enough, he's wearing a seaman's jacket with brass buttons. You can see where there's been a big gash on a thumb and there, 3 feet from the head, the bandage.

Now, that body belongs to someone and it's still freezing weather so we've a few days' grace. We get hold of a cart before the tide floods and we bring that poor soul above the tidemark. He's placed decently in an outhouse and the word is sent out to try to identify the fellow.

Sure enough, an answer comes from Appin, Argyll. This is a man by the name of MacPherson. He comes across on the ferry, as soon as he can.

'That's the body of my son, John MacPherson. I'm very grateful to you for looking after him. This will make it easier for us all to bear.'

The father's face did not show any trace of shock. Someone asked that poor man when John was lost.

'My son was mate aboard a merchant vessel, the *Fair Holm*. She failed and went down off Tory Island. North-west of Donegal.'

'And when was that?'

'That was over two weeks ago.'

Everyone goes quiet. I'm sure that poor man knows there's a story but no one wants to tell him it.

But if you go to the cemetery in Fionnphort you can see for yourselves. There's a stone that stands out – it's black slate. It's engraved with the name of John MacPherson, mate of the *Fair Holm*. It says how his body travelled all those sea miles and fetched up on the sands of Erraid. How he found his way back this way. How his father buried him here.

Sound of Mull

THERE WAS NOT A RAISED VOICE THE WHOLE WEEK, on the boat or in the classrooms, except when Kenny went into showman mode. I saw our skipper in full flight when I rejoined the boat at Salen. That village is set about halfway up the Sound of Mull, on the island. You can recognise it from the remains of an old wooden pier reaching out from a small peninsula. Kenny took up a rope and taught a few of the kids to tie a bowline. 'The fox comes out of the hole, goes that way round the tree and then goes back down the same hole again.' That's how a loop is made. One that will not close in on itself. But then he said, standing on the stern platform as if it was a stage, 'Do you know why a skipper is called a skipper?'

'Oh yes,' the youngsters answered, 'Margaret told us it's from the Gaelic word, *na sgiobair*.'

'Aye,' says Kenny, 'but it's also because…' And he started skipping, like a boxer, on his stage.

Another time we put a few socks down into the thwart pump – that's the timber box from the aft bench to the bilges, which has a simple steel handle. There's a bit of froth when you pump fast. 'Do you know what that is?' he asked our pupils. 'No? Well, I'll show you.' And he pumped fast enough to get the froth, fished out the socks and said, 'That's the boat's washing machine.'

The village of Salen, Isle of Mull, was my home for a year. I was about 18, then. I'd hoped for a berth on a ring-netter working out of Tobermory. Big hauls of herring were being landed at Oban or Mallaig. These vessels took shape at Nobles of Girvan or Nobles of Fraserburgh; Millers of St Monans; Blackies of Port Seton. They came along the sea roads or through the Caledonian Canal with their purring Kelvins or Gardners. All these pistons in all these cylinders powered a flush carvel skin of varnished boatskin larch. Their distinguishing feature was their slightly raised canoe stern. The round of it and the rise at the end of the boat's whole sheerline are features of a simple shape that seems drawn without effort but impossible to improve.

There was money to be made at the herring fishing that year so my job was snapped up. I did not get to chase the herring, as my Lewis grandfather had done in his day. Instead, I planted trees and drained ditches working for the Forestry Commission. The job I liked best was draining, which was a team game with hand-driven tools made for that job. The sharp rutting spade cut the edges and the bent fork, which I remember as the 'hock', laid the divot at the side of the new ditch. Then the man in his wellies followed, 'bottoming' or cleaning out the channel.

When we were not on piecework it was the lowest wage in the country but there were other compensations. I met people such as Roddy MacNeil, a native of the off-lying island of Gometra, and a Gaelic speaker. One lunchtime, Roddy showed me how to pluck a twig of hazel and carve out a whistle. I listened to his yarns and passed him the newly published songs of the Melbost bard, Murdo MacFarlane. I now know that Murdo was a great friend of my grandfather who became a road labourer when herring markets crashed between the wars. The Melbost bard was a maker of songs with a basis in village life and a worldwide outlook. These songs are lasting well and travelling far.

Since then, I'd completed my year in the forestry and my five at uni and 15 in the coastguard. Roddy MacNeil, retired now but still very sprightly, joined us for the sail across to Lochaline. He had been recorded by the School of Scottish Studies and he and Margaret were already good friends. We pulled the *sgoth* out under oars then found the breeze to take us over the Sound. On both sides, farms snuggle, or 'coorie in', between the hills that are mostly more gradual than those of the west side. There is a huge variety of landscapes within an arc of good visibility. In some ways, this more gentle beauty has its drawbacks.

Even when I lived on Mull, back around 1973, holiday homes were a real issue. Many of my mates in the forestry were forced to leave the island because they just could not compete in the housing market. The days of an employer or local authority providing housing, for that reason, were already in decline. But there were also new settlers to this island of depleted population. Many were committed enough to be caravan dwellers, winter as well as summer. James Hunter, writer on the social history of the Highlands, talks of 'the new crofters'. Most locals now accept that 'incomers' have often been essential to the survival of outlying communities. Winters of severe gales can be a hard test. Those who stay on have proved their commitment.

Many have also brought new skills and enterprises. Mull now produces one of the tastiest Cheddar-type cheeses I've yet discovered and biscuits that melt in the mouth. The Mull Little Theatre was run by a couple based in Dervaig but has gone on to develop into a new form, a generation on.

Still, there was a sad note in hearing how few names of local origin were on the class registers of the schools we visited on the island or mainland sides of the Sound of Mull. In comparison, my home island of Lewis still has a higher proportion of residents who can trace their family roots in island settlements.

Somehow *an Sulaire* made all her appointments at piers near schools. Between oars, sail and the generosity of those who drove boats that did have engines, all the pupils had a share of the experience. Margaret and myself had to keep them talking and drawing and singing a few times but the boat always showed up.

Roddy demonstrated the art of tying a bowline behind your back. I was not allowed to sign off from my first watch as a regular coastguard until I could do exactly that. It's not just show. If your fingers learn a certain movement it happens as if by instinct. Then you can tie that knot in the dark with cold hands. As we sailed the few miles, easy and steady, with the banter going all the time, I was looking over to plantations of spruce, pine and hybrid larch. I had planted plenty of them myself, though I never did hit the rhythm that could regularly reach a tally of over a thousand a day.

We're on an eggshell with a fin below.
The wake meets our linseed sheen.
Our breasthooks hold our ends together.

Ribs are fastened to follow their bent.
A quarter should be a full measure.
The yard stretches out the cloth.

You lever the rudder to impress sea.
Salt heals saw-cuts.
A hull is a scuffed chart.

The Great Snowball

I'd spent some hours in the hail or shine around Stornoway harbour, packing herrings. I had that in common with one Morrison of a different generation – the cooper, storyteller and collector of the lore gathered as *Traditions of the Western Isles*. He worked in the herring industry in the early 1800s. I was engaged in casual labour in the early 1970s before I went to Mull to pick up that job in the forestry.

Morrison was a schoolmaster in the Uig district of Lewis before moving to the bustling town. He does not seem to have been successful in business but he had an appetite for stories. These were as plentiful as herring in the trade between east-coasters and islanders, the Baltic buyers and the itinerant gutters and packers.

There is still a pile of *olacs*, or big stones, lying where they were jettisoned, close to the new ferry terminal in Stornoway. You can see this 'Little Russia' when the sea falls back at big spring tides. Morrison's catch of stories was written out in manuscript over several volumes. One of these has been lost but the others were typeset and published in the 1970s.

That's the same decade that saw a brief revival of the herring industry, when Faroese and Norwegian buyers came to deal directly with the drifters and ring-netters. Their small ships always looked fresh in oiled pine, offset by white-painted deckhouses. They arrived with a stock of empty white-wood barrels and departed with these filled with the sweet-cured catch. I had just left school and was swithering between hunting for a job on a fishing boat and going on to university. The herring-packing was good money for the time but working conditions were hard and everything depended on the market. The basic forestry wage was poor but steady. I could even save a bit for my student days to come when we moved on to piecework rates for draining or planting.

You didn't have to work outside when it rained. It rains a lot on Mull. I talked about this with one Ian Campbell a couple of years after I left Mull. He was driving a van and a group of students to a drama festival in Dundalk at the time. I was riding shotgun. I told him a yarn I heard from Donald MacKechnie in Dervaig, Mull. This is how I remember his telling:

'One time a deer came galloping down the track, demented. It dropped at this fellow's feet, stone dead. It had been shot.

So he just nudged the carcass into some bushes. Then the toffs came running up, in their tweeds. "Did a stag come past you just now?" they asked. "No a stag did not come past me," he said with not one word of a lie.'

One story suggests the next. I'm going to retell you the tale that was Ian's reply. People kept saying, 'What part is that Campbell fellow playing? He's your star.'

Our driver with the wild, straggly beard had no official involvement in the production, but Ian would produce a whistle from his pocket. He might even dance. Mostly he was just himself. I wasn't surprised when I caught up with his work a few years later. He made the scaffolding set for a trilingual play, *Craobh nan Ubhal* or *The Aiple Tree*. The set and staging raised the whole show, in more ways than one. The design made the idea come alive. He was the star of that show too. This is the story Ian Campbell told me, on the road to Dundalk.

Did you hear about the year there was a big snowfall on Mull? No? Well, it lasted and lasted. Usually snow is gone in a day or two in this part of the world. Anyway, one time, it just lingered on. You couldn't do a thing. The ground was frozen. No one had tasted fresh food for long enough.

Donald's in by the fire. There's plenty of peat but his wife is getting fed up of him hovering about the house, getting in her way. 'Is it not about time you got out and found us some fresh food?'

'How am I going to do that when the snow is so deep? We'll just need to wait it out for a thaw. There's plenty meal yet.'

'Never mind meal. You take down that ornament hanging on the wall and go and shoot some fresh meat for us.'

True enough, Donald hadn't been out with the gun for a while. She kept on at him until he took the rifle from the hook. He was soon trudging and moaning. Only thing for it was to get up the hill a bit. There might be a hare darting out between the stones or a starving deer searching for a blade of grass.

But the blizzard came down again and he couldn't see a thing. He reckoned on staying on the rise of ground, that'd be the safest thing. If he followed the slope down he could end up somewhere dangerous. So it was a slog, one boot after the other. It cleared a bit and he knew he was near the top. He'd forgotten about looking for something to shoot now. He just wanted to be home safe.

The blast of wind hit him on the ridge. He started to roll a snowball, just to keep warm. You know the way it all just gathers and gathers. He kept it going and damn it, soon it was just about rolling itself. Not only that but it was clearing a path for him as it rolled down. The walking was easier and everything was a bit more cheery. But it was getting that bit faster and it was leaving a track behind it you could have got a horse and cart along.

Donald broke into a run behind it and the sky was clearing all the time. Things started to look familiar. Would you believe it, the snowball was rolling down towards their own village. His own croft, in fact. But the snowball was moving really fast now. And then there was that feeling, you know the one when something has started and there's nothing you can do to stop it. The machine is moving and that's that. That's what tragedy is and sure enough, as soon as Donald realised the great snowball was heading straight for his own house, there was a mighty crash.

That was only the start of the noise. His wife came out and saw the stone walls of their barn were all caved in and there was even more snow and ice everywhere. She was shouting at him. 'I send you out to get something for the pot and you destroy our own croft.'

She said a few other things too. But Donald was a bit distracted because he'd seen a small movement coming from the snowball. He just reached out and took a hold and pulled. Here was a rabbit. His wife was delighted. But he'd seen another movement. It was a horn. An antler in fact.

Now it was Donald himself told me this. He told me he started digging into the heart of the remnants of that one snowball. He pulled out, so he said himself, no fewer than two stags and five hinds. There was three brace of mountain hares, one brace of ptarmigan and no fewer than ninety-nine rabbits. That was where I had to butt in.

'Donald,' I said to him, 'ninety-nine rabbits. Good story but could you not just as well have made it a hundred?'

He looked at me then with great pride.

'Ian Campbell,' he says, 'Do you think I would make a liar of myself for the sake of one bloody rabbit?'

Another volunteer skipper took over from Kenny at Tobermory. *An Sulaire* made a safe passage home to Stornoway via the island of Eigg. Since then, Kenny Morrison took her on another expedition to Mull, with a strong representation of musicians in the crew. There are iconic images of the vessel inside Fingal's Cave, out at Staffa. Recordings of reverberating whistle tunes.

Over the years it has been a struggle to maintain *an Sulaire* and find younger people willing to take on the huge responsibility of skippering her. For me, with a background in education, it's clear that the motivation and training of volunteers, with safeguards and support, is the most crucial issue. As volunteers' skills develop, more responsibility can be delegated. *An Sulaire* is still in commission, now 20 years after her launch. That might not sound like much in the history of a vessel that could last for a hundred years, but it has been a long haul of maintenance, fund-raising and negotiating. You forget about that when her cloth is stretched and she puts her timber shoulder to the weight of the steep North Minch.

Her planks are painted now, in a deep blue-black, more like a working-boat finish. She still has one upper plank or 'strake' in oiled larch to show the grain of her boatskin. For some years now I've been doing my own share as one of her volunteer skippers. Everything is heavy, sail spars and steering. But you can pair a strong and a not-so-strong person at each position. Even if the crew is fit, the tasks have to be shared or she just doesn't sail. Maybe my awareness of her sailing qualities has increased as we've met a range of conditions. Most would say she can take more than her crew. I don't think I ever take her workings for granted. I watch that heavy yard as it pivots on her ironwork, heel first, to dip around her mast of Douglas fir. As skipper, you repeat the warnings, at regular intervals. So far there have been no serious injuries. Recorded accounts of the history of the winter great-line fishery read like descriptions of battles. Some vessels simply never returned and some were seen to fail, swamped and broken, within a few long cables of a home shore.

Moonspinner

I DID NOT THINK OF MYSELF AS BEING UNFAITHFUL to the old *Broad Bay* when I crewed on the powerful *an Sulaire*. You could argue that these are horses for a different scale of courses but really from the same stable. They are Scottish island working boats, along a line of Norse boatbuilding culture. The shapes are very similar even though there is a clear divergence in the way the sailing rigs have evolved. This is due to a combination of local conditions, the main functions of the craft at different times and the number of able crew available. There is also the inescapable factor of preference.

Eric McKee's *Working Boats of Britain** proposes that there are two main factors in the evolution of the shape and rig of a craft developed, over many generations, round the coasts of Britain and Ireland. The task to be carried out is a huge influence on shape and size. The localised conditions they would encounter day after day, he argues, is the other main issue. Prevailing winds and their interaction with tidal factors generate the seas the vessels had to deal with. Underwater geography also affects the waves they will meet, close to home or out at distant fishing grounds. Would the vessel return to a deep-water harbour or would it have to be light enough to be hauled over boulders by the men, women and children of an isolated village?

I've often held on to the iron railings by Butt of Lewis lighthouse and looked out to the meeting currents. You can study the changing tideline and the rise and fall of standing waves, as forces are in opposition. You guess at the eddies that might have allowed the sensitive helmsman to take his charge out to hook their share of a harvest. You imagine her buoyant stern rising to a breaking wave and hurtling towards the dog-leg route into the tight harbour at Port of Ness. Maybe you would elect to hold her out and ride on the bare poles in the hope of finding a quieter shore on which to make your landfall. North Lewis and Orcadian craft had to carry men and fish through such conditions on a daily basis.

In contrast, a yacht would be drawn in response to the wants and tastes of a client or a likely owner. It's a strong argument but I don't think it's that simple. Some historic working boats were

---

* *Working Boats of Britain – Their Shape and Purpose*, Eric McKee, Conway Maritime Press, in association with The National Maritime Museum, London, 1983.

also designed for their commercial purpose by a team or by a naval architect. But of course they would have borrowed from proven features of previous types of craft. In the same way, yachts – for racing and for cruising – have often been based on the proven hulls and rigs of working vessels. This can be traced in the sailing lifeboats of Norway, designed by the Scot, Colin Archer, and the generations of double-ended yachts they have influenced. Then there are the slope-keeled herring-drifters of Scotland's Loch Fyne and the yachts the same yards built when the fishing was quiet. The Morecambe Bay prawners showed their paces when they flew regatta rigs and their crews had a busman's holiday. More than one Bristol Channel pilot cutter went on to carry mountaineers to new discoveries in high latitudes.

The intended purpose is also a huge factor in the development of yachts. Did she have to turn on a tanner to gain advantage when a flock of sails approached a racing mark? Or would she have to hold her course and punch into huge seas, even though she could not be much bigger than 25 feet, if she were to be affordable? My new obsessive study of the lines of small yachts was not simply a fancy for a change of boat. I wanted to sail through the settings of stories, further from home than I could safely reach in an open boat.

The relationship between the evolved or 'traditional' in boatbuilding and the innovations of individuals is as complex a mix as it is in music, song and story. A tale of riddles, recorded from travelling people and thus considered 'traditional', might have its basis in a poetic dialogue such as that in one of the 305 ballads transcribed by Francis Child in the 19th century. The ballad might in turn have borrowed from the riddles embodied in the poetry of John Gower, a contemporary of Chaucer. And that might have been distilled from wise tales attributed to both Jewish and Islamic tradition or influenced by other European literary versions, reached through the common medium of Latin.

If you read such a ballad out loud you might well find yourself adapting a word or two to suit your own voice, as in fact I seem to have done:

What is greener than the grass?
Smoother still than crystal glass?
What is louder than a horn?
What is sharper than a thorn?
What is brighter than the light?
Darker than the black of night?
What is keener than an axe?
Softer still than melting wax?
What is rounder than a ring?
Us to you, our answers bring.

Envy is greener than the grass.
Flattery more smooth than any glass.
Rumour is louder than a horn.
Hunger is sharper than a thorn.
Truth is brighter than the light.
Falsehood, darker than the night.
Revenge is keener than an axe.
Love, more soft than melting wax.
The world is rounder than a ring.
Thus, we now, our answers bring.

The number of replies is nine
and so we never shall be thine.

So it is eloquence that has saved the soul from the devil or the maid from the lecherous knight, according to the version. Just as eloquence or wit frees a crew from the grip of the blue men in the lore of the Outer Hebrides. And I would argue that the shared form of this eloquence is often a blend of literary sources and the moulding of language over generations but passed by word of mouth. Just as boats are shaped by drawn lines, transferred to moulds but also by the hand and eye of their builder.

I was still in love with both *Broad Bay* and *an Sulaire* when I became conscious that my eyes were straying to the images or lines of wooden yachts. I still appreciated the sweetness of the shape of my early love, *Broad Bay*. Looking side on, the dip from bow to midships then rising again to the stern forms a subtle curve. That is called a sheer line on a working boat as well as on a yacht. When I cleaned her bottom on a sloping shore I would pause, not for a rest but just to observe the fullness developing upwards from the sharper V at the keel, close to her rudder. Some might call this same shape plump or judge it lacking in grace.

To the eye of this beholder, that shape is simply beautiful. The aft aspect of *an Sulaire* is brought to a very similar curvature from the well-steamed planks of larch, clear enough in their long grain to take the bend and twist into a rebate in the sternpost. The main difference between the two boats is not the shape but the scale.

Despite her age, the old *Broad Bay* still seems lively and petite. This is a boat you can banter with. *An Sulaire* is more the diva. She can scare you a bit as well as impress you with her capability to charge on through huge, clashing seas. She has the power and buoyancy to venture from the bay to the ocean.

Yet I returned again and again to images of small, affordable yachts, which could shelter you from the rain and wind as well as take you out to the fishing. My roving eye settled on a class of yacht known as the Stella. Then flirtation became compulsion. It is not that I undervalued the attributes of two cared-for examples of working craft, now used for pleasure. My lustful daydreams settled on a type of craft that is greatly influenced by the construction of the type of working boats we've so far met.

The technology of overlapping clinker planks was put to use by designers of small racing yachts and dinghies. They saw the advantage of a high strength-to-weight ratio. A boat with a smooth skin of 'carvel'

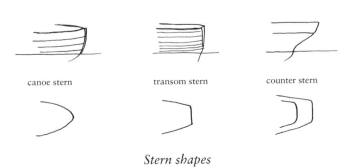

canoe stern   transom stern   counter stern

Stern shapes

planks needs to be heavier because there is not the structural benefit of the overlapping 'clinker' planks. The framing is also usually heavier because it is built first and the planks are moulded to that skeleton.

Just like a racing car, a lighter yacht will be faster than a heavy one of similar attributes, as long as she can take the power used to drive her. The first Stella-class yacht borrowed from the Scandinavian experience of transferring the skills of designing and making working boats to leisure craft. A competition across several countries, pre-World War II, produced an agreed design for a simple and affordable class of yacht that could meet for regattas. Some thought the Folkboat too functional, with a transom board for a stern instead of a graceful canoe or counter shape.

The winning design provided more volume within its 25 feet and was simpler and cheaper to build. But the original Folkboat is really for racing on an equal basis and for camping on for a weekend or two. Kim Holman, the designer of the Stella class, drew a boat that was a similar shape but had a bit more volume inside and was a plank higher and a tad longer. She had a heavier ballast keel of iron, bolted on underneath so she could carry more cloth. The result was a successful inshore racing yacht that could also cross from Essex to the Netherlands and house four people who could cope with a very basic level of comfort.

That sounded about right for a family of four. My research showed that we could afford an example of this type. A more recent fibreglass yacht of similar capability was beyond our reach. Our

Stella-class yacht would be 'all there' but in need of a bit of tidying and improvement. Years of crawling around *Broad Bay* on the shore with scraper and paint had given me the confidence to take on such a responsibility. We offered for *Moonspinner*. She was moored in a small marina off the Clyde. By this time, all the family had gained a little more experience of sailing small yachts. We should have the hang of this one by the time we reached the North Minch.

Clyde to Kerrera

THE PREVIOUS CUSTODIAN OF *MOONSPINNER* POINTED out the half-model of the hull on a plaque of wood on a wall. One half lengthways is of course all that is necessary to document the hull shape. This was the trophy given by the Stella Association for an exceptional cruising log. There had been a revival in the class as older boats were restored and fitted with new diesel engines and crisp sails. Most of the active owners raced in the Essex and East Anglia areas, but others remembered that a part of the design remit was to draw a simple but safe cruising boat.

We hoped to round Ardnamurchan Point and set a course home for Lewis. This route takes in some challenges. I had studied the pilotage that would take us down the Clyde from Helensburgh and then on to Loch Fyne. I spoke to a friend who had made that trip in a similar boat and I'd done a bit of reconnaissance, onshore. The Crinan Canal cuts off the exposed long limb that leads to the Mull of Kintyre.

Thomas Telford was not only an engineer who took on huge missions but also a designer with a consistent aesthetic. The black-enamelled ironwork and woodwork of locks on the Crinan Canal is matched in style by the stone and slate of the lock-keepers' cottages. There are no twiddly bits. Telford also designed the Manchester Ship Canal and innovative huge-scale bridges. These were great days for engineering challenges linked to a neoclassical style that most would say has worn well. As in boat design, everything has to function. The locks are still manually operated. The attendants still work the gates on the sea pools at Ardrishaig and at Crinan. Apart from that, you now have to turn your own handles. These cast cogs still move easily. The handles are easy on the hand, worn in over generations of users.

When you clear Crinan you are into a tidal cocktail of swirling waters. The departure time is crucial. I took notes from the conversation with the man who had made this passage before in the boat we now owned. As the tides turn at a slightly different time as you head north, it is possible to have a run of fair tide that will take you clear of the Sound of Jura and then well up the Sound of Mull. But that of course also requires favourable wind.

Not even a Stella can point where she wants. There is a no-go zone, very rarely less than 45 degrees, either side of the point from which the wind is coming. You can do as much passage-planning as you like, but you still need a crystal ball to forecast the wind accurately more than a few days in advance.

Most Stellas were painted with a white top plank. *Moonspinner* was coated in a rich and constant yacht enamel of La Rochelle red. This carried all the way to her mahogany toerails at her sides. Her low cabin was also varnished light mahogany. Her decks were cream painted. Her recently replaced mast was in Douglas fir in an oiled finish. The long steady grain pattern, broken only with a very few small knots, ran as high as you could see.

Down below there was good sitting headroom but you had to stoop if you stood. There was a simple gas cooker opposite a plywood board as a chart table. The vinyl-covered settee benches were the main two bunks. The mast was housed or 'stepped' on a reinforced deck area so there was no spar going through the cabin to hinder you from going through a curtain to the low front section or 'forepeak'. A 'pipecot' of canvas stretched on a coated steel frame swung down to make a simple berth at each side. A chemical toilet was wedged in at the centreline. Ropes, sails and tackle were stored in slatted sections. You could see how everything was designed for simplicity. Elaborate yacht joinery is expensive because the lines are seldom straight and working space is tight. It also adds weight, unwanted in a boat that will race others of like design.

This was to be our family mobile home on the water. Sean, by this time, was quite tall but the pipecots were full-length though narrow. He was happy with that. Ben was not so lean but nearly as tall. They both installed their stock of books, brought along for the journey.

Their mother, Barbara, had completed a dinghy-sailing course in Hamburg when she was a student. She had gone on to crew on her father's dayboat and been trusted to take it out on her own. She is German and in that country you need some form of qualification to drive any boat on any waterway. A strong swimmer, naturally stocky in build, she moves about a boat very easily. She has a good sense of where the wind is coming from and can take her share of chartwork as well as a turn at the tiller and tie the necessary knots without thinking about it. Barbara can calculate a course and sail it too. But, like many people, she is nervous when it comes to running under engine in a tight harbour.

The Dolphin petrol-driven motor has a distinctive feature. If you want to put it in reverse, you have to stop it first. After an intake of breath it restarts when you pull a switch that tells it to run the other way round. At least it did, every time this was demonstrated by the previous owner.

Our departure, under engine, from Helensburgh was smooth enough and Sean and Ben made a game of ticking off the buoys. The Clyde channel is clearly marked by red and green markers. Usually this is orientated towards entering a harbour so, now we were heading out to sea, we would leave the greens to our port or left side and the reds to our starboard.

There are other buoys called cardinal marks. These are yellow and black, in different combinations, to indicate the point of the compass they direct you towards. So, for example, a south cardinal will point you to pass to safe water to the south of the mark. It has a shape at the top, two cones downwards, in case it is in silhouette and you can't decipher the colour code. At night a specific light sequence will distinguish it from a north, east or west cardinal. This is part of an international system adopted late in the 20th century.

The rules of the road are logical. When you are examined for any seagoing qualification you have to demonstrate a full knowledge of them, just like the highway code on land. The difference is that, in the UK at present, you can take a powerful boat out to sea without any qualification. Harbours often insist that those who rent their berths show proof of insurance but again it is not normally yet a legal requirement. We could all repeat the main rules of the sea road and our family yacht was fully insured.

The wind was light and behind us. On a delivery trip you often run the engine unless there is enough wind to get the boat going faster under sail, but the weather was fair. The hills were rising. It did not seem possible that there could be a city with a history of shipbuilding and world trade not far upstream. We soon had a mid-blue spinnaker swelling out ahead of us. Sean's own dinghy-sailing skills were showing as he adjusted the wooden pole that set, like an extension of the boom out front, to keep the balloon-like sail full. I nodded when the pole was horizontal. He made the control rope fast without any hitches that could jam.

There was a light hiss and the chuckle of water on clinker that was enough to tell we could cover the miles today, without the engine. We made good progress but the wind failed just as we were considering heading up the Kyles of Bute. That passage takes you through a dog-leg channel with the Burnt Islands at its turning point. I reckoned on running the motor for a while before committing to that route, in light airs. It gave its own quiet hiss before it died, not long after it was warmed up. This was the first year I carried a mobile phone and I had the previous owner's number. It rang. He answered. But he could not help. We had already tried the usual check on the plugs. The battery could not be flat because the starter would turn and the motor would indeed come to life. It would only run a few minutes before stalling. There was a good flow of cooling water and at a touch you knew it was not overheating. There was no trace of water in the filter and we had topped up with fresh fuel, mixed with the correct proportion of oil.

When some people say there is no wind they mean there is light wind. We looked towards the bay at Rothesay on the Isle of Bute. This was where I had planned to turn to round the north end of the island. I did not want to risk these twists and turns, in flukey wind, in an area where there is significant tide, without a back-up engine. Instead we rounded the south tip of Bute. *Moonspinner* ghosted along under sail. It was a fine evening and we looked to Goat Fell on Arran and its companion peaks. Our angle to these landmarks altered very slowly. I remember the skyline of the Isle of Arran as the graph of an unreliable pulse.

The boat's gas cooker did work. I planned to replace it with a simple spirit stove as the combination of gas and petrol aboard put fear into my bones. For now, though, we all repeated the checks of switching off every valve once the job was done. Soon we had heated soup and made sandwiches.

Sean, Barbara and myself took turns steering, with a large, light genoa driving us slow and steady. It was a very striking shade of red to match our planking. Darkness came slowly but the course was simple and the lit marks were winking in their different sequences. Our batteries would not last long if we were to run the tricolour navigation light at our masthead all night long.

Before long, the boys were bleary eyed. Both went down below to test their new bunks. We found that a hot bouillon kept the sudden chill at bay. Barbara was at peace. I thought she might be disturbed by the failure of the engine on our first day of ownership. We took turns to catch a doze, sleeping bags round shoulders. When you keep a boat moving through the night in the right direction you tend to cover the miles, unless there is strong tide against you. Two knots for eight hours brings the same result as a speed of 4 knots for only four. This arithmetic is within my grasp but this is a lesson I've needed to relearn over the years. We had to anticipate any wavering of the light breeze to keep way on the boat.

Barbara was relieved when I decided against anchoring in a bay that was cluttered with the outline of fish-farm cages. Neither of us was keen to attempt to sail in to Tarbert harbour in such fickle conditions. Better to sail on, through the night. We steered on the compass or on a visible star held against one of the rigging wires. Mostly we steered by our angle to the airs you could feel on a cheek. The changing outline of the land and the disappearing lights of Tarbert proved we were progressing up towards Ardrishaig.

Just when the chill was beginning to cut through our layers of cloth, the waters exploded around us. Loch Fyne was a famous herring fishery. There must be the remnants of continuing migrations or at least a run of mackerel because these dolphins were chasing something. There was a feeding frenzy of scores of broaching mammals and diving birds. Barbara woke the boys and they did not take long to emerge.

These were common dolphins with their yellowish stripe. We did not have enough speed to entice them to bow-ride for long but they were out to play. Some leaped clear and it seemed to become a competition. Others sorted themselves into formations, to leap in tandem, turn by turn. Our lads squatted on the foredeck, mesmerised. Then our companions were gone.

It took the dinghy paddles, one at each side of the narrow yacht, to cover the last cable – only one-tenth of a nautical mile. We arrived at the sea gate of the canal about the time they might start to open and shut. A larger yacht motored up behind us.

'Are you fanatics or have you engine trouble?' They offered us a tow through the system. It was tempting but I knew we should take the chance to repair this engine, new to us, before venturing out to fast-flowing tide, out of Crinan.

Breakfast helped. The batteries were being fully recharged, ashore, while we got busy with the frying pan. Then I put emery cloth to sooted plugs and checked the timing again, as per instructions. We did manage to reach the other end of the waterway but it was stressful, never sure of forward or backward momentum at the right moment.

Rain came down in sheets. Crinan was a huddle of dripping people in summer coverings supposed to be waterproof. No signal for the mobile. No battery left anyway. I wedged myself into the phone box. Barbara and Ben were due elsewhere. I would need to tell our next, hopeful, crew member that we would not be picking him up at Oban tomorrow.

His number was ringing but right then there was a thump and bang at the phone-box door. Here was the one and only Ken Linklater – a member of our Stornoway sailing community. He was down for a spin in the car with his wife and he'd been amazed to recognise me though the glass.

No preambles. 'Did you get the boat then? How you getting on?'

This is the only other person I know who sails a boat that is also driven by a Dolphin motor. He swears by it and had his sleeves rolled up at the slightest mention of a small issue. He also rechecked the basics of ignition and timing. Then he calmed down. This was their holiday, away from boats for a while. I was too tired to think but Ken spoke on the phone to my friend, neighbour and prospective crew, Norman Iversen. Ken's patient wife, Isobel, would drive back to pick up Norman, now in Oban, and we'd make a start on the diagnosis.

Barbara took the boys away from the yacht, which had become an engineering site, while Isobel carried out her mission. Ken sat down to consider the whole engine system. He is a thinker by nature. He remembered that his own exhaust had sooted up once, so the motor was choking on its own fumes.

Norman said 'hello' on arrival then rolled up his own sleeves. Now Ken and Isobel drove off to continue their holiday. They dropped Ben and Barbara at Oban so they could catch their own train connection, as planned.

'Run it now,' Norman said. It was Sunday. Even the church bells were subdued here. The convertibles were silent in the hotel next door as their owners were prising langoustine meat from pink shells. I turned the key.

There was plenty of noise and plenty of smoke. 'Bit more revs,' Norman said.

The motor did run when the exhaust was not attached. Ken's diagnosis was right. We removed enough soot to create a route for the poisonous smoke to leave the vessel. We could still catch the evening tide that would send us out the Dorus Mor or Great Gate, a swirling channel that would give us access to the Sound of Jura and the sea road north. The updated forecast was not ideal but we now had limited time. That's not the best reason for deciding to sail but we were fed and rested, and we were certainly not the most popular yacht in the basin.

The Dolphin engine is a very quiet unit with little vibration, when it is running properly. Another couple of boats were chugging in to the sea lock. We seemed to be in agreement on the tide times but these yachts were not planning to go far. I sniffed the fresh breeze and knew why. As forecast, it was mainly northerly with a bit of east. We would have it on our beam as we turned to sail through the Dorus Mor. The tide would then carry us north but the wind would be mainly against us. Sound of Jura. Sound of Luing. We were at the start of the system when a huge volume of water has to fall slack before it gains momentum to return whence it came. With luck, the seas would not yet be built up by wind in opposition. The sooner we got through the gate the better. In a few hours it would be strong wind against spring tide in a waterway confined by islands, broken by skerries, not all of them marked. And it would be dark.

We hoisted a white jib, a crisp sail, heavier and smaller than the red genoa, now neatly stowed below. It was time to put in a reef, to bring the mainsail down a size, before we were out into the more exposed waters. Norman helmed while father and son shared the tasks on deck. Our neighbour does seem as if he were born to steer a boat. He spent what he called a ten-year holiday crewing for his own father, skipper of a sturdy but shallow-drafted vessel that went into all the nooks and crannies of north-west Scotland. They collected rafts of seaweed, gathered for processing. Norman was used to guiding a vessel into tight channels. He showed no anxiety as our speed rose suddenly and we were into the tideway with no more chance of changing our minds.

'She's good to windward,' said the son of a Norwegian father and Lewis mother. His father, Fred, had once appeared at our door pulling a sled containing a box of live hens. His son's wife had put her foot down after her bedding plants were scratched out. Fred knew that Barbara was looking for some laying hens. The snow had lingered and here they were. We might have had a dram. I thought it was a big step, though a small distance, a Norwegian pulling live cargo through the rare Lewis snow to bring a present to a German woman, now settled here.

I wanted to ask Fred about his wartime experience and how he had met his own Lewis wife. I never did but I knew he went for a pint at the British Legion to meet other veterans. That would have been the place to hear the story. Fred is no longer with us and the Legion is closed now as the veterans have dwindled to a last few.

Aboard *Moonspinner*, our roles were clear. I was looking for the courses and for the buoyage, identified in advance. Sean, very strong for his age, ground the winches as we found our angle, hard on the wind. Norman is of medium height and medium build. He wore a close-cropped beard, near grey, and smoked very thin roll-ups. He spent a lot of his life astride a formerly grey Fergie tractor, also now painted red. Sean and Ben had once taken pleasure in telling him we'd seen that model of tractor in a museum in Holland.

Some would be disorientated by *Moonspinner*'s angle of heel. Her waterline increased when she leaned as she was designed to do. 'She's taking it all,' Norman judged. We had been provisioning, repairing and preparing for long enough. Now we were away. Three rounded Paps of Jura were fast falling away astern to merge into a blur of snowy quartzite. Seas swirled but had not yet risen against the strengthening breeze. It was dry and clear and I sensed a faint roar, more like a river than the sea. The log of our way through water stayed steady, nudging 6 knots – a good speed. But the hand-held GPS told another version of our progress. It measures from one position over the seabed to the next in a given time, so that includes the effects of any currents. We were making close to 9 knots and the speed was climbing.

The north-going stream shoves some of its weight into the narrow Gulf of Corryvreckan, north of Jura and south of Scarba. We should not tack too close to that entrance. It was already roaring in the distance. Through the binoculars I could also see the first signs of significant whitecaps on the seas ahead. This was where our route narrowed. I was not yet ready to trust the repaired motor, working against the wind. We could make our zigzag route if we kept the legs short between each 'tack'. You may remember, that's when you turn the bow through the wind so you fall about the same number of degrees off the wind, now on the other side of the vessel. The principle is the same, whatever the rig, working boat, dinghy or yacht.

Norman and Sean were both grinning as our tacks became sweet. I was concentrating on the compass, checking that we had a safe clearance of the obstacles. I also had an eye on the numbers displayed on the echo sounder. I related these to a folded chart. We always tacked when there was still some margin of safety in case the boat, still new to us, failed to come through the wind. She always did. Still, it was a relief when dusk fell and the sector lights appeared. Our route was between the rocky islands of Fladda and Dubh Sgeir (one of the many reefs of that name, which simply means 'dark rock'). Both these showed sector lights, so you see white, red or green, according to your angle of approach. Navigation is sometimes easier at night. You look only to the lights or compass and can't see the intimidating rocks.

Once through the narrows, we could hold our tacks for longer. The boiling white of tidal interaction was still prominent against the slate black of Seil Island, now to starboard. Out ahead, the high jabble was flattening out again. I did consider clearing the south end of Kerrera, leaving it to starboard and pointing on up with the Isle of Mull off to port, but that area is open to a groundswell from the open west to pour into the cocktail. Our progress, to windward, had taken complete concentration. The few other yachts that had departed Crinan on this tide had all veered off to seek the shelter of Shuna or Loch Melfort. I felt we'd do well to follow the buoyage up the Sound of Kerrera and find anchorage in a vantage place for our entry into the Sound of Mull the following morning.

Norman reminded me I had to gain confidence in our engine. It started first time and took us the last half mile. We found a wide fish-farm boat on a huge mooring buoy. That would do. It was about midnight when fenders and lines were secure and the kettle was on. I switched off the steady motor and it was then I heard the water lapping over our floorboards. Norman looked at me. I wondered if I could have misjudged a tack. Had the keel touched hard ground at speed?

Then Norman moved. He took off the covering board and went straight to the engine sea cock. 'I'm kicking myself,' he said. 'I was going to put a second jubilee clip on the cooling-water hosepipe but it went out of my mind.' He did it now. Sean pumped her dry. No more came in. We all hit our bunks and were asleep in minutes.

Even a corrected course,
allowing for our own
magnetic field,
is affected by isobars,
the stationing of satellites
and anchored responders.

Recorded ephemera
and hands on helms.
Previous history
and the tense present.

But a lee shore
is always
implacable.

MacPhee's Black Dog

Only the bare bones of stories are writ in stone. These usually come with an outline of a human skull and an hourglass, in case you have not yet discovered that life is a breath. When it comes to detail, even the most established of folk tales exist in contradictory versions. In fact, this was a main criterion for collectors. JF Campbell (1821–1855) was influenced by the work of his friend GW Dasent, translator of Norwegian tales collected by Asbjørnsen and Moe. Campbell supervised a team of Gaelic-speaking collectors working in the Highlands and Islands of Scotland. He considered multiple versions, with their regional variations, as evidence that a story did in fact have vernacular origins. A single instance could perhaps imply that a story was the recent invention of a single author.

The tale of MacPhee's black dog is just the sort of story we might have told at anchor in *Moonspinner* had we not all been exhausted by preparing our vessel for sea. The black dog story is linked to locations ranging from Colonsay to Benbecula. One version, preserved in a written form by an enlightened minister of the church (one JG Campbell), brings the story to the skyline I had been studying for several hours. The three Paps of Jura had taken over from jagged Arran as the shape scored in the sky. The ridges of Jura and its neighbouring Scarba were now drawn by ink on the tail of a leaping hound. Colonsay, Tiree and Benbecula, all also associated with the tale, have milder, lower-lying skylines.

They say that MacPhee was from Tiree. That's fertile land, with wind-blown sand from its long beaches to sweeten the soil. Like its neighbour, Coll, it looks more like a continuation of nearby

Ireland than the rocks and scree and moorland of Mull, Jura and Islay. In MacPhee's day folk might spend all their lives living and working on one small piece of ground. He became a wanderer because small crofts were being gathered together. He lost his tenancy but he had a skill that was in great demand. He was knacky with dogs, training them and getting them to run to round up the growing flocks.

Once he was asked to choose one pup from a litter as a payment for a great favour. He was led to a cave by an old man who pointed to the finest hound with her litter of pups. MacPhee pointed out a strong-looking black dog. 'Take any other but that pup,' he was told. But MacPhee insisted. The old fellow relented. He could return to take that one, when he was weaned. 'Be warned now. It will only ever run for you the once.'

'Maybe that once will be enough.'

Everyone thought MacPhee had made a bad error of judgement this time. The shepherd and hunter had to suffer many a comment on the dog, which grew to be the finest-looking animal but also the laziest. The bitch did all the running. 'Why do you feed that dog?' he was asked, more than once. The reply was always the same. 'The black dog will have his day.'

There came a time when MacPhee was hired to lead a party of 16 gentlemen on a deer hunt on Jura. They were to cross by boat from Islay. The black dog rose and crossed with them to the door of their lodgings. He sniffed the air and returned to his place by the fire, though MacPhee's bitch trotted on to the pier with the men. 'You should shoot that dog and save yourself its feeding,' said one.

But that day the winds blew too hard against the tide for any crossing. 'Maybe the black dog can sense something, after all,' the same man said.

Next day they got across, dog and all. The chase took them well into the hills, up at the north end of the island. Not a shot had been fired but no one was ready to give up. So they gathered bracken and heather and bedded themselves down as best they could in a cave. As each of the young gentlemen lay down, he wished that his companion were a woman rather than another hairy male. MacPhee said it was poor luck to cast a wish like that. Better to think of the good woman at home.

He stationed himself nearest the mouth of that cave so the dog and bitch could have a last stretch and relieve themselves. But he became alert, not long after they had all settled for the night. I can't say if it was a sight or a sound or the rising hackles of the dog that woke him. The shadows were stealing through the cave. A strange thing on a cloudy night. There was only a flicker of embers but MacPhee was sure he could see the glint of white bones or beaks. He blinked and made out a long line of small figures, cloaked. These glints showed, under grey-black hoods. He had no need to count. He knew there would be 17.

Now both dog and bitch had teeth bared and hackles up. MacPhee followed them back into the darkness of the inner cave. There was not a sound from any of the hunters. MacPhee knew it was already too late for them. Right then the nearest shadow moved towards him. 'Run now,' he said to the black dog. 'If you only run once, run now.'

The dog ran ahead of the bitch and all his power went into it. It was as if the stone slab of the cave shook from the impression of his paws. The shadows bolted. It was then the thunder sounded from above. But it was not thunder. MacPhee looked up to see the sweep of a claw. It was reaching for him through the chink where the shapes that had done for his companions escaped like smoke.

MacPhee's black dog was already in the air, all his strength in his great leap. Dark jaws locked and the dog held on while the bitch crouched to keep guard over her master. Now MacPhee discharged his gun, upwards, above the dog. There was a roar never heard before or since on Jura. A hundred rutting stags.

The dog held on, though there was only a mess of splintered bones left to hold. His master took his chance then and called him in. He left the scene with both dog and bitch. The dawn was coming to the sky and they were met by nothing. Dog and bitch followed MacPhee to the boat. They would need to cross the fast-flowing sound again. They would return with strong men to recover the 16 bodies from the depths of that cave.

They say the black dog never did run again. They also say that MacPhee continued to feed him and care for him till the end of his time.

Sound of Mull

TWO MEN AND A BOY WERE SNATCHING SLEEP aboard a red-painted clinker yacht with a high rig. I'd made the great skipper's mistake. We'd been wakened, before 6am, by the clatter of the fish-farm boys starting up their engines. I'd been ready for the off but given in to pressure to tie up for a minute or two in Oban. Norman was short of tobacco. We put two reefs in the mainsail of the red Stella as the ferry cleared the buoy. No other boats were departing Oban bound for Mull today. We'd need every hour to punch into heavy breeze.

Tack after tack produced a fine speed through the water and plenty of spray. It was excellent sailing with my two crew, taking turns to grin, at the helm. But I knew we'd be lucky to drive through the narrows, out from Cragnure, if we were not through by the turn of the tide. Sure enough, I could see ahead to a white wall of water. That was the result of a 30-knot wind against several knots of contrary tide.

Sean and I clipped on lifelines to the strong point on our lifejackets. These are attached to webbing straps running along the sidedecks to the bow. If you stumble and trip and go over the low guardrails at the sides of the boat, at least you are still attached. I feel it's better to keep the lifeline short by passing it once round the webbing and then back to fix the second clip on your lifejacket or harness. This makes movements awkward but the idea is to stop you from going overboard. It would be no easy matter to recover someone, even of my weight or Sean's. We worked together well to get the third and final reef in the mainsail, and the same white jib would also help. *Moonspinner* had a tiny storm jib aboard but there is a risk of reducing power too much when you are trying to work upwind. I guessed the wind would give us 5 knots' speed, on our best angle, with a safe amount of cloth up. But the tide would wipe 3 knots off that. A 'speed made good' of 2 knots would inch us through but then you have the effect of turbulent water slowing progress. There is also great pressure on boat, rig and crew.

We had a look at it, more in curiosity than hope. You can't get back those two or three hours you lost at the start of the day, but Norman and Sean were taking pleasure in the sailing for its own sake. We punched on into the funnelling wind, working between the bleak Duart Point and the white-painted beacon on the reef out from low Lismore.

We were now beating against a gale in a small yacht, looking for that extra few metres of safe water that would give us the angle to sail clear. You need to catch each other's eyes and work as a team. The fellow on the tiller gives the nod but you don't want to release the power from the foresail or jib till the turn towards the wind reaches the stage where it flaps or 'luffs'. Then you want a smart transfer so the controlling rope (sheet) on one side is released and the strain is taken up by the other.

It is very satisfying when each turn is made in a positive way with the sail going neatly over and not a word needed. If the boat is turned too far downwind you lose the ground you've gained on the last leg or 'tack'. If you keep her too close to the wind the sail will continue to 'luff' – the boat will drift sideways rather than drive forwards.

I stopped looking at the chart and the tide tables. I already had the period of slack water pencilled beside it, corrected for British Summer

Time. No amount of strategy could change that simple calculation. We would not be transiting the Sound of Mull till tomorrow.

My two companions tuned in to a banter that crossed the years between them. Norman had become like an honorary uncle to Sean. They were just as content when we picked up a buoy at Craignure rather than sailing the detour to find a more pleasant anchorage off Lismore, in the Firth of Lorne. We were a bit exposed to a swell but we were in a good position to beat on up the Sound on the morning flood. Sean took his first dram (to my knowledge) that night. I made our usual spicy pasta sauce. Norman had been cool as any cucumber as we'd driven through white spray, working all day to cover the distance the Oban ferry sails in less than an hour. 'Is this all right for you?' I'd asked, though there was not a lot we could do to change things. 'This is what I came for,' he said.

Something had happened between the three of us. I knew it to be worth even more than catching the tide. If you've made the wrong decision, you make it worse by going back to the 'if only' moment. That's history and the bow has to move forwards, usually, when you're sailing. But that evening the sweat poured from our neighbour. Norman was not used to the sprinkling of chilli I'd nonchalantly thrown into the pan.

I went to my bunk with the realisation that sailing is not only about objectives. I had not intended to study the small area of geography at the heart of the story of Lady's Rock quite so closely, but the observation would be in my telling of the story ever after.

The deflected winds
paw their way
closer. Still,

tides will turn
as the borrowed waters
must return through Sounds

but the bulge of their curves,
will always alter
just a bit.

Lady's Rock

I've now sailed close to Lady's Rock, off Lismore, more than once. My strongest memory is that first occasion. It was no time for sightseeing, yet the quality of that turbulent water is still held in my mind's log of remembered sea conditions. It was like mutton broth on the boil before the fat is skimmed from it. Visibility was good. The skyline of mountains was a sharp, wavering line, over the Firth of Lorne. The island of Lismore squatted low by the whiteish water.

MacLean and his lady were not on good terms. Folk wouldn't be in a rush to accept an invitation to dine there. No matter the quality of the food that graced the board, there would be silences and tension.

The marriage had brought an alliance between two powerful families. MacLean's wife was one of the Campbells of Argyll, but her husband spent less and less time at home in Duart. That's a stout castle out on a promontory of the sheltered and fertile east side of the Isle of Mull. But what good is wealth and beauty if there's no warmth to be had? They say that MacLean was often away on his best mare on the long road north.

A galleon remained at anchor in Tobermory Bay. MacLean would dine there more often than he did at home, drawn in to the cheer and wit in the great cabin of that ship. They said there was a Spanish lady, of exceptional beauty. They said her conversation was sharp but full of learning. They said more than that.

You might think Lady MacLean would be glad to be free of her gloomy man for a while, but her husband's absences were an affront to her and her family.

The Spanish ship carried gunpowder, deep within her holds. One night there was a great roar, over the bay. Splinters of European oak rained from the dark grey sky. There was one survivor. His adventures are at least one more story, also collected and written out by the hand of Donald Morrison. That tale's for another day.

MacLean wasn't on board when the ship was destroyed, but that cultured Spanish lady was. He was sure his wife had paid her own servant to lay a slow fuse in the hold of that vessel. They say this, they say that. But, on Mull, most people were sure Lady MacLean was behind the terrible event. England was always at war with Spain but the complicated reasons behind that struggle did not mean much to the people of the Scottish islands. It's possible that the Campbell family were looking to show their support of a distant court in London. They might have been seeking rewards in land and power.

In his rage, MacLean had his own loyal servants take hold of his wife, whether she was guilty or not. Her hands were bound and she was taken aboard a small craft. They rowed her out from Duart into the Sound of Mull, taking her right up to the lonely rock that's off Lismore Island. There's hardly space for one person to stand on it. The tide was rising. The water would cover the rock and rise a fathom more. There's no force in the world can stop that rise and fall. MacLean's men left her there and rowed quietly into the fading light.

The water crept higher. It was still calm and she was able to hold her footing. This was during a warm spell of weather so she did not give way, at once, to the seeping cold. When the water was lapping at her breast, that poor woman let all her fear out in a terrible wail. If you've heard seals calling from a rock, that sound is not so different from the cries she made that night. But there was something human left in her voice. There must have been, because a boat, out to seek herring, heard her cries. They came close and were able to haul the sobbing, shaking woman aboard.

She revived enough to tell them who she was. They knew that on no account should they land her at Duart. Instead, they took her to a shore in Lismore itself. They found help in a house where a fire was blazing and water was soon boiling.

The rescuers sent a message to Campbell, her brother in Appin, Argyll. It was not long before she was brought home to her own people. However, her brother had received a letter from Mull. MacLean had written to say how a terrible fever had taken a grip of the people of the island and that Campbell's sister was among those who had succumbed. Because the weather was so unusually warm, so far into the year, they had been forced to act in haste. They'd proceeded with a proper burial, with no time to wait until her family heard the sad news. He was sorry the family could not have been there to pay their last respects.

A coffin, weighted with stones, wrapped in cloth, had been interred at Duart. The body of Lady MacLean had been left to the sea. So they thought. Campbell wrote back to say that it was a tragedy but what could they do? Except of course to meet and join in taking food and drink together in memory of the sister of one and the late wife of the other.

MacLean suspected nothing and made arrangements to travel. Soon he was seated at the long table in the hall at Appin. The finest claret was decanted for them. They sipped and ate. There was herring, dipped in oatmeal and fried in its own oil, then well-seared venison from the hill followed by pressed white cheese from the best farm in the territory.

At last, each man sat with a deep glass of brandy. MacLean said what fine hospitality he'd received. There was of course only one thing missing from the gathering.

'If it was possible, to have one more glimpse of that fine woman, your own sister and my late wife,' he said, raising his glass to her memory.

'Well, I don't think that will be too difficult to arrange,' said Campbell. Then he drew aside the heavy drapes that had been drawn behind them all through the meal. She stood, tall. There was colour in her cheeks. This was no ghost.

Lady MacLean's brother was for putting steel into the ribs of the man who had left his sister to die. He had to be stopped from doing the act there and then, against all laws of hospitality. Strangely, it was his own sister who appealed for the life of the man who had left her to drown.

I can't say if it was because there was something left of the affection they had once held for each other. Or, more likely, a sense that she too had been responsible for the intrigue. But she pleaded for him and Campbell relented, releasing his brother-in-law, against his better judgment.

That made little difference. Not long afterwards, there was a ferocious clan battle that changed the colour of the sea, lapping on a shoreline of Mull. Indigo water turned maroon. MacLean met his end at the battle of Bloody Bay.

Through the binoculars, we could see the white wall of tidal disturbance fall low. It was a fine day's sailing and Norman and Sean took her higher up the track line than we needed, to get an angle on the wind to take us into Tobermory. After the previous day's hard work, under deep-reefed sails, they wanted to see her run. Like MacPhee's dog.

We did that and they saw the needle climb to over 7 knots, on the dial. Sean had his weight out as he held the foresail sheet, going to the winch. Norman controlled the main as well as the tiller. 'No weight in it,' he said. A rudder is also a brake. He did not need to apply it because we had the sails balanced for the force of the wind and because rig and hull are well designed. This was about the maximum speed for the type of craft, unless it's surfing, free of the physics of wave and waterline lengths.

The northerlies were due to continue and Norman was obliged to get back to work. We had to leave her on a mooring in Tobermory for a week or two. Then we took her safely home to Stornoway harbour, as a family. Barbara went along with my decisions on very early starting times in order to make the most of strong tides. We all had to take a share of helming and we all had to catch some sleep. Barbara's confidence grew enough to take *Moonspinner* through a couple of tight turns as the rest slept.

Yet we did not keep the yacht for long, though her sailing performance was excellent and her motor gave no further problems. Already I was restless to venture further into open sea. That would take a steadier boat with a smaller, self-draining cockpit, in case a wave decided to join us aboard. There was strong interest in *Moonspinner* and we accepted an offer from someone who would keep her near Gairloch. I offered to sail her across with a mate of mine and her new owner also aboard.

The farewell voyage was one of the best Minch crossings I've experienced. There was snow on the Torridon mountains as we sailed hard, bound for Badachro. She made a steady 6½ knots. Strangely, it was easier to part with the vessel after sensing that she was sailing close to her best. A few years later, it was painful to see her ashore, near Gairloch pier, neglected for a while. Equally, it was a joy to see her, after another few years slipped by, afloat in the new marina at Wick. Her red enamel was renewed and she had kept her name. I knew that because it was painted on in an illuminated script.

Sandra

I CAN NO LONGER AVOID THE DELICATE SUBJECT of sharing a vessel between friends. This has not happened often in my life. One rare instance brought me to the geography of stories I might have missed. Even if I have come to know the bare bones of a story, I feel that

I cannot bring it to life again unless I can picture a route through its terrain.

I was still working towards my seagoing ticket at the time. Ken Linklater's work had him travel all over Scotland so it was not fair to ask him for a hand with the Dolphin engine during his time back on the island. Another friend helped me make sure the motor installed in *Moonspinner* was serviced and safe. Then he met complications in his life. He was returning to his home island of Skye, to spend more time with a daughter who needed him to be near, but he could not bear to leave his boat behind. He was in the middle of his own intensive training course for a job he could not afford to lose. But he had also invested his money and his time into a project yacht and he couldn't afford to lose that either. I wanted to repay his time but there was some self-interest, too. I was also curious to sail a type of boat new to me but now one of the most common kinds of leisure vessel you will see round British coasts.

Stornoway is blessed with a deep-water harbour. Hence its history, from Vikings to Klondykers* to oil-associated industry and developing renewable energies. Many harbours lose their waters, on each and every tide, leaving mud or shingle for boats to sit on before they refloat when it all comes back in again. Their owners may have to time their comings and goings with that cycle. They are in thrall to the moon.

This is where a bilge keeler is a very suitable craft because it will stand, even and steady, on its two matching keels, rather than falling over. It does not need to perch against a wall on a single deep fin. There is much snobbery in sailing and I've heard devotees of more streamlined craft say that a bilge keeler will sail like a bag of nails. There is a bit of 20th-century sailing history that proves it's not as simple as that.

---

* Term given to generations of vessels involved in the herring trade – a rush for silver.

There will now follow a small digression that will take us to *Sandra*, the blunt and buxom vessel I was given charge of for one voyage. She is of a class modestly called the Invader. But, like the family of working craft of Norse origins, or the yachts these influenced, the design did not just appear from out of the blue.

In the late 1960s, sailing achievements were being taken further and further. Names such as Sir Francis Chichester were spoken as often as those of soccer stars. He held the world record for the fastest solo circumnavigation. The holy grail was the solo non-stop transit round the world. A race was established to provoke designers and single-handed sailors into joining the attempt. That's why it was the Golden Globe.

The story has several different endings. The happy one is *Suhaili*, built in India, of teak. She was strong rather than streamlined and was kept on going by a merchant navy officer called Robin Knox-Johnston, to win the prize. Then there is the thoughtful tale. The mystical Frenchman Bernard Montessier did not turn up back towards the start line in the English Channel but sailed on round again, until he reached Tahiti. He was in a strong position but did this act 'for his sanity' rather than playing along with the rules of a competitive race. He lived on for many years, to sail, think and write.

There is also the tragic story of Donald Crowhurst. He staked his reputation and business as a designer of marine electronics on his own attempt. When his ill-prepared trimaran failed to cover the miles after a late start, he composed his own imagined log of miles not sailed. That could be seen as a great work of the imagination, but he was in trouble when a boat, also a trimaran, out ahead of Crowhurst's fictitious position, fell apart 1,100 miles from the finish. It is possible that Crowhurst's broadcasts of false positions spurred Nigel Tetley to drive his boat beyond its limits. Crowhurst's theoretical position would now be placed under the scrutiny of sailors such as Chichester, who really had made the journey before. What there is of Crowhurst's true log indicates a suicide. Knox-Johnston donated his race winnings to a fund for his widow.

Another contender became a legend. Chay Blyth was an ex-paratrooper from inland Hawick. He began with almost no sailing experience and no knowledge of maritime navigation. He took an example of a 30-foot fibreglass boat, a bilge keeler already in production, as far as the southern tip of Africa. By that time he had become competent in sextant navigation and was making good time. The vessel and sole occupant met huge seas and the boat did not have enough grip on the water to cope. Again and again she would 'broach' or turn side on to waves big enough to roll her over. He knew he had taken this type of craft to its limits after broaching 11 times in one day. This man, who was already one of the legendary pair who had survived storms to row the Atlantic in an open 20-foot dory, was now a husband and father. He judged it suicide to take *Dytiscus III* on to the Southern Ocean. He had cleared the Cape of Good Hope but retired from the race and put in to a South African port to make repairs.

Despite this, he made a triumph out of his adventure by inviting his wife to join him in the quest to return the borrowed craft to Britain. Their story is told turn-about in an entertaining account.* You have to read between the lines to detect the times of terror.

That vessel's survival, voyaging way beyond the conditions it was built for, prompted a flurry of boatbuilding. The bilge keeler had coped with more than anyone sensible thought it could. *Sandra* was clearly one example of this line of development. This Invader 22 was a smaller boat, of that family of bilge keelers, designed for coastal cruising but capable of standing up to a bit of sea if caught out. She was not blessed with an inboard but had a recent and well-maintained petrol outboard motor. She was bought as a project and my mate had concentrated on structure and engine and rig first. There was almost nothing down below decks.

This is a guy who was always there if you needed a hand with timing, points or fuel systems. In return, I'd try to pass on what I'd

---

* *Innocent Aboard*, Chay and Maureen Blyth, Nautical Books, Lymington, 1970.

learned about setting sails and passage-planning. Some days we did a 'sail for a sail', jumping over to *Moonspinner*. I was keen to build up experience of how different types of craft handled. This could be a main factor in tumbling into affairs with other people's objects of desire.

This is the most personal of issues. I have seen vessels built of glass-reinforced plastic that are of a streamlined and sinuous shape. But when I viewed their exposed inner selves, bare of 'headliners' of stretched vinyl, I felt little curiosity to look closer. Their painted matting does not interest me the way a craftsman-laid skin of clinker or carvel, timber planking does. Yet I know there will come a time when I will be impatient with all the care a living wooden structure requires. I will want to sniff breeze and feel movement through water, rather than scrape and rub until every one of my muscles aches.

No material is really maintenance-free. It must have seemed a wonder when the alchemy of resin on matt, aided by a few drops of catalyst, gelled to form a smooth skin over a shaped mould. A gelcoat of finish makes that exterior surface even more smooth still. Nordic Folkboats are now moulded to the shape of an original wooden example to form a near-perfect hull. This is done at a fraction of the cost of a craftsman-built timber version. However, once the integrity of that finish is chafed or scraped, water can enter the very fabric of the wonder material. 'Osmosis' is the new disease that has replaced wet rot but is also to do with moisture content. Telltale blisters can appear and require treatment. Or perhaps no urgent measures are required. The surveyor advises the owner that the fibreglass boat is no longer perfect but should be safe for some years, so long as her condition is monitored.

Analysis can only take you so far. It's just not possible to be objective when you attempt to probe into why a vessel in one material excites you and one of another skin type does not.

My friend had lifted his pride and joy out of the water for winter. He was going to work on the interior and install a diesel engine. Then everything changed. He needed someone to take *Sandra* to Broadford, Isle of Skye. He could then live aboard her for a while. The separation from his wife was going to be messy but the boat was his own. I didn't ask any more personal questions. And I needed no second asking. I did take a close look first, in daylight, to be sure of what was there and what was not. As she swung on the 'high-up' hoist of a flatbed truck, I was surprised by how pleasing her shape was, if you looked above the neat and trim waterline. The exterior was well cared for. I knew that she was beautiful to him. I did not desire this vessel, which is just as well, but we could be friends.

It did not take long to fix her deck-stepped mast in position. Like that of the Stella class, the rigging was not much more complex than that of a dinghy. The majority of it was new, in shining stainless steel. The fittings were up to the job. 'Don't look inside,' I was told. I did not, but I had to ask the key question. This might seem strange but, according to my coastguard experience, the most usual cause of vessels sinking is due to the holes in the boat. Accidental holes from hitting rocks or from gas explosions do happen, but most boats have holes deliberately drilled in them to compromise the integrity of a perfect skin. There might be an intake and an outlet for a toilet. Another for the waste water from a sink. One to let cooling water in to circulate round an engine and another to let it out in a wet exhaust. There might also be a couple of drains to let rain or seawater run from the steering area – the cockpit.

If the pipes detach from any of these, seawater will enter the boat at speed. I had already experienced this, first hand. If fastenings perish or the 'sea cock' (usually a tap of bronze) corrodes, you might also let in the sea. My mate told me there was no toilet. No sink. No inboard motor. The cockpit was not self-draining. Good. No gas. Good. We'd bring a camping stove.

I helped tension the rigging, by feel and by eye and by sound. We did not use a measuring meter of any kind. We went round every connecting shackle and put a twist of monel wire round the eye so none could work loose from vibration. We had an anchor and chain, warps to tie up and fenders to prevent chafe against other craft when in harbour. I brought a hand-held VHF radio so I could hear forecasts and get a message ashore, if need be. Together, we improvised a simple way of reducing sail. That's another factor essential for safety, whatever the craft.

We took her for a spin. The motor started easily and ran well. Of course she sailed very well downwind but she was also not that bad upwind. I knew, in theory, how many degrees of leeway (side-drift) I should allow if we had to beat across to Skye. (That's when the wind is well forward of the midpoint of the boat.) But it would be smarter to wait for a wind that would drive us from behind that midpoint or 'abaft the beam' as we say in the trade, when we're showing off.

Stornoway to Portree

THERE ARE TWO KINDS OF DELIVERY TRIP, by sea. One is when the owner is aboard and the other is when he or she is not. This was of the second kind, though I would have been very happy to sail with my pal. I would have consolidated my own passage-planning by asking him to do it, independently, and then comparing our results. This time, Barbara was keen to come along. We were between boats as we had just made an offer for one, presently far from our home in the Outer Hebrides.

We brought along a chemical toilet, going spare, from a campervan we'd now sold. We'd leave that aboard as a donation to the ship when the job was done. You'd be bound to get a comment from the crew if you carried a spare anchor home on the ferry. 'So you don't really trust us then.' But the crew would never let us forget it if we brought our own toilet up the gangplank.

Barbara had seen to provisions and I had a small folio of charts. Tide was not a huge factor at first but it would kick in at the north end of Skye and we would work our passage to get some help from it. The wind was fresh. I knew the dangers of underestimating the speed we might achieve in this small but beamy craft. That can be dangerous if you arrive into an area of hazards sooner than you've calculated, in poor visibility. I also know that you sometimes need to slow down a sailing craft as well as push it to its best speed in the breeze experienced at the time.

The wind allowed us to point the boat in the right direction. A bilge keeler will make more leeway than a comparable vessel with a single but deeper keel but that is not a major factor if the wind is with you. This time the forecast held true and the steady west to north-west wind drove us at close to 5 knots through the water.

Soon we were about 3 miles to the east of the Shiants. This archipelago was becoming my first reference point once the Stornoway 'roads' were left behind. From this distance out there is nothing to show that there is no longer a bustling croft on these islands, or that the west-lying Eilean Mhuire, though bright green, is only visited by shepherds, geologists, archaeologists and occasionally even its 'owners', the Nicolson family. The thorough research, evident in Adam Nicolson's engrossing *Sea Room**, proves that the relationship is more complex than 'owning'.

You might just make out the hints of raised ribs of land. These remains of backbreaking 'lazy-beds' were built up from years of collecting 'tangle' of nutrient-rich seaweeds. These ribs are often the only signs of former settlements.

A route by sea will often take you by a landmass or archipelago seen from a different angle to the one you sailed on a previous voyage. That is one reason why I've never experienced boredom on an uneventful passage. Even if I have set out from a port I've departed from often and arrived at an anchorage I know well, the route always seems new to me. Maybe it's like returning to a complex piece of music. There is pleasure in the familiar and an equal pleasure in

---

* *Sea Room*, Adam Nicolson, Harper Collins, London, 2001.

experiencing the rise and fall of shapes unnoticed before. Gaps open and close. There is a continually altering relationship between air, ground and sea. This has been best described in another time, another language, another ocean:

> 'Tall islands point to the sky and level ones prostrate themselves before the surges of water. Islands are piled above islands, and islands are joined to islands, so that they look exactly like parents caressing their children or walking with them, arm in arm.' *

There is probably a detailed log of the main twists and turns of our passage in *Sandra* but I am not going to hunt for my written account. Instead, I'll trust the imagery that has lodged in my mind and the remembered mood. Perhaps it is because we were well prepared and the weather was clear but I remember a very close spirit of cooperation.

The outlook to one series of islands gave way to another. Off the north tip of Skye there is the high island of Eilean Trodday with its significant lighthouse. There is the lower-lying Fladda-chùain but there are also the lesser islands and covering skerries. Further headlands play hide and seek with you. I could identify Duntulm but was also conscious of the drama of Dunvegan Head lying further out along the coast that faces the Outer Hebrides. Is it possible to separate sightings recorded on a documented date from your previous and subsequent memories? My first experience of navigating a yacht, under the eye of its owner, happened to take me by these islands but on the opposite side, between them and mainland Skye. The skipper was Ivor Horton, my mentor in coastal navigation. He worked me hard as a trainee coastguard and he worked me hard on that passage. I had to apply the methods learned

---

* *The Narrow Road to the Deep North*, Matsuo Basho, translated Nobuyuki Yuasa (1966 edition), Penguin Classics, London, p115.

first at a stationary chart table. Plotting a criss-cross of two or three compass bearings is a simple matter but it's trickier when the boat is jumping about.

That day the rocks glittered. Other times they have remained hidden behind dense droplets. This is a traffic lane, a recommended route for major shipping bound northwards up the Minches. It is an eerie place to be in when you have lost your sight. Darkness is fine because there will be lights in helpful sequences. In one version of the ballad of riddles it is 'thunder' that is louder than a horn. When you nose your way near the edge of a shipping lane in fog, you know the better answer is 'rumour'. My strongest connection to the line of Fladda-chùain goes further than the observed shape or the memory of its silhouette. My elder son, Sean, was the youngest paddler in a group of kayakers who crossed the Minch at about its narrowest waist. They rested and made a brew on that island. Sean knows I like to sense the stories behind found timber, so he told me how I couldn't imagine the stockpile of generations of driftwood, piled up by the tides, in that place. He handed me a piece he'd prised from the rocks that held it for years. Timbers, once bent by steam, were still riveted together. The parts are probably oak. I don't want to scrape the weathered surface to inspect the grain. The fastenings are iron. The found object is certainly older than me and probably older than the two of us put together. There is no way of knowing if the relic is from a vessel that was left to fall apart peacefully or if it met a sudden end in this tideway. It has now followed me across different thresholds. It makes me think of the skills of those who design and build and thus allow our explorations, whatever their range.

When we began our relationship, Barbara was the more experienced sailor and by far the more experienced photographer. She did not seem to feel a compulsion to extend the range of either of these. I think I did, at that time. This often led to tension between us.

Looking back on that day, I think we were free of that, in the neutral territory of someone else's boat.

I'm grateful to *Sandra* for bringing me back across a line on a chart – one I'd drawn first on that voyage with Ivor. It remained a peaceful day, for Barbara and me. And it had its epiphany. Close to the Skye mainland we both glimpsed a long, shining blackish back following a small, curving dorsal fin, to fall below a surface.

It is a fairly common sight in the Minches or the Sea of the Hebrides. This was a huge animal and its long back glistened. The designed hull of our charge slid through the water but we could observe effortless grace in this mammal, up to draw breath before diving to feed. I think I said, 'A minke' rather than, 'A whale.'

When I was a coastguard, I learned that many species of whale were sighted or were stranded in our area of jurisdiction. A fin whale has a very similar back profile to a minke but it is more rare and there is a huge difference in scale. Perhaps there is an analogy between the goshawk and the sparrowhawk, similar in appearance but vastly different in size. But at sea, in differing visibility, it is very difficult to judge both distance and scale. It is possible that sightings of cetacean are simplified because we tend to assume we are seeing the more common species. A marine biologist advised me that it would be easy to confuse a minke whale with a sei whale from its appearance, though the tone of its 'blow' is different. I'm not the first to quote a succinct sentence from JA Baker's ten-year study of falcons, *The Peregrine*:

'The hardest thing of all is to see what is really there.'*

And when a Northeasterly
comes off the Tundra

a rippling tendency
in wind-driven current

---

* *The Peregrine*, JA Baker, New York Review Books, 2005 edition (first published, 1967).

will swither as
an onshore wind approaches

high shale skerries.

A Cow and Boat Tale

If you can kayak across from our Long Island to Skye, you can see how a story could cross, given the right breeze. Donald Morrison, that cooper again, says that this story is from Skye. When I say 'says', we're both writing but we're trying to speak. In the edition of Morrison's manuscript, edited by Norman Macdonald 'under the direction of Alexander Morrison, District Librarian, Public Library, Stornoway, Isle of Lewis, 1975', the story is titled *A Judge who Pleased Both Clients*. I want to retell it because it has lodged in my mind. That's not a matter of learning it up. For me it's more like allowing it to become a part of you and reimagining its landscape, its characters, images and tone. Maybe a phrase or two will remain nearly intact, each telling, like a refrain.

There were two crofters, neighbours. Each had a great passion in his life. I'm sorry to say that we're not talking about the crofters' wives, though both of them were married, happily enough. One man was very fond of a particular boat and the other had a very fine cow.

We like a bit of beam in a boat on the west coast and this vessel had ample. She'd looked after this man, all their lives. Many's a thumping lythe came over her gunnels. She'd always found the way home, through the reefs, to the geo where she was kept safe.

The crofter did not venture out to sea as often as he used to but he'd be content to take a stroll in the evening. He'd just stand back from the cliff, admiring her lines.

His neighbour would pat his cow's rump in the morning and she'd wander out and find her own grazings. He never even had to send the dog. She'd be home in good time in the evening and give a good yield of quality milk. She'd never kick or bump the pail. You knew what to expect and it would be the same every day, whatever the weather.

But this night the cow did not appear home, back at the croft. Right away, our man knew something was wrong. He went out along the cliffs there and then. He was stopped in his tracks, just at the edge of his own ground. There was mud and hoof marks and signs of a struggle but the cow had slithered over the edge. Now these are gradual grassy cliffs and she might have survived but she'd gone stumbling into the very spot where his neighbour's boat was kept. She must have panicked. There were split planks and broken timbers everywhere. The splinters of the boat had finished her off.

Pain often shows itself as anger. This man, who had never had a bad word with his neighbour, went shouting and banging at his door.

'Your boat has killed my cow.'

'What are you talking about, man? You're making no sense.'

But then, when the other fellow realised what was behind the words, he said, 'And what about my boat. Is she all right?'

'Of course she's not all right but it's my cow we're talking about here and your boat has done for her.'

First there was an argument, then silence and then a court case. Neither of these men had much money behind them but it looked as if they would ruin themselves at law. There was no legal precedence for this case and no court could decide who was responsible for the losses.

The case was much discussed and gained the interest of MacDonald, the laird of much of Skye at the time. It was due to go to the Court of Session and we all know how long that would take.

'Gentlemen,' said MacDonald, 'Do you not think there's enough men putting claret into the mouths of the Edinburgh lawyers without us contributing more?'

He suggested putting the case to an independent man – a factor on the neighbouring estate. It wouldn't cost them a penny. This man was respected. So they all agreed to meet.

'Now,' said the factor, 'I've no letters after my name and no legal qualifications whatsoever. But may I suggest that there's no point in having this discussion unless we all agree to abide by our finding.'

They all nodded their understanding. Each told his side of the story.

The factor looked to the man who had lost his cow. 'Remember our agreement?' He nodded. The factor said the same thing to the one who had lost his boat. He nodded too. And then he asked MacDonald, the laird, if he would also abide by the finding.

'Well, I do not see what that has directly to do with myself but yes, of course, I'll abide by what's decided.'

'In that case,' said the factor, 'I can see both sides of the argument. The cow might well have survived her slip had the boat not been in that exact place. And clearly the boat would still be intact had the cow not fallen. But we must look deeper into the very cause of the accident. It seems to me that a section of coast like this has inherent dangers to man and beast. Therefore, a dyke should have been established to offer protection. And so I find against the laird for the value of a replacement cow to this man and a boat to the other. And for the cost of erecting a suitable dyke so that an accident like this may not happen again.'

And to his credit the laird did pay.

Portree to Broadford

THE BREEZE CONTINUED TO DRIVE US on as the tide took a hold. We steered *Sandra* down the inside route. First there was the visible rugged Quirang up ahead on the Skye mainland. Then we could identify the old man of Storr, high up on a ridge, to starboard, shoved back from sea. The name is derived from its Gaelic original, which could refer to an old man but also to his penis. We planned to leave a chain of islands to port – Rona, Raasay, Pabay and Scalpay. We had made good time but I wanted to be alert when we sailed under the shadow of the Cuillins. We could afford to break our journey in Portree.

The Black Cuillin range ahead of us was more than the 'serrated blue rampart' that the Raasay poet Sorley Maclean feared they would be reduced to, were it not for the redeeming passion a human might feel for another. Strange how often we try to cope with landscape by liking it to the human. We passed by the point of The Brothers then Barbara ticked off an outlying starboard mark and we were into the wind eddies that dash back and fore across the bay at Portree. You see painted buildings and wooded shores. You are tempted into thinking that this harbour is filled with tame water. But I had been well warned by those who had visited it more times than myself. The wind can shift from giving you a friendly pat on the back to cuffing you from ahead in a matter of seconds. A sudden quarrel with an obscure cause.

All the moorings were occupied and a couple of larger yachts were rafted up outside fishing boats. They might have to do a very early morning shuffle. We came sniffing up close now, under outboard, in a cheeky fashion. One of the fishermen gave us the nod. 'That pontoon is only really for pick-ups and drop-offs but there's plenty of space for dinghies if you just tie up at the end. As long as you're away early in the morning.'

I said we'd be up early to get a rising tide through the narrows, down the inside. 'Decent tide for you the morro. There's a wee box for the Harbour Trust, up top.' We slipped our mooring fee into it and strolled off to seek a couple of bunks up the town. It was hoaching with folk, locals as well as tourists, judging from the accents and the occasional greeting in Gaelic. It was Skye Gathering Day and there would be a song and dance but no chance of a berth ashore. Thoughts of venison casseroles faded. We might be clutching at hamburgers from a van.

After Barbara had her dram of Talisker and I'd downed some Isle of Skye brewed ale, that didn't seem to matter so much. Pipers held their duels outside but the drummers fought it out on pads on the tables in the bar. It was like walking into a folk tale, adapted by Ealing in its heyday. The banter was fast and it was as friendly a riot as you could hope to enter. I was thinking it was not every day Barbara would be up for this mayhem. Now it was in balance to our long peaceful day on the water.

We had another drink in a pub with a very good singer-songwriter holding sway. Ballads are not yet dead. Then we braved the interior of our floating accommodation. Barbara heated up soup and I threw down lifejackets and jackets and anything that would provide a small barrier between our sleeping bags and the temporary flooring. She rubbed a towel over the condensation on the exposed glass matting. Our friend had a bit of work to do.

I slept sound but woke before the alarm. I looked at a detailed chart, bright in the early morning light. Neither the topography nor the soundings had changed in the short night. The passage down the Sound of Raasay is straightforward but I jotted down the few buoys in a sketch, just the same. We could take a detour round the outside of Scalpay (not to be confused with the island of the same name out from East Loch Tarbert). But we had no need to do that as we'd have plenty of tide. The calculation was simple. The sounding at the narrowest point of the tidal channel between Scalpay and the mainland is 0.1 of a metre. That means there will be virtually no water there on low-water springs. That also means there would be the full range of tide at high-water springs. This morning we should be able to navigate through safely in a much deeper boat than this one.

The rise and fall of tide is not regular but it can be averaged into an approximate calculation of the height of tide at a given time in the daily rise and fall. You can do this more accurately by reckoning first of all the difference between the nearest station with recorded data (Broadford in this case) and the standard port (Ullapool, for example). Sometimes this involves interpolation. You then enter a graph of height of tide and time for that standard port, making adjustments for the differences between it and the secondary port. Then of course you allow a safety factor to make sure you have a margin. Sometimes a tide will be 'held back' by strong contrary wind or boosted higher by an Atlantic low-pressure system but usually the predictions can be trusted.

When you are required to prove your competency in coastal or offshore navigation, you have to demonstrate a firm grasp of this by calculating the height or time to a very fine margin. In practice, today, anything close to half tide would be plenty. It was still a thought, aiming for the narrow middle of the tidal channel. The chart showed diamond-shaped markers ashore on either side of the narrows. We identified them so there was no need of a GPS. You know that you are passing over sea that will only be damp ground in a few hours, but this was the ideal boat for the venture. If I did make a mistake she could just sit on the shingle till the waters returned.

We came smoothly through Caolas Scalpay. Now we could lift our eyes from compass and chart and visible marks to enjoy views to more distant features. We had a line of sight to the five sisters of Kintail, still another landscape with a narrative made human. Really my own thoughts were still on tidal waterways. One of the strongest versions of the waterhorse legends is linked to the brooding Isle of Raasay.

Before the morning was over we had my friend's boat tied up on his mooring, as described to us. His dinghy was ashore with the lifejackets under it. I rang his mobile to say the job was done. He was relieved. One worry less. But it was he who had done us the favour.

You can't assume symmetry
in plotted curves of rise and fall

the upturn of tracings
on a calibrated sensor

a jagged graph of soundings
hitting on a datum
passing it by.

The Waterhorse (An t'Each Uisge)

You might think a Lewisman would have no need to cross over to Raasay to experience the habitat of the waterhorse. The Morrison manuscript records not one but two accounts of a great battle with the last of these, both on our own Long Island. In that respect they are like the last wolves killed in Scotland.

I'd heard of the waterhorse but had no idea of their malevolence. My first boat was called *Cymru* when I bought her for 30 pounds. She was a plywood catamaran, with the hulls joined with slats of painted whitewood. This small platform was bolted on to plywood lugs on the canoe-like hulls. It was difficult to find stainless-steel bolts then, at any price. And I was on a very tight budget. I bought new bolts in mild steel and used light spraying oil that now came in an aerosol can.

My father got hold of a shed for me to work in and I sanded and primed and painted till she shone. He lent me two trolleys from the small supermarket he ran. Soon she was primed in metallic pink, undercoated grey, then finished in Donegal green enamel. That's not a lucky colour if you're on the east coast of Scotland. But we were on the west. She came, piece by piece, to the end of Kenneth Street, Stornoway. My mate helped and we assembled the whole thing and figured out how to step the mast and make the rig secure with lanyards. The sails were hardly used. Someone must have had a scare and left the recently made boat to fade into the rushes.

When she was in the water, you didn't see much. My father called the construction 'a fish-box with a sail'. I couldn't bring myself to screw the nameplate back on when she was complete. *Cymru*, the name of a whole country, down the wet road, seemed a bit heavy. I asked my mother for a translation of 'waterhorse' and that's why she was then called *an t'each uisge*. She told me that my grandfather would have told me plenty of stories about them. She did say she thought they could be dangerous.

Norman Malcolm Macdonald, the playwright, told me that he probably wouldn't name a boat after one. Once you were on its back, it had you. You were stuck there and it would gallop back to a deep pool. It would go under with its victim fastened on.

But it was too late to change the name of the first craft I ever owned. I had never sailed a boat, only driven one under motor. And I could just about row and paddle. My mate was a very strong swimmer and I was a bit more heavy in the shoulders then and could cross the harbour, at a push, as long as I didn't inhale any of the oily water. We sometimes borrowed buoyancy aids but not often. I had one sailing lesson from another pal who had joined the Merchant Navy. That was that.

I now know that this is called experiential learning and is the normal technique used for teaching beginners how to sail, although in those situations there is a safety boat to pick you up and an instructor to tell you why you capsized and how you might avoid it next time.

One night, she dived. One hull just went under the water and she accelerated and dug her bow down till it seemed she would dive on. My brother was crewing and his face showed that this was more than he'd bargained for. We had no toe straps or other means of clinging on. Instinct prevailed. We must have got our combined weight out far enough to bring her head back up. There was nothing but our feet holding to the craft as we each held a sheet rope. Our bodies were still under the water level but the craft was sailing on and we were still aboard.

The simple craft gave me a fascination with sailing that still persists. Between my mother's conversation and the bedtime stories I heard from her brother and the reported tales from her father, who died when I was three years old, I also gained a lasting love of stories.

Some say that there are two distinct types of waterhorse. A kelpie is a creature that lives only in running water. It has the power to swell the burns – increase the volume of water till it can drive anything away in its path. But *an t'each uisge* lives in deep pools, fresh water usually or brackish. If you get on the back of such a creature it will dive down and drown you, if you're lucky, before it devours you. Some say a human liver is repugnant to the waterhorse and so that will be washed ashore after the rest has been eaten and the bones have sunk to the bottom.

Some also say that a waterhorse often takes the form of a handsome black stallion. One Donald MacEachen of Benbecula recorded several traditions relating to sightings of the waterhorse in the Outer Hebrides. One man saw what he thought would make a fine ploughing horse but then saw it again with two strange riders on its back. A woman at a shieling sat with her sewing on her knee and was amazed when a strong and very handsome young man entered and laid his head in her lap. But he had weed in his hair so she took her shears and cut her sewing from under that head. Otherwise she might have been lured on the back of *an t'each uisge* into the depths whence he had come.

They do say in more than one place that such a creature can be harnessed for work if a bit is placed between its teeth. WG Stewart reported meeting a drover on Rannoch moor who possessed a very rare object. This was the bridle of a waterhorse, which he'd hung on a crook of rowan. Its fabric was the leather from the skin of adders and its buckles and bit were of silver. The touch of metal is feared by all creatures from worlds below the surfaces of the ones known to us.

Martin Martin, one of the few Gaelic-speaking travellers, who commented on his voyages to the more remote Scottish islands, reports a tradition from Raasay. It took a blacksmith to get the better of *an t'each uisge* – the touch of iron again. But it was only after he lost a daughter to the creature that the Raasay smith and his son forged heavy hooks to trap the thing on land, where it could not live for long. Only a strange jellied substance was left.

My father had a way with stories too and his family was also an eloquent one. He'd slip to Doric, telling us of his grandfather who broke difficult horses, and not by whispering to them. And when I lived in Aberdeen, as a student of education and literature, I met Stanley Robertson, a weel-kent storyteller and singer of the travelling people. I'm sure he told me some of his own family's versions of kelpie and waterhorse legends. I'm also certain that something from all these versions of stories stays with you. Your mind mixes traces from forgotten tellings into a rendition you've only just heard.

There's many an inland water runs deep. Some lochs, they say, are as deep as the hills behind them are high. Then you get these fertile green strips between the rough high ground and the water. That's mainly grazing land but some of it is ripe for the plough.

There was a crofter once, struggling to feed his family. There were acres of very rough ground to plough, if it could be done. He was already like an old man, worn out by years of trying to make the best of those hard patches. One night he failed to return from the loch. His boat was found at the far side of the water, broken by the boulders at the edge. A rope was also found there, broken and fraying at one end. And there was an old blanket – a close-woven cloth you might huddle in to try to keep some warmth if you were out fishing or hunting.

No other sign of this lost man was ever discovered. Some people said that he had not gone to the water's edge to fish, that night. They suspected that he had gone, in desperation, to try to harness the waterhorse. There had been more than one sighting. The old ones said that it took the form of a strong black stallion on land. It had the power to pull the plough, if you could only get a bridle on it.

That family would never have the money to buy a strong young gelding at market and feed him and keep him. They'd not been able to keep any horse since the old mare had died, years before. But everyone said that you should never get astride a strange horse, no matter how it might promise you strength and speed.

Whatever happened that night, there was a woman left as a widow. There were mouths to feed and her eldest lad was still only a boy. He was very willing, though, and fit and strong with it. The widow heard her son talking about the waterhorse – that's what they'd need to pull the plough. She shushed him right away. It was enough to lose one of her family that way.

So life went on and they all did their best. The lad tried hard. One day he was down at the shore trying to snatch a fish from the loch but the boat was beyond repair and he could not reach the best lies. He sat on a stone and wrapped his father's old blanket around him to try to keep out the chill. Right then he saw an old woman from the village hobbling along the hard banks. She lived on her own out beyond the rest of the houses and some said she was a strange one.

'Not a bad day,' the boy said.

'It's a dry one but I'm feeling the chill of it in the marrow of my bones.'

Sure enough she was shivering.

'You'd better take this,' he said. In one way he treasured the cloth as a sign of his father and in another the memories it brought were too painful.

'I've a wee something for yourself,' the old woman said. She took off what was left of her own thin shawl. It had been finely made once.

'Cloth can cover more than skin,' she said.

He took it, so as not to offend her.

A day or two later, the boy was higher up the hill, trying to snare a rabbit. He had about the same luck as he'd had at the fishing. Who should come along but that same woman. He'd just brought his bannock out of his pocket. His mother had ground some of the last of their meal to make sure he had something in his belly when he was out trying to find food for them all.

'Not too bad a day,' he said.

'Could be worse, could be worse,' she said. 'It would be a lot better if I had a crust of bread to bite on.'

The boy looked at the small bannock that was in his hand. He looked at it one more time then he broke it in two and shared it out.

She reached into her pocket and took out a small leather pouch. She handed it to the boy. 'I'd keep that with you. Salt can kill as well as cure,' she said.

It wasn't long after that when the boy was up on the moor. He'd stacked the peats they'd cut earlier in the year but they knew of no one with a pony they could borrow to carry them home. The boy had patched up an old willow creel and tied it round his shoulders with that frayed old rope from the wreckage of the boat. He was sweating with the effort.

He wasn't that surprised to see the same old woman he'd met twice before. 'It's dreich but the wind is down,' the boy said.

'Aye, but it would be a better day if I had a blazing fire to go home to.'

The boy felt the weight of the dry black peat on his back. He put his bundle down for a minute and looked down at the old rope holding it all together. It was a keepsake of his father but it was a sad reminder.

'You can take this creel of peats,' he said. 'We've plenty more, out the moor. The rope will keep them on your shoulder.'

This time she dug deep into her bag. 'I thought I might be seeing you again,' she said. 'I brought this for you.'

It was a bridle for a horse, an old one but sound leather with an iron bit. 'Iron holds fire and blood.'

The boy took that from her and went back out to take as many peats as he could carry in his arms. His mother was pleased to get those, and the very few rabbits and the thin brown trout he took home, but they all knew this would never get them through the winter. His mother and the rest of them had done what they could with the *cas-chrom*, the foot plough. But none of them were that strong, really.

The boy said nothing at all but he knew that there was only one way to find the beast of burden they needed. If he was going to try it at all, this would be the night. It was cloudy now but the moon was up and it would shine on the deep loch soon enough. He knew what to take with him. He crept out of the room where his brothers and sisters were asleep.

He soon saw the ripples that made a different pattern to the others on the dark water. Soon a noisy thing was stamping its feet and gasping air in through its nostrils. It took the shape of the finest horse he'd ever seen, dark as black. He allowed himself to be seen. Sure enough the animal came trotting close to him.

I don't know if it was the boy or the horse luring the other but soon that boy had his fingers in the thick mane and he was about to swing himself up on its broad back when he stopped and heeded the first piece of advice he'd been given. The boy threw the light shawl over the withers of the horse, where it stuck firm. There was now something between the dark skin and his own self.

That lad was no great size but he was nimble. Soon he had the nails and fingers of one hand deep in its mane. He was up and they were cantering. But the horse was heading for the water. The boy pulled to one side at the mane to swing the horse the other way. Then he felt smooth skins between his fingers. There was the glint of tiny eyes and the writhing green of a host of serpents.

But he remembered the advice he'd been given and clutched with his free hand for the bag of salt in a pocket. In one movement he flung it all over the hissing mane. Sure enough he found that salt kills. The mane was thick hair again and he could grab it with both hands.

But the stallion gave his all now. The more the boy clung on, the harder the beast galloped for the water. He would need to turn it now or never. His fingers were so deep and tangled in the mane that he could not let go, even if he could slide off the back of this animal.

But even the waterhorse was tiring. He'd to open his mouth wide to take in the breaths he needed from the dry night air. The young rider saw his chance. He had the bridle slung from his belt and he wrestled one hand free as he clung for dear life with the other. He bided his time and waited for his moment, even as the hooves were striking on the stones at the water's edge. As the animal gulped in air, the boy simply dropped the bridle over its head and the iron bit fell into the open mouth.

The stallion clamped his teeth but he bit on iron. The hot-blooded animal was under the boy's control. Now the rider could turn his powerful mount in the other direction, the way of the land, away from deep water.

As long as the bit was in its mouth, the waterhorse was nothing but a strong stallion. It was fed and it was rested and it was given water. The very next day, the lad led him to the old ploughing tackle that had belonged to his father. The buckles were tight and the leather was oily and strong. He pulled and pulled as no other horse had ever pulled in that parish. Folk looked on as strips of brown became waves of black loam or rich roan red. Each one was tilled and the lines were as true as you'd find at any contest of the best in the whole island.

When all their ground was tilled, the boy led the stallion back to the water's edge. He took the bit from its mouth and watched it gallop for the water. It could be that he wanted the challenge of seeing if he could harness it or its like another year when he was in need of it. But maybe that smart lad just knew that he could not keep all that power harnessed forever. He'd fared well this time and he might not do so well the next. Not even with the help of cloth and salt and iron.

I'd like to be able to tell you that they found some more traces of the lost father. Or even that he'd been a prisoner somewhere and broke free at last. But I'm sorry, I can't do that. All these stories, from all these places, say much the same. If you're stuck on the back of a waterhorse and it dives, you'll never be seen again.

My personal relationship with this tale might strengthen the argument that there is not always a hard line between the oral and the literary, the devised and the evolved aspects of a form, whether it is a vessel or a story. I have tried to tell the story of *an t'each uisge* the way Norman Malcolm Macdonald told it to me, fleshed out with elements noted in the two versions Morrison the cooper transcribed. It just seemed as if something was still missing. Then I heard the writer and storyteller Janet MacInnes tell a version similar to the one you have just experienced. I asked for her source, expecting to find a link to a recording or transcription I had so far missed. She pointed me to Theresa Breslin's adaptation in her wonderful *An Illustrated Treasury of Scottish Folk and Fairy Tales*, superbly illustrated by Kate Leiper (Floris Books, Edinburgh, 2012).

It seems to me that this literary reworking is now finding its way back into the oral tradition. It is inevitable that some of the author's interventions will not be separated from earlier preserved forms of the story. I have tried to list the varied sources in all the stories retold in this book and I am grateful to Janet for bringing me to Theresa's new written version of this one. The author gave permission to include some of her interventions when I tell it now. A more detailed discussion on sources can be found in *Notes on the stories*.

The return to Skye, his home island, worked out well for my friend and for his relationship with his daughter. We are not in touch often now but I did drop him a message to see what had happened to the boat that had carried us so peacefully through the territory of stories.

It turned out he sold *Sandra* when he needed some cash. She is not in the water now. Her present owner probably does not see a project when he looks at her, only an ideal. People seem to take turns to be lost in their admiration of a boat. But my friend is keeping an eye open in case that owner decides to let her go again. He would like to lead her back to the sea.

Whether they are made of solid wood or plywood, fibreglass, polyethylene or carbon-fibre, working boats or leisure craft have always been built to different budgets. If you pick up a magazine such as *Yachting World* you will get the impression that the only yachts now, around European coasts, are vessels of more than 36 feet, whether driven mainly by sail or by power. Training of professional yachtmasters is increasingly geared to managing these 'industry standard' types with their sprinting performance and wide, roomy interiors. It's a fine line between taste and prejudice. There are disadvantages and advantages in the choice of material, length, beam and draft.

You can still thumb through *Practical Boat Owner* and learn from other people's projects. Yachts like *Sandra* continue to be discovered and renewed and given a new lease of life. Many modest craft have taken their owners on adventures while many expensive boats seldom go further than a course from one marina to the next. But of course some of the roomy modern boats have brought the pleasure of sailing to a large number of people who have taken a training course aboard or chartered one, to take them further than they could otherwise sail. Again, it's horses for courses.

Boat designers, like authors, will often unknowngly take vernacular solutions on board. Let's return to the shape and function of the bilge keeler. For centuries, Yorkshire cobles have been built to a form that allows them to sit on the shore between tides on two projecting bilge keels of oak. Additional resistance to leeway was provided, for sailing versions, by an extra long rudder, placed in position once the boat was out from the shallows. The principle is not really so different from the various lowering keels and daggerboards, rediscovered by designers of contemporary racing craft.

Sealladh

IF YOU THINK HEBRIDEANS HAVE AN INTEREST IN BOATS to the
point of obsession, just wait till we get on to the subject of family
genealogy. Then there is the genealogy of boats, where both passions
are compounded. We're not unique in this need to trace where a thing

has come from. For example, cruising and racing sailors will often be aware of the details of the career of Chay Blyth, after he learned navigation by taking that small boat to its limits in the 'roaring forties'. As Knox-Johnston had now completed a non-stop solo circumnavigation, Blyth set out again, to claim his place by achieving the same result by doing it the 'wrong way round'. A slim steel machine, drawn by the designer Robert Clark, showed that pedigree in her lines but was so practical that it enabled him to achieve one of the last great 'firsts' in yachting. Blyth took *British Steel* westabout, solo and non-stop, against prevailing trade winds and currents.

The elegant racing yachts of earlier dynasties are now restored, with huge budgets, to vie for positions at Cannes or Antigua. Professional crews, in matching white or cream, form orderly queues on their weather rails. A complex cloud-pattern of sail can be carried in the fast, warm breeze. William Fyfe passed his name down generations. An ornate dragon motif carved into the hulls of these grand designs was also transferred, as a hallmark. Most Fyfe yachts were built on Fairlie slip, on the Clyde estuary. But, for now, let's think of inshore routes and the Hebridean boatyards where the builder was the designer and built by eye.

In contrast to the builders of racing yachts, drawn by naval architects, island boatbuilders produce, in clinker timber, the shape of a boat already in their minds. The Macleods of Port of Ness, Isle of Lewis and the Stewarts of Grimsay, an island just off the east side of Benbecula, built working craft for contrasting conditions and for different purposes. This is the time to rub a hand along the planking of a strong Grimsay-built craft by William Stewart. The vessel now called *Sealladh* (Vision) was taken into the ownership of the community of Berneray. That island, to the north of the Uists, is now joined to the group by a causeway.

The vessel's origins are in another joined-on island in the Uists. Unlike most coastal villages in the southern isles of the Outer Hebrides, Grimsay is blessed with a safe small harbour. The route westwards is tricky and tidal. Now that Grimsay and Benbecula are joined by a series of causeways, the Grimsay boats have to lower their masts and duck under a bridge to head out west. The two main types of working craft built on Grimsay, over several generations of the Stewart family, appear to prove Eric McKee's theory on the major influences of location and function.

I was allowed to share in adventures aboard *Sealladh*. She was known as the *Royal* when she was first built. Many of our Hebridean boat names of the early 20th century are patriotic in a British sense. This may be linked to the fact that our islands suffered proportionally greater losses than anywhere else in Britain during World War I. Like most of the Stewarts' vessels, she was built for a trade plied along specific routes.

You could imagine the endless criss-cross wakes of the craft that have taken generations of hopeful lobster-fishers out through the ford at Benbecula and over the shifting shallows to the exposed archipelago called Monach or Heiskeir. You might think the name of Heiskeir is confusing enough, as there are several islands of very similar names, though varied spellings, in the Inner and Outer Hebrides. Haskeir (east side of the Hebrides) is the foundation of a major Stevenson light. Bear in mind that the origin of the majority of these names is Norse, then the name was transliterated to reflect Gaelic pronunciation and then again to a cartographer's best guess at how the sound of the name might be written for readers of English. The reoccurrence of identical or very similar names round Scotland's west coast is a coastguard's nightmare.

So we have to be specific. From now on I will refer to this group of low-lying islands as the Monachs. Look out from the west side of Benbecula and you can usually see their interruption of the horizon. They huddle snug in the shallows, about 5 miles out. Their own high lighthouse is built of brick but from this distance it is a needle. On a fine day you might say the islands are reclining. In a storm you'd say any occupants were as vulnerable as the poor lads sent out over barbed wire to test the strength of the mechanised rattle of deaths ahead of them.

The weight of an incalculable fetch of Atlantic sea has to go somewhere when it meets these shallow banks around the Monachs. These days, our forecasts make an educated guess at the highs and lows of wind and waves, hour by hour. Remember, though, that even a barometer was rare in coastal villages a century ago. Yet, men and boys were sent, west of the Uists, to pluck indigo lobsters from the green and maroon and white of all that seething brine. It was only after huge losses of crews were suffered in open boats that public barometers were installed at harbours all round the British Isles. That was around the turn of the 19th into the 20th century.

By that time, the double-ended form of the Grimsay-built boats was already well established. They would be moored in a bay at the Monachs and return to harbour in Grimsay after finding their channel through the ford. They had to be stout to take the pounding that is inevitable even if you are not caught out in a gale that was never forecast. The boast of the Stewarts is that their vessels were 'never broken in a sea'. They could never be deep-keeled in shape, as they had to dodge as close to reefs as possible to win their catch. Their area of operation abounds with tidal banks. Thus, the more V-shaped planking up from the timber keel, before a flare to fullness, had to extend for most of the length of the boat. That provides a similar total underwater area to a deeper shape that is not carried over the whole length.

If that sounds complex it's because the shape *is* complex. Yet it was built, time after time, without a drawing and with maybe a rough mould or two to check that the planking was lying the way it should. Of course, two planks would be cut at the same time. Symmetry might not be necessary in a sail but it is essential in a hull.

As they did not have to be hauled up shores, they could be built with heavy sawn frames, closely spaced. The lateral benches or 'thwarts' are also a bracing structure. These are stout, like the reinforced 'gunnels' at the top plank, which protects the shell from the chafe of hauling lines and the buffeting against piers of piled stone while landing the catch.

There were several variations over the years but these could fall into two main types. Before engine power became common, these were driven by a single dipping lugsail. The mast was taller than that of the North Lewis boats because it did not need to be dropped for beaching. So the sail had a different shape – it was carried higher and more of its area was to the front of the boat. The sailing hulls were double-ended and beamy, with rounded sterns. They could not risk saving too much weight for improved performance but they had to be able to surf for home when steep seas built up over the shallow sound. Everything aboard a working boat is a balancing act between different requirements.

Sealladh (fishing number CY210) was built in the 1950s. She is thus an example of this hull that was developed first as a sailing vessel. Later examples show how the shape and build changed when inboard propulsion became the norm and the sail was a back-up. The boats could be even stouter because the propellor could drive them to their hull speed even if they were on the heavy side. In addition, the floors and stern post had to be heavy enough to stand up to the vibration caused by a huge turning flywheel. This was easier to achieve in a craft with a transom (or squared-off) stern.

Early motors would have been a miracle of sparking and petrol and paraffin, to be protected at all costs from a drenching of salt. There is an authored Gaelic poem, sometimes also sung, celebrating the internal combustion engine that took the lobster-fishermen to the Monachs. Here is a translation of one stanza, but the whole poem is about energy, through a sea-route mapped by identified marks:

> 'Copper and cast iron smoothly riveted,
> bolted on top to ensure total stability,

a liberal supply of petrol, timbers resounding bravely,
and the battery emitting green sparks.'*

The same poet is best known for his realistic depiction of the mechanised World War I, in his native Gaelic.

The restored *Sealladh* has a neat light diesel, a Japanese block with British-made marinising parts on rubber mounts. Her tiller would need to be thrown away over her rounded stern in any serious race. It is a superb shape of doubled curves, immensely strong and steady in the hand. But it seems heavy to someone looking for a craft that will sail in light airs. It is solid timber, painted white, like the gunnels, over a ground colour of a maroon shade known as 'Bounty Red'. Her lugsail was built by the community, of natural cloth, proofed. It is also heavy but it has a quality and a smell of its own.

This is not the best craft for tacking round a bay, seeking zephyrs. It is, however, the ideal craft for making safe short passages between our islands, in good conditions. I became friends with Donald MacLean, through our shared interests in boats and stories. He works on the ferry that pirouettes through the tortuous passages of the Sound of Harris. When we took the Lewis *sgoth an Sulaire* down that way, Donald got involved. So did a few more of the Berneray and Uist boys. They set up their own club and began work on the old *Royal*. The restored boat was renamed *Sealladh*. This is one of these words that has many connotations. Maybe 'Vision' is close, if we have to fit them into one word. I took time to see the restored boat and admire her lines and her colours and, most of all, her strength.

'Would you be up for a trip to the Monachs with us?' Donald would ask, almost every time I was on the ferry. Donald always seems cheery. He is lightly built, wears thick glasses and usually also wears a grin. 'If I'm free,' I'd say, time after time. I couldn't tell you his yarn

---

* Dòmhnall Ruadh Chorùna: *Orain is dain le Domhnall Domhnallach a Uibhist a Tuath*, (Taigh Chearsabhagh, Loch nam Madadh: Comann Eachdraidh Uibhist a Tuath, 1995). See also www.scottishpoetrylibrary.org.uk.

of the day the tractor ended up on the roof of a barn but I remember holding my sides to ease the pain of laughing. Then one midweek in June the phone went. 'I suppose it's too short notice for you. Aye the Monachs. That's what we're planning, anyway.'

Berneray to the Monachs

SEALLADH POPPED HER NOSE ROUND THE corner out of the Sound of Harris on a very fine evening. Donald was at the helm with seven other souls aboard. Some of the team were his regular crew of Berneray residents. Some were visitors and one of them was me. Both sexes and several nationalities and languages were represented. This was not a crowd in the stout, roomy boat. We were able to proceed under sail but the motor was running for a time. The evenings were long but we hoped to enter Griminish harbour to pitch camp ashore before the short night fell.

Visibility was excellent. The light northerly was just enough to push us clear of the sandy shores of Boreray, left to starboard. These islands, out from the Sound of Harris, are all capped with rich grazings, in comparison to the rocks and heathery turf that root on most of the east side of the Outer Hebrides. Donald knows the Sound of Harris, every reef and rip of it, like the back of his hand but he'd never been in to Griminish. He forgot to mention that. I had been out with him in the Sound several times and got used to him navigating as if by instinct. This trip, I had not thought to study the pilotage in detail, nor key in some waypoints to our hand-held GPS.

The skipper asked me to dig out the pilot book and eyeball the chart. It was the last of the evening light. My eyesight isn't that great any more so I found my specs and read out the description of the two painted posts we were looking for. These would guide you through the rocks if you kept them in line. Of course, we should have had an electronic waypoint to aim for on the hand-held GPS and a compass bearing to back that up.

The two watchers up front said, aye they could make them out now, white marks. Just as described. 'That's them in line now.' Donald and myself didn't like the look of the line very much but his eyesight is no better than mine. We inched forwards. I went up to the bow and saw the boiling at a reef not very far ahead and just said quietly, 'Back her out Donald. Hit reverse now.'

That's what we did and then we all had a close look, clear of the hazards, to take a new line of approach. The daylight had faded so the leading lights on the true marks became visible. We'd been lined up on a couple of random telegraph poles. Our bowman's eyes were not much better than my own or our skipper's. We came in safely then and camped ashore. It was a fine night. We could all cope with the romantic cliché of Eriskay ponies strolling through the sunset until they began to nuzzle the stays of our tents, looking for our sandwiches. The stark shape of the abandoned tall house on Vallay, the tidal island across the bay, stood near-black against the impossible range of burned and bright orange shades. I had crossed over to Vallay before, at low water. There are enough remnants of teak and Oregon pine, ceramics and bronzework to reveal that this was once someone's dream-house.

We made a chain gang in the morning, passing all the gear back out to *Sealladh*. Well, nearly all of it. We were away in time on the tide. It was a good passage with a fair breeze and we were able to sail most of the way. The mood was at first one of bright anticipation. We were to visit territory that is more than a landscape. It has its own songs and tales and archaeology.

The famous turquoise waters of the west side of North Uist yielded to infinite variations of dreich and dull grey. There was a substantial swell and a little chop on top of it coming in, even though we took the deeper route to the anchorage. We came the longer way round, west of Shillay, with its unmistakable tall lighthouse column.

The seas were not so smooth when we came in close. Our heavy lugsail kept us steady enough but it was an uncomfortable motion. I knew it would have been much worse in a boat that was not designed for this very purpose. A few of the team spent the last hours of the passage bent over the heavy gunnels, heaving up from time to time and shaking their heads. No one made any fuss. For some, this is the price you pay for visiting offshore islands. Others leaned back to try to take in the full height of the brickwork that once lit a warning to great liners or North Atlantic convoys.

This time we were very cautious and well prepared, threading her into the shallow water to drop anchor off Cean Iar, the westerly island. We ticked off our waypoints to take us clear of the hidden reefs and the shallows. It went off very smoothly, checking the depth with a lead line. Then we noted our transits, visible points in line, as a check on the rate of drift.

We landed on the Monachs. This meant a tiring row back and fore in the rubber dinghy, taken turn-about by Donald and myself. All eight souls and all their gear now had a foothold on this abandoned archipelago. Not a lot was said. Everyone was gazing at the bare land that had provided a home over the centuries. There were voyaging monks. There was a nunnery. There were crofters and lobster-fishers. There was even the exiled Lady Grange, held here against her will before she was taken further out to Hirta, St Kilda. She had heard too much of her husband's plotting in the Jacobite cause.

The expedition cook, Ursina, asked for the gas cylinder. It was only then we discovered that we'd left it ashore at Griminish. I was for taking *Sealladh* back for it, alone or with one other as crew. I don't mind doing without wine or beer for a few days but the thought of doing without tea is a challenge. Instead, we all spread out to gather driftwood. We started to build a simple drystone shelter, to contain the fire. There was no drawing in the sand but different voices contributed to its design. Most of the elder folk, including myself, had done some building work at some time. The youngsters went running for material. Flatter stones were wedged to provide a level platform for the next layer.

The top was being brought in to form seats for both kettle and pan as our fuel arrived. We had to range quite far but all hands contributed to our wood-burning oven. This was now the focal point for our gathering. We looked out from it to our vessel, at anchor in a calm bay, before the loom of Shillay and its lighthouse. The deep red hull became less and less prominent till all was in silhouette. It had to be near midnight and no one could say where the time had gone. Tents were all pitched and we were well filled with the stew that Ursina had brought along for our first night on the Monachs. She is from Switzerland but has lived on Berneray so long that she speaks like an islander.

Our fire became brighter and higher as the visible tower darkened before us. Then came the blink of the minor navigation light, recently established beside the redundant one. There were plenty of stories. Those who had been quiet when they were squeamish at sea were lively again.

Someone had found a ready-made frame that might have once held window-glass. It was placed a few metres seaward of our domestic installation. You looked through it to observe the outline of the craft that had taken us here. *Sealladh* was now in the same frame as the original lighthouse. The Northern Lighthouse Board brought additional families to the Monachs over the years. They would have made a significant contribution to the congregation and to the school role.

The shape of the tiller, in outline, now seemed perfect for this craft. Of course, there is more than one kind of love. The lines of that solid but hollow shell of *Sealladh* were not imprinted into my memory at first glance. Now that she had taken us and all our gear out over the shallows and swells to these Atlantic islands, though, I could not imagine a bonnier craft. It was another Grimsay poet who reassured me that it was nothing abnormal to have feelings for a boat. I lost one, dragged ashore in a hurricane-force wind, once. Mary Macdonald phoned me to say she was sorry for my trouble. 'Remember I'm from Grimsay,' she said. 'I know what a boat means to the one who has cared for her.'

Now I will attempt to lightly sketch our bootprints on land. Next morning, we explored singly, in groups or all together. Being low-lying, this island group has a completely different character to volcanic

St Kilda, west, or the grey-green and rounded Isle of Scarp to the north. Think of the Paul Strand photograph of wading horses on the Uist shoreline and we're getting there. But there's also the perspective that has you looking from the islands eastwards to dominant Eaval, rising from the flatlands of mainland Uist. Another turn of the head opens up the jagged ridges of North Harris, if the visibility permits. Looking from the Monachs, rather than to them, the reciprocal bearings bring you to view a significantly different landscape in each of three quadrants. Out westwards and a bit to the north you might just catch the suggestion of St Kilda, a smudged thumbprint near the top of the frame.

We used *Sealladh*, under motor, to range further around the archipelago of the Monachs. On the west side you felt vulnerable before powerful desolation that you know continues until the Americas. Stepping back from marram grass to cropped grass and rushes, it took a bit of looking to realise that massive, storm-rounded boulders had been cast so far inland by natural forces. This was my first sight of the evidence of that fearsome power. Now it is difficult to separate which of my lingering impressions of this land and seascape were glimpsed on this first expedition and which were experienced on subsequent visits. Perhaps the line between a story retold and an attempt at a factual traveller's narrative is also a smudged one. I know that my verses that have now found their form have been shaped over more than one visit and more than one sitting.

machair spills
a rough greening
to the sandline

gets eroded
but kicks back
on the other side

repels
falling boulders

tosses them
like pups
a long way in

Sometimes I would go ahead in the rubber dinghy, sounding with a long paddle. Our best chart was sketchy. On the east side you saw signs of habitation, layered over years. One ruin revealed a brickwork storey laid on top of the first one of stone. You could imagine the lightkeeper's families trading the board's plentiful butter for crowdie. The shallow pool, which was all that separated the east and west parts of the main island, was warm enough for wading to be pleasant on your feet. The three main islands in the group are all still really connected, once the tide falls to its lowest point. It was difficult not to think of running children.

We saw the restored schoolhouse. Other remains of houses saddened us all. I looked at layers of improvements, now exposed to the eye by the action of weather.

the harling's gone so
you see the join –
bricks over stone

maybe one shift of scale
was enough –
market, catch or temperature

improvements crumble

will most of our developments
look like this
accidental balance?

the trapped fall and jamming
of three chimney stones

a still dance
without people

One person voiced the feelings of us all. There was a phone signal on the higher ground so a couple of folk had to make their call. That was all that was needed to let us spend an additional night. Instead of sailing on north, back to Berneray, we gained time to explore further. We could stand for a while by the old schoolhouse. This is now a bothy, in community ownership, thanks to a generous family who had once had deeds of ownership. Families with connection to Grimsay and to the Monachs can now book a bunk here. Shepherds can rest, between the 'fanks' or gatherings, to clip or cut.

We motored on round to the north side of the group, to line up two white-painted cairns that take you into the anchorage before the lighthouse on the island of Shillay. Moorings here were still in use by the current Grimsay lobster-fishing fleet. Stone and tin bothies ashore appeared to be in occasional use. The fishermen could spend a night or three out here if they were getting results or if they were caught out by weather. I wondered at the stories told in these, over the years, to make the waiting game shorter and thought back to a conversation with the Harris boatbuilder, John MacAulay. John was the coastguard volunteer in charge of the South Harris team for some years. He told me he had worked on a Grimsay boat for a while before he served his time as a shipwright. It was indeed story after story, in the bothies out on the Monachs.

The artists among us envisaged an international retreat, developed from the accommodation buildings, built to Northern Lighthouse Board standard. They were so strong that the structure was still essentially sound after so many years of abandonment. Then we motored out of the pool and took a short cut we had not dared on our first arrival. *Sealladh* had now completed a circumnavigation. We reclaimed our first anchorage. Ashore, we also reclaimed our campsite and our stove of stone.

The skies were more bleary. It took longer to get our fire going and we used some of the stack of found and broken timbers we thought we'd left for the next visitors. We were still a crew, brought together by one vessel. Our island of departure, Berneray, still holds its own small but strong community, thanks partly to another causeway. Perhaps we were all conscious of the lost communities of the other islands we had looked to on this one journey – Killegray, Ensay, Boreray, the Monachs and of course Hirta. The St Kilda group lay sheltering under a high cloudmass, this day.

Donald and myself shared the same tent. We took turns waking that night, going out to look at the sea and to feel the wind and check on our charge, out at anchor. The wind was howling at times, way beyond what was forecast. The rain had come so there was no chance of keeping our driftwood fire going. What had we done? But in the morning, the front had gone through, as forecast. We gathered the gear one last time and clambered over the rocks again to pack the boat.

Between motor and sail we made the trip north in one hop till we were round Griminish point and well clear of Vallay. The skies brightened and we were glad again of that last day we had been able to share. We got a good sailing angle for the last leg and the boat came into her own. Her engine was stilled. The full sail filled till she heeled slightly. The clinker chuckle told us we were tramping on, over the small shining seas.

'We're cooking on gas now,' I said. But Ursina said, 'No, better than that. We're cooking on driftwood.'

> that muddied turquoise
> across from stolen mountains
> – mist and gale together
>
> seals are putting their necks out
> the return of the hills of Harris
> – we're all curious
>
> scurrying legs, wings
> a pale cluttered clutch
> – wound-up sanderlings

tidal tangle tints
from the belly of this bay
– every shade of sailcloth

we're clear of undertow
but Berneray is underway
– her sail is cottongrass

Black John of the Driven Snow
(Rubh na Marbh)

One of the strongest versions of the selkie or seal-wife story is most closely linked to the shore at Balranald, east of the Monachs. A hard-edged form of the same story was gathered in Nova Scotia from the Gaelic-speaking descendents of emigrants from the Uists. Its brutal beginning is firmly set in the Monach islands. Several voices have contributed to the text of an edited version, published in its Gaelic original. It has strong similarities with the form taken by this story in the Faroes, which has the scale and intensity of Greek tragedy.

But this is not the story that feels right for now. The one for this moment is a naming tale, in the same way as *Lady's Rock* gives you the legend that lies behind the name. This one refers to one specific point on Ceann Ear.

The words are not mine but those of a man who was born and raised on the Monachs. He was generous in allowing me to record him and share his telling.

A story from Angus Macdonald, Knockintorran
It was from Lewis, these people were from. There's a few years gone by since people like that came to steal beasts and food and whatever else they could get a hold of.

But this time they were wanting to get out to raid Heiskeir. They knew there was plenty animals and food out at Heiskeir. But what they didn't know was how to read the water. The seas between North Uist and Heiskeir.

But they got hold of this young boy. I think he was from Houghgarry. And he was to show them how to get to Heiskeir. But some not very good weather came along. Squalls of snow and hail. And this boy was to take them through it. That was their plan.

But when the boy found out what they were really interested in doing, he wasn't that keen to help them. But one way or another, they were coming pretty close to Heiskeir. A shower of snow came on them. And the young boy said, keep going out towards the rock over there. And we'll get in round it. The young boy well knew they wouldn't get round that rock. But when he got near to the rock he jumped out of the boat and landed on it. But he left all the others, the raiders, in the boat. So the boat went on to the rocks. And that's where they were drowned.

So he got on to the land and I've heard that he was a good while on Heiskeir after that. He stayed out there, that young boy. But the men he sailed out with, they were all drowned.

Their last shout was, 'Where are we now?'

'I don't know what that point was called,' said the boy, 'but I know what they'll call it from now on. It's the Point of Death.'

I recorded the tale told above during a second excursion to the Monachs, in *Sealladh*, about a year later. It is a transcription from my video recording of Angus 'Moy' Macdonald speaking in the restored schoolhouse on Ceann Ear. Angus told both an English and a Gaelic version. A friend, fluent in Gaelic, provided the translation on which this is based. The same method was used to transcribe another story from Angus, which is included in the next section.

A Second Crossing

MAYBE A YEAR AFTER OUR FIRST TRIP TO THE MONACHS, we took Angus 'Moy' Macdonald out in *Sealladh*. We departed from Berneray, in good weather. At the same time, a group of children involved in the Scottish Children's Parliament were preparing to make a shorter crossing to the islands in a fast inflatable craft. Angus was not too keen on bouncing over the waves at speed. He smiled at the prospect of covering a longer distance under sail or propelled by a steady diesel-driven pulse. This time we had a man aboard who knew the shallow areas well. Duncan MacLean had helped his father work this very boat for several summers. He was confident he could remember the marks. We also had a more detailed chart, copied from the engraving of an old edition, with depths in fathoms. These often publish lines of detailed soundings, 'by lead line', which are not transferred to new editions.

Duncan pointed the way for Donald, the skipper, and we approached close to the outlying Stockay, on the east side, avoiding two shallow banks that are clearly charted. Then Duncan guided us in, though we could see the swaying strands of kelp beneath us. This would have been the route for the raiders in the story of *The Point of Death* if the sharp-witted pilot had not directed them into the deadly rock that still carries the name he is said to have given it.

We had no sooner helped Angus ashore in the rubber dinghy than we heard the roar of the inflatable craft's twin engines. A boatman and a team of carers saw to the business of the safe transfer ashore of a lively group of youngsters. We were at a sandy bay looking out towards a visible hill of Benbecula and the higher blue-grey summit of rocky Eaval, on North Uist. The headland to the north of our bay and several outlying reefs all provide some shelter. I could see the bay would be exposed in easterly or south-easterly winds. It is not a mooring-place you could leave a boat on in a gale and expect peace of mind. But now the sun was out, the boats were bobbing gently and Angus was thanking us for taking him back to a place where he had known great happiness.

He was born on the Monachs and had been a pupil in this very building we were strolling towards. Lichened stone and a tidy roof of blackberry-hued Ballachulish slate made the building look far from oppressive, in this light. Time and again, the stereotype of the harsh Presbyterian ethos of the northern part of the Outer Hebrides is belied by first-hand accounts. This visit had a clear educational purpose. It was the concept of an artist, by the name of Alexandria Patience, commissioned to work with the Uist area's representatives in the Scottish Children's Parliament. I had introduced her to Donald MacLean. The community boat association responsible for *Sealladh* was keen to support the idea of bringing the young people out to hear the reminiscences of a man who had lived here when he was about their own age.

That night, Angus stayed in the converted old schoolhouse along with some lobster fishermen who had left their boat at anchor. Tents were pitched outside and children, carers and boat crews all cooked and ate together. Stories and memories happened all the time, with our skipper contributing his share. There was also time for us to stroll and imagine past lives and for the children to run and let off some steam. It happened quite naturally. The children gathered together in the old schoolroom while Angus described coming to school with a bit of bannock to keep him going through the day. An impression of a close community was formed. It was no idyll. There was work to do before and after classes, in those days.

This man has a gentle but compelling voice. All the listeners were drawn in and I don't think anyone had to call for quiet. I can't explain how the move from remembering came to the telling of the story you have already encountered. I may have guessed it might be the time and asked Angus if he knew the legend. The act of crossing to an island in a craft that has its own story can bring you to an ease with each other that might otherwise take a lot longer to find. His telling of *Rubh na Marbh* (or *The Point of Death*) reminded me that 'fleshing out' a tale with additional detail does not always improve it.

The tape spun on. When does a personal account of a remembered event become a story? We might have our own stories of this trip to tell by the time we reached the twisting channel that would take us through the ford to a safe anchorage in Grimsay. Before we packed up our tents and gear for the return, Angus had another recollection for our gathering. He began by saying, 'This is not a story. This is something that happened to me.' These are his own words, recorded, transcribed and translated. I'd like to introduce them, briefly, with some lines that came to me from looking closely at a lugsail, similar to the one made by the Berneray community and carried by *Sealladh*.

A whole history of repairs
in the articles we use
– the planking and
the cloth that drives it.

One person's debris
is another's material.

We get where we need to go
by short, tacking stitches or
the long lope of
homeward bounders.

We can't calibrate the fade
of patches on patches.

A sail has its own memory.
We call it, stretch.

An Incident Remembered

There was a horse we had, Tommy. Tommy was his name. And my Dad, he wouldn't let us yoke that horse. He didn't want us to be handling the horse at all, as there was something wrong with him.

There was one certain place on the island where the horse wouldn't go down to the seashore – the track going down there. He would always stop at the dunes. As soon as they would come on to the shoreline, the horse, Tommy, wouldn't pass that way until my dad would go and take him by the head and he would walk him past the seaweed. And then the horse was quite calm, just as quiet as any other animal.

But when the boys from the lighthouse were drowned, one of the bodies came in on the cart track. In the seaweed. But the horse stopping there – that had been going on for years before the boys from the lighthouse were lost.

The dry and bright wind, from the north-east to east, freshened steadily. We aimed for the break in the causeway that connects North Uist to Grimsay and Benbecula, joining up the stepping stones of smaller islands. Angus was well prepared, in his oiled-wool gansey and a crofter's jacket of oiled cloth. A few of the others didn't manage to get their waterproofs on before the first spray broke over us. They would soon be shivering but there was only about 6 miles of open sea to cover before we'd get some shelter from the land.

At first we were able to carry the sail but then it had to come down as we began to punch right into the wind, under engine. Angus showed no signs of anxiety or discomfort. This was a man used to being out in the elements all his life. Donald kept the jokes coming, shouting over the thump of the diesel. Even with the visibility diminishing in spray there are usually signs of coming closer to land.

In the seas around the Hebrides there are nearly always diving gannets, several species of gull to be identified, sharp-beaked guillemots, shag, cormorant and curve-beaked razorbills. A pair of skuas will often haunt your stern. As you close on the land, the variety of species of bird widens further. Several species of divers, grebes, duck and geese may be sighted.

We came in to the lee of Baleshare. This is another island that is now a peninsula. The drying flats of mingling mud and sand host the walkers and runners, curlew to sandpiper. I never tire of the impossible sight of sanderling groups with hidden method in their mad dashes, in formation. These are the wound-up, fluffy birds that dash and peck in shallow waves of themselves. I once listened to a scientist outline the interdependent species in the flora and fauna of a shore near this one. Her informed enthusiasm brought me to jot down a few lines that I don't think I ever altered:

Eyebright and kidney vetch
but it's ladies' vetch
that thickens milk
by rye and bere and
cousins of buntings.

Dulse dulls in dry warmth.
It will shine maroon in broth
as residue of other
seaweed tribes
filters to ragworm
and in turn
to dunlin.

When we reached the winding but unmarked channel through the saltings at the North Ford, our pilot came into his own. It was difficult to see what Duncan was using. The islets – drowning banks of grasses – all looked alike to me. At least in the Sound of Harris there were cairns and beacons, necessary before the buoyage was improved. Duncan had learned this route by crewing for his father. Perhaps there was a safety net of Gaelic words that would steer you through, if you memorised their syllables.

Then we all put our shoulders to the task of lowering our mast. It was secured along the length of *Sealladh* as we chugged through the gap that could now be seen. A single diamond-shaped marker rose from a few stones, like one of the old passing-place signs. And then I could recognise the mass of Grimsay to port. This is an island that still holds its population, thanks to its harbour and now its causeway.

Donald was to leave the boat here so the Berneray community could take part in the Grimsay Boat Day, a gala and parade to be held in a week or two. I heard they carried off the prize for the best Grimsay boat that has been to the Monachs.

Later, we shared a few more excursions and projects. Then some of the 'leading lights' in the team moved to other interests or other places. One member died. *Sealladh* has now been sold on to Duncan and so has been returned to the family who commissioned her. The proceeds were used to launch a new club. The Berneray folk are now building a Saint Ayles skiff, a clinker plywood design, for competitive coastal rowing. They will be able to participate in a water-going movement that has spread far from its Scottish start to involve communities in many countries.

Kennary

YOU HAVE TO BE BRAVE TO EXPOSE ANYTHING you have made to public view. When the making of poems and stories became a need, I was fortunate to be able to share these first with trusted friends. I laughed once, during a writers' residency in France, when a friend talked of an exhibition of visual art as exposing yourself (*exposition*) but now I think he was dead right. You have to be braver still to launch and sail a boat you have built. I'm not talking about any issue of safety. You need to have a bronze neck. Brass is not sufficient.

I have never built a boat but I know a man who has. I watched it take shape, in his shed. A boatbuilder has to be thick-skinned, unlike the vessel he is constructing. Visitors will drink your tea and then just say what they think. 'Is she not a bit high in the bow?' Or even, 'She's like a flipping iceberg, down below. How are you going to ballast that?'

Archie did a lot of standing back and looking at the developing shape. He has the scale and build of a ship's engineer who might reach into tight corners. He has a late crop of curly white hair and still speaks with a Glasgow accent. He could be cast as Dougie in *The Vital Spark* except that he has a wit more dry than gin. Until he breaks into a short laugh. He drinks a lot of tea and thinks things out while he is doing that, or smoking roll-ups. He is one of the most original thinkers I know, curious to discover how things really work and sceptical about solutions offered without proper scrutiny of the question. When he asks *why* a boat sails – one of the mysteries of physics – he is not satisfied when you suggest *how* it sails.

'Think of it as a wing. When you pull the sheet rope you change the shape of the cloth to make it more flat or more full. Tight to go into the wind and full when the wind is more behind you.'

'Aye but why does that make the boat sail?'

That was a long way ahead of us. First there had to be a hull. It was clinker-built. You may remember that this is when the planks overlap. It is their cut curves that compose the shell. Strengthening lower 'floors' are fixed to join both sides at an early stage. The first few planks or 'strakes' of Archie's boat were fairly straight and then the curvature increased so the cut shapes had to be steamed before being bent into place.

Archie worked alongside a friend who was building his first boat. Neither man has had any formal training in this art but both are skilled at sharpening tools and working with wood. Archie is also adept with metalwork and is a qualified electrician and plumber.

I visited to take photographs, stage by stage. Archie grew up in Glasgow but spent summers with his relations on Grimsay island. These happened to be the Stewarts (builders of *Sealladh* and countless other working craft) so he was clenching copper nails soon after he was past the toddling stage. When he showed willing, he was trusted to do a bit more. He said that the boatskin larch, sent from the mainland, often varied in quality. They had to make do and use everything they could, so he learned to join planks or ribs with scarf joints very early on in life.

He married a Lewis woman and they left the city for her home island. Like many people out of town, at that time, he did most of the building on their own house. He also found time to renovate a clinker boat that had been squeezed by a visiting ship and written off. He built a boat or two of his own. These are strong and practical and look similar to the later boats built by the Stewarts of Grimsay.

However, this one was different. Archie had studied the building of *an Sulaire* and he had sailed in *Broad Bay* a few times. He really started grinning when he came out in a Stella on a gusty day and we were all standing vertical in the cockpit as she leaned and accelerated, the way they do. He set out to build a sailing boat. To my knowledge there was never any plan. There might have been a sketch on the traditional back of a brown envelope but that was about it. As the planking developed, it became clear that Archie had an idea.

There are specific knacks you have to be able to do without thinking – planing a constant bevel; making a rivet tight but with allowance for the swelling of the plank to come; reading the grain of a slab of tree. But then, unless you are working to follow an architect's drawings, the shape is the thing. And his companion in the shed also produced a well-shaped boat, with a nod to Archie's but with something of his own. To me, the process of developing these vessels seemed familiar. Perhaps this is because it reminds me of the way the shape of a poem emerges from the dust of words.

He used steam-bent strips of oak to brace the shell. This is less time-consuming than sourcing timbers with the right bend in their grain. These have to be cut to complex templates, joggled to sit tight on the inner side of the planking. Steamed-oak ribs, however, are simply bent over the planks and fixed through the overlaps. Once the timbers are riveted in place with staggered copper nails, you have a very strong construction. This method has the benefit of lightness. This is called 'framing up' and is easier when done by two people. So, each boatbuilder helped the other and the work was done in a couple of Saturdays.

Archie wanted this one to be a sailing vessel, first and foremost. Yet one day I arrived to see a hole bored for a propeller shaft through a strengthened sternpost. On this size of craft (21 feet overall) I would have suggested an outboard motor on a lowering bracket. If we got the rig right we should be able to sail into tight places and the outboard would be adequate, in a calm. But Archie nodded over to a corner. Under the tarpaulin was a metal thing of beauty. It was a Volvo engine, but a very early model. 'My uncle told me that one never did much work. "Take it, if you ever finish that boat of yours," he said.'

Archie's sons and nephews got on the internet and the missing parts appeared. Those he could not source, he made. Then he had to remake the timber floors to create the space to install it. These are an essential part of the structure. It was as much invention as fabrication. He realised that bent steel could provide the strength where there was no space for timbers of sufficient weight for the job. He had reached the same conclusion as the designers of timber-built racing yachts in the latter part of the 20th century.

There was a significant dip in the shape of Archie's boat from the bow down, and then a more gradual rise to her transom stern. This 'sheer line' is one of the main points of discussion when a boat's shape is judged, without mercy. Most of the visitors said that this one was bonny but would present some challenges when it came to decking it. Then there was the low cabin, perfectly in keeping with her overall shape. He must have drawn that out first, but if he did I never saw his sketches.

It began to look like a viable pocket-cruiser. A small yacht, of working-craft origins in her seakeeping lines but with space for two decent berths below. Now it was me who was on the spot. What about the rig?

I looked back on the measurements and drawings I'd once done, before ordering a standing lugsail rig for *Broad Bay*. That would be a suitable rig, easy to handle, and it seemed in keeping with the lines of the boat that now existed. I scaled up my sail plan and smudged it and drew it again until it looked good. We would need a jib and I thought maybe a small bowsprit so she would be well balanced.

There were some figures but mainly I was trusting my judgement, though not far enough to go to the expense of ordering a new set of sails. Then we had our stroke of luck. We had a tip that the navigation department of the local college had given up on any pretence of offering sail-training and had sold off an Orkney-built launch. The new owner had no interest in the standing lug rig that came with it.

We went to have a look. The sails had never been out of their bags and the varnish was unbroken on the mast. We stretched a tape measure. The tan terylene sails, from William Leitch of Tarbert, Argyll, were as if made to the plan and dimensions I'd sketched.

Next, we had to decide the positions for the 'chain plates'. These are stout bands of bronze or steel or cast metal that distribute the strains of the rig through the wire stays to the hull. We had to establish the position of the mast and estimate how far aft the wires of the supporting 'shrouds' would reach on each side. Then

I was for fixing a mast step, rooted to the keel, so the mast would go through the deck and down. Archie reckoned it was not quite long enough for this and was worried about creating a constant drip in his newly fibreglassed plywood deck. He produced his own calculations to argue that the downward thrust from compression was not the major force. Despite that, I persuaded Archie to customise a larch fence post, placed to form a removable support under the deck-stepped spruce mast.

After deconstructing a fair part of his new boat to install the vintage engine, Archie had to make tankage and plumbing for two fuel systems. This was a unit designed to start on petrol and switch over to paraffin – a cheaper fuel in the olden days.

There comes the time when you have to lift your head from details to see what has been made. Archie did the painting himself though I owed him enough favours to offer help. He mixed a few colours of yacht enamel together. It came out close to Baltic blue but with maybe a touch more grey in it. Only Archie could produce a warm blue-grey.

He arranged the low-loader and I turned up with rigging gear. When you put a dry clinker-built boat in the water you expect some leaking until the overlapping planks swell to make watertight joins. She was not taking in much but needed a huge amount of ballast because of her deep shape. There was an argument for an external ballast keel but we were too late for that now. Another mate and I sourced the roundest stones we could find to supplement bags of shingle. We may well have been reusing part of 'Little Russia' – the ballast piles cast by Baltic traders in Stornoway harbour when the weight of the cargo of herring was sufficient.

Next year we could cast lead to the shapes of the bilges, with channels for drainage. For now, she could sail with shingle and round stones packed low down. Only a day or two after her launch we were able to hoist the crisp sails and catch enough breeze to take us clear of the harbour. Archie takes more pleasure in sailing than anyone else I have ever met. That grin came on as we moved easily through the water, in very light wind. She tacked and she gybed and she could keep sailing surprisingly close to windward. She got moving in a gust and then I could feel the 'weather helm' we expected. This is a tendency to turn up towards the wind – a good thing in a very small measure but a flaw if significant. She would need that bowsprit and the jib out front but then she should be balanced.

Archie had come up with a vessel that could sail and one that would shelter us even though of course she had not yet been fitted out, down below. My friend's compulsion was to navigate his creation back to the anchorage that gave her a name. By sail, or by his uncle's engine, we would need to take *Kennary* down the Hebrides in time for the Grimsay Boat Day.

The Witch's Pool

THE GUSTY BREEZE WAS FRESH enough but on our shoulder, where most sailors want it. Mr Leitch's standing lugsail had a good shape, even with both reefs in. With this smaller sail area she was balanced with just the small jib up front. We had not yet got round to fixing a bowsprit to take an outer 'flying' jib.

The Shiants are pretty much due south when you clear the buoy at the entrance to Stornoway Approaches. You could still make out their cloudy and darkening loom from the steep falling curve of Kebock Head. Home territories, experienced often and in varied conditions. But it is never exactly the same vista.

We had the tide with us, so a night sail was a possibility, to take advantage of that and the strong wind. It was still June so there hardly is a night, more like a few hours of twilight. This was an electrician's boat so of course we had no navigation lights. We could point a powerful torch at our sails though these were tan, not white.

The new boat went sweetly through the flat water of the harbour area. She was still comfortable when it got lumpy outside.

I'd thought the drag of a large, three-bladed propellor would hold us back, under sail. You could feel it was there but the waterline is carried along most of the length so *Kennary* is not what I'd call a slow boat. The boatbuilder looked uneasy. Following seas or no, they'd be big enough in the Sound of Shiants. We had only been out in his creation a few times, in sheltered areas. She was not yet well tested.

Archie took the tiller as I had another look at the tidal atlas and the charts. We had no fixed navigation equipment but a hand-held GPS with plenty of spare batteries. We also carried a sounding lead with many metres of knotted rope to record the depth under us when we were slow or stopped. My pal looked tired. He is self-employed and he'd been finishing a lot of promised jobs, to allow him the time to take the new boat 'home'.

'We could do worse than the Witch's Pool,' I said. 'In from Dubh Sgeir. Before Loch Mariveg. Get the pick down. Grub, sleep, early start?'

'Yeah, we'll go for that.'

'Aye but we might need an engine to do it.'

Archie had fully explained the witchcraft involved in starting the motor on petrol and judging when to make the changeover to the paraffin tank. I was relieved when he said, 'But we'll do that wee hop on petrol.'

Strange thing is, these engines are known to start better when cold than when warm. We had run it to know it was alive, leaving the berth in Stornoway, even though we had not needed to engage the prop to sail clear. We swapped positions.

I made sure of the line between a conspicuous dark bun of rock and Glas Sgeir, the next small island, in towards the Lewis coastline. It was plenty bouncy but we would be entering a lagoon, sheltered from most winds. We could just about sail it, if the engine cut out, though we might lose the breeze in the narrow channel between high rocks. Normally I would spill breeze from the sail, one way or another, to give a slow, controlled approach. This time I'd keep her speed up, so we had enough way to get through if the engine cut out. I had no confidence in the antique. The anchor was already fixed to chain and rope. It was ready to drop.

The modern metric chart and its electronic versions do not show the same level of detail as my photocopy of an old chart. The lines of soundings are listed in fathoms. Lights have changed their marked characteristics. Some have been removed and some have been installed. But the rocks have not shifted far. You keep slightly to the south as you approach Caolas na h-Acarsaid to avoid a reef close in to Rosaidh, to the north of the channel. Then it's down the middle till you veer to the north side to enter into the lagoon. The route is sketched in the Imray-series pilot book, compiled by Martin Lawrence. (His input is incorporated into the Clyde Cruising Club's guide *Outer Hebrides*, from 2013 editions onwards. These are now also published by Imray.)

From there I usually keep my line till well clear of the charted boulders on the southern shore of the channel. You need to make another pronounced dog-leg to make sure of avoiding reefs that are usually hidden but are as shown in the pilotage guide. Then you hug the steep-sided southern coastline till you enter the inner pool. I had a couple of waypoints in the GPS in case the fog fell but I've been in here, in different craft, often enough for fluency.

The engineer did his duty and the big flywheel turned with very little vibration. It was a well-mounted unit, even though my own preferred option was to sink it as part of our mooring. We kept the sails up till we were in. We swapped positions again and I used the simple signals that are all that's needed to guide from the front to the back of a small boat. Watch fishermen enter harbours. A finger nudging right or left. A palm up or a palm flat. It's little more emphatic than the gestures buyers used to adopt at auctions, over rows of fish boxes in our markets. Now most of the business is done on the mobile phone, before the boat is in.

Although the east side of the Outer Hebrides is blessed with many sheltered natural anchorages, some would say the landscape does not have the drama of the exposed west side. To the eye of this beholder, the lines of islands and promontories have their own quirky beauty. There are more charcoals in the shades of rocks but still great variety, moving from the basalt seams at the Shiants to the salt-scrubbed gneiss. Rowan, grey willow and eared willow keep their tenacious toeholds. The Western Isles Native Woodland Restoration Survey Report* suggests a far greater range of trees and flora than you might guess. Study of a location easily accessed from along our route listed lungwort, old man's beard, bracken, calluna, bramble, dog-rose, blaeberry, great wood-rush, common polypody, hard fern, broad buckler fern, wood sorrel, bog myrtle and primrose.

Often you meet a local yacht, doing just what we were – making the getaway from town but grabbing some rest before sniffing the Minch proper. I tried not to look at the naked gas flame on a camping cooker, with no flame safety cut-out. 'We'll need to close it at the bottle and put it outside after?'

We did. Then I slid the hatch fully open. This was only a couple of years after resigning from my job managing a coastguard watch. In terms of safety at sea, I was now a gamekeeper turned poacher. We were both tired out from all the preparations. We would start out fresh and early in the morning. I wondered how my friend must be feeling to be sleeping for the first time in a vessel that had emerged from his own head, built by his own hand.

Slow the tree and let the timber ring.
Sap-damp planking needs to breathe.

Lines will run behind the spraying dust.
Boatskin is supple straight from the steamer.
Copper clenching lets the membrane stretch.

---

* www.north-harris.org/wp-content/uploads/2012/11/Native-Woodland-Report.pdf

You learn to trust the keel that's under you
but don't scrimp on the ballast
unless you can shift yourself fast.

The Tale of the Flounder

Loch Erisort district

An hour or two out of Stornoway harbour and we had passed abeam the mouths of Tob Lierway, Loch Grimshader and Loch Erisort with its offshoot of Loch Leurbost. All these places provide good shelter in suitable conditions. If we'd had the time to explore we could have sailed up to Peacam Bay, to allow us to paddle our rubber dinghy ashore to walk on Eilean Chaluim Chille – or St Columba's Isle. There is an old stone jetty on that same island and a cemetery with carvings in stone. Up the rise, there are much older marks left by humans on this ground.

We were on the first leg of a route from Presbyterian Lewis to the borderlands in our archipelago. At Grimsay and Benbecula we are at the limits of the Protestant territories. I think the only recent signs of any tensions were a few loud-toned letters to the local papers. But it would be fair to say that a reminder of the religious past, pre-Reformation, is not always comfortable in Lewis. Since we were at anchor, just over the rise from Eilean Chaluim Chille, a tale linking the saint to the flounder comes to mind. But this is not the way it is told on Lewis so I will first give you our local version.

The fish were meeting to decide who should be the King of the Sea. The flounder fancied its chances because of its great gift of altering the colours on its back, to blend with the nature of the seabed. But it is not the fastest of fish, over a long haul. It hugs the bottom when it swims.

By the time the flounder crossed the seabed, to reach the great gathering of fishes out in the Minch, it was all over. The matter was decided and the fish were dispersing.

This flounder hailed a passing dogfish. 'Who was chosen?' he asked, expecting to hear it was his own self.

'It was the herring.'

The flounder was not too pleased to hear that.

'Why the herring?'

'Because the shoals travel the waters of the world. They suck in plankton. They never prey on other fish. They shine with silver but you can see every other colour in their scales.'

'The herring it is then. I suppose that's it all over now,' said the flounder, crossing one lip over the other in disgust. Which is why you might notice the mouth of that fish still has that twist, to this very day.

A Hidden Anchorage

THE SEARCH FOR THE IDEAL ANCHORAGE is like the search for the vessel that will come close to meeting your list of demands. You will find yourself returning, again and again, to study the shape of a boat. And you will want to return to a place that has provided shelter when you needed it. You may think you are looking for adventure but you are also hunting for some form of security. I felt safe in the body of Archie's boat, as long as neither the motor nor the cooker was running. When both were operating, I was uncomfortable. Thinking out our route, in the light of the new forecast just received, it seemed to me important to stay clear of any course that would make us dependent on that motor.

We went out the southern passage, clear of Mariveg, dodging another covered reef. There was Kebock Head ahead of us and the ebb tide helping us on. We wolfed bacon sandwiches on the way and sipped from insulated beakers of coffee. We were on full sail now and Archie was smiling. On this point of sail (a broad reach – with the wind a bit aft of the beam), the balance was not too bad. 'Good decision, stopping last night,' he said, and I knew he was right. It might be a slower passage, with the breeze less strong, but we still had enough of the northerly to push us along. My friend was developing a sensitive touch on the helm of a sailing boat. Best not held too rigid.

You can refer to *Approaches to Stornoway* to start with and then consult *The Little Minch*, both Admiralty charts. The Imray pilot book will also be a good guide but it would not be sufficient for our next anchorage, after covering a good number of miles in a gentle manner. We could have made Kallin harbour in Grimsay but our arrival would have been at an unsocial hour for descending on Archie's relatives. Also, we would have woken up to a hell of a bustle of shunting lobster-catchers, old and new, in that place, thankfully still a working harbour.

I wasn't ready for that yet and asked Archie if he was now confident in his motor – the temperamental mistress. 'It's a bit like sailing with Bette Davis,' I said.

'I never knew you did,' he said. The much-maligned engine was cold now so she started fine and I pointed Archie towards Flodday Sound. From the sea, the islands on the north-east side of Benbecula are not distinct. You have rising, heathered territories, best identified by their relationship to the dominant hills. Eaval lies to the north of them and Rueval is south-west. When the land is not high, a sudden rise to 123 metres is significant. I used an electronic waypoint to be certain that we were indeed working our way between Flodday on the seaward side and Ronay, the island made memorable by a great Gaelic song of exile.

Archie was a bit surprised when I asked him to slow her down. 'That's the way in,' I said.

'No?' he asked. 'Sure it's not that next one? That's a bit wider surely.'

It is, but it is also strewn with stray boulders, just covered by tide. The way in to this pool, one of several places I know as Acarsaidh Fhalladh, or 'Hidden Anchorage', is like a parable. You take the narrowest of paths. Like honesty, the tightest to steer but the one that brings rewards.

'You're flipping joking?'

I had to reassure Archie that the fine small ship he had created was not likely to sink within a stone's throw of her return to her spiritual home. The engine spun and thumped in a regular pulse that took us towards the high-sided passage. 'We'll be fine as long as these rocks don't squeeze any closer together,' I said.

Martin Lawrence's notes are rightly guarded but suggest that reefs indicated by the current chart are simply not there and that local knowledge also points to possible access at any state of tide. When I sailed *Broad Bay* to Lochmaddy, I took a chart to the pub one night. Several local folk, fishermen as well as cruising sailors, pointed out this entrance, as a possible excursion. 'It's clean,' they all said.

There might be space for two small craft but probably not three. The anchor was soon deep in the mud. The engine was stilled and the cooker rigged. I could hear the burn flowing down from the high ground of Ronay. The slow beat of the wings of a wide heron. Later, there would be the fingerlight bodhran beat of snipe. Our inlet formed a rounded bight in this island. Landbirds could cross the paths of seabirds.

We could take *Kennary* on to the bays of Grimsay in the morning, at our leisure. We had made a good passage and had time to be sociable and to explore further before the Boat Day. We were both tired out. Archie had come a long way since laying a keel in his shed. There was a lot going on in my own life at that time. I thought back to the feeling of relief when we were no longer joined by lines to the harbour pontoon. Underway.

Now we were 'made fast to the ground' in a secluded anchorage, round the corner from Archie's true home in the world. I wondered what diversity of species flourished ashore, within the protective coat of heathers. It was one of the most peaceful nights I've spent, at anchor.

It's only one clear line.
One of the unwritten rules
between the sharp upper shape
and the lower

probably

a reflection.

In this light now
the rocks in air and water
are strong, white, equal.
The little green's gone.
Maroon is a tint
in the charcoal blacks.

Chaluim Cille and the Flounder

Since we are now at anchor in the islanded borderlands between the Presbyterian north and the Roman Catholic south, it seems appropriate to tell that other version of the story of the flounder. Ashore, the carvings on gravestones and the style of churches change significantly. A few miles further south and you will stumble on roadside shrines with the brightly painted figure of Mary. There does not seem to be noticeable friction between the different religious communities here. Neither the landscape nor the moving waters show any traces of the dotted lines on political maps.

These muddy-bottomed sea lochs, with their inlets to fresh water burns, are, in season, the routes run by migratory sea trout. You can sometimes see their fins cut the calm. Small, silvery herring-fry boil at the surface. Down below, you have the flounder.

This is a clever fish because it can change the colour of its back to take on the hue of the bottom. It can lie still and become part of the sand or gravels. So much so that you can hardly see it, even if you are wading, hunting for its shape in the muddy sand of a shallow pool.

So it's nothing so strange that Chaluim Chille trod on one. This flounder had no respect for that saint. 'Can you not watch where you're stepping?' she said, twisting her mouth.

'You might watch your own temper,' said Chaluim Chille, looking closely at the angry fish. 'Your mouth might stay like that.'

And so it did. Not only that, but you might have noticed that this was passed on to all flounders ever since.

We sailed on next morning, taking *Kennary* up the tidal pools which provide good anchorages round from Kallin harbour. The motor did cut out on us but we were able to tack upwind to drop the hook within sight of the boatshed that meant so much to the builder of this vessel. Boatsheds are famous for remembered conversations. I once recorded Norman Macleod, son of the boatbuilder at Port of Ness, wondering how his father built a single boat there, given all the visitors, stories and cups of tea. Over the next few days, I got the feeling that it was similar in the province of the Stewarts of Grimsay.

Archie joined his relatives ashore and his wife drove down from Lewis to be with him. I slept aboard the boat, at ease when the engine was not running. I remember looking out through the round bronze porthole, crossed by the telephone lines running across the village skyline ashore. I had a plate with a soft-boiled duck's egg, pale blue on the outside, coral white and a yolk of orange. Sided by a floury bannock. The crew was being well provided for.

We usually took the boat out for some time each day, not going far but exploring the tidal waterways under sail. Curious people would come down to study her. I remembered another phrase from a conversation with the Grimsay poet, Mary Macdonald. When it became clear that I would not be living with Barbara, my wife, for evermore, she offered some advice.

'Ian, you need to find yourself a Latin woman. She'll understand you have other loves in your life. She'll know for sure she'll be sharing you with all these boats you're in love with.'

One day we had four or five other souls aboard. The handy little craft took us all along on our small expeditions. Once or twice someone asked what was under the bonnet. Archie would lift the lid to show the bonny but silent, green-enamelled engineering. There would be a sniff. 'She's not petrol, is she?' and we'd have to admit it wasn't even as simple as that. I think Archie could have sold his creation a few times over if she'd had a compact wee diesel motor or even a recent outboard.

At the Grimsay Boat Day we paraded round the circuit, mostly under sail as the others chugged along. There were older double-enders and newer creel-boats with transom sterns. They were all painted-up to the highest standard. A decorative line was highlit yellow standing out from black. Maroon and flag-blue were favoured but Donegal green was acceptable. My friend won the prize for the best boat not built in Grimsay.

I knew we would have to wait until there was a reliable westerly or southerly airstream. A few pressing matters would bring a return of stress if I left them much longer. Archie stayed down, catching up with his relations while I darted home by buses and ferries.

These done, I consulted forecasts and it looked like there would be a short weather window if we were fast off the mark. I caught the bus that connects with the Sound of Harris ferry, southbound. Archie's cousin put us up. We talked over the tides. It was agreed, we'd maybe have to stem a bit on the road back north. If we kept further out in the Minches, we'd be clear of the strongest of the contrary ebb.

Our host was now just about retired from the lobster fishing. He'd made a decent living at that but he was not yet ready for slippers by the fire. He seemed very sorry to see *Kennary* shake off her Grimsay mooring.

I was tired, from arrangements and travel, at the start of this trip. Archie is not really used to the gruelling watches required when two people take turns to steer a boat without any automatic system. We were both exhausted by the time we'd cleared the port-hand buoy at Arnish to enter Stornoway harbour. Still, it had been a very good passage, assisted by tide where it mattered most.

We were sailing as a team and it showed in the Stornoway week of local boat races. There was a section for luggers and gaffers. A local sailing instructor devised some complex formulae for handicapping a very varied fleet. The breeze suited us – strong but shifting. Archie helmed and I adjusted the sail trim. It blew and I tightened everything up. Soon I had to get everything but my feet out over the side to keep her level. I clung to a mast stay. She carried all her cloth. The weather helm eased a bit when we allowed the mainsail right out and sailed her free, knowing we could change tack easier than most of our rivals.

We came second across the line and were judged second on corrected time. Archie was a happy man, accepting another prize.

Dunderave

IT USED TO BE THAT A WORKING BOAT was priced by the foot. When you placed an order you would pay, in stages, according to the length of the vessel you wanted. Costs went in proportion. Local yards would usually be building craft of a very similar type.

In contrast, sailing yachts could be of very different characteristics and varying volumes, according to the designer's drawings. Vessels designed to cope with voyaging far from land will usually be deep-drafted. They will carry a significant part of their weight in the keel, to counterbalance her when she is driven hard to one side by the forces of wind or waves. The space inside her is another issue. There is a formula called 'Thames Measurement', which gives an estimate of the tonnage based not on displacement but on length and breadth. Thus it indicates the volume of the craft. Yachts with a bigger useable space usually cost more.

I came to know this when I first hunted for a suitable family yacht, within our budget. I did consider the South Coast One Design (or SCOD). I had seen a good example afloat on a mooring at Stornoway for many years. Because they are a bigger-volume boat and deeper in draft, they are thought capable of going further afield than a design like the nippier and lighter Stella. But at that time they could be about double the price. Charles Nicholson's aim in designing the South Coast One Design was to meet demand for a fleet of cruiser-racer craft of fairly basic fit-out. They had to be reasonably affordable but capable of taking part in cross-Channel dashes or cruises to Brittany or Holland. The first was built in 1955 and a further 105 followed, the last in 1970, when fibreglass production of rival craft was well established. Although not much longer than the Stella they have much more headroom, because they are deeper. They are heavier built, of thicker planks laid flush (carvel) on a frame of closely spaced ribs.

John Macbeth asked me if I'd take a look at one for sale in a yard south of Oban. By this time my lads had completed their studies and were finding their own ways in the world. I no longer lived with their mother, Barbara. The divorce had not yet come through but we had been apart for some years. Now I lived in a townhouse by the harbour. I shared part of it with a colleague of John and sometimes we were joined by friends and even by our respective partners.

Now and again I sailed for money, crewing on a larger boat or delivering a small one. Usually, I preferred to teach sailing in my own time, between paid projects in the arts. As a volunteer skipper of community boats, I enjoyed watching people gain practical skills. My young son Ben was living far away, following his creative passion for music, and his elder brother, Sean, was working all the hours he could find building up his skills as a teacher. I did not see enough of either of them. I was conscious that the sailing community had become my alternative family.

John made an offer for the SCOD. It was accepted because the owner was paying yard fees and insurance and the other costs that mount up when you are unwise enough to own a vessel of any kind. She'd been out of the water for a couple of years. She seemed sound but there was a list of jobs before she would be safe for sea. John grew up in France and still has the accent. He has tight curls of short fair hair and blue eyes. He also has the gift of the gab, as we say.

He was doing research for a PhD in the field of alternative energy. John thought he could finance his new obsession with sailing by living aboard a boat and saving on rent. He had made a good choice of project. The volume was just about enough for a tall, fit fellow. It had good headroom in the raised part of the cabin.

Looking back, I don't think I found the SCOD, *Dunderave*, beautiful though most would say she was attractive, given a fresh lick of paint. Her mahogany doghouse adds additional headspace so even John did not have to stoop upon entering the cabin. To me, it seemed a little out of proportion to the blunt hull.

This is part of the compromise between living space and sailing performance that is inevitable in any cruising yacht. John could stand at the galley and at the simple chart table. He was besotted and this was before the design had its moment of glory. The actor Ewan McGregor appears to be sailing an example in a Woody Allen film. There is probably an experienced sailor aboard but hiding from the camera.

There was no love-rivalry between young John and myself for this vessel he would rescue and live with. Thus I can now be objective, stepping back to see why I wanted to help in this project, even though I had already sailed most of the route that would take *Dunderave* to Stornoway, where John was studying. The challenge of helping to make the vessel seaworthy, in the time, appealed and it was a chance to pass on what I'd picked up to young lads who were good company. I can now look back to see myself becoming involved.

We start at Kilmelfort. It's January. A young man and an older one are building a temporary polythene tent around a small yacht so they can do some work on it. The temperature is a few degrees below zero but there is electricity to the stance. They have two heat-guns for stripping paint and some other bits of assorted electrical gear to produce heat and light. These are rigged so there is a localised environment. The two-part epoxy mixture needs a minimum temperature for the chemical reaction that will set it. The atmosphere also has to be dry.

A few parts of the hull have been stripped back to bare wood so the epoxy, sometimes strengthened with other fabric, can fill small holes or heal an area that has been deeply chafed. The zinc-rich primer paint, which will protect the epoxy when it sets, also needs a minimum temperature. That is achieved, within the improvised tent. The two work steady hours but dark and cold come early. They can put on a heater in the boat's cabin and cook food on a camping stove. This will also take the chill off the saloon area, which contains a bunk on either side.

They have time to clear up properly and plan the jobs for the next day. One of the forged bolts that keeps the iron keel attached to the timber will be driven downwards. This is the one furthest forwards, where there is a cutaway in the hull shape deep enough to remove the bolt completely. It can then be checked for wear. Most surveyors will insist that this is done from time to time.

They use a patent bar, which accepts a three-quarter-inch drive socket, to remove the nuts inside the hull. This was made for the older man by the Stornoway blacksmith. When he asked about payment, the blacksmith, Calum, said to take it back when he was finished with it and he'd make it into something else. But his customer, who was and is me, paid him something and let it be known around the harbour that the tool was available for this job.

The keel-bolt inspection went quite smoothly until it came to putting it back. There was no sign of any corrosion. Often the natural acid in oak corrodes steel, once the sacrificial zinc galvanising degrades. But these were of quality iron. The threads were cleaned and a little grease applied so it would drive back in place. But it failed to lock in its recess in the keel. The nuts at the top could not be fully tightened until the bolt locked in place. The two men would take turn about, suggesting solutions from their different experiences. They listened to each other. So far, they'd been able to complete all the jobs on the list by pooling their skills.

This time they positioned a bottle jack under the bolt head but it did not have quite the reach to apply enough pressure to stop the long bolt from turning. So the older fellow picked up some of the many wedges that were lying all about the yard and drove one against the other until the bolt lodged tight. Then the interior nut and a second locking nut were torqued up.

They studied the weather forecasts on a laptop computer, up in the pub. Off-season, it was only open for a few hours in the evening. They would go there after eating large meals of local haggis or sausage or other filling things. Then they'd check emails and nurse a pint. The younger was fed up because the elder one was always typing away instead of swapping stories. He was emailing back and fore with a woman he had met on *Guardian* personals. They were discussing literature rather than boats and they were also flirting in typed language. She was American but had lived in France for some years. He had recently sailed to Brittany, crewing on a small yacht, and had made good friends with the owner. He was due a visit to France. The younger man had recently ended a relationship he had been in for a year or two. His life was filled with his PhD project and the idea of the live-aboard boat.

At last the two men saw the prospect of clear weather and the rise in temperature they'd need to complete the paint job. They had detached every element of the wire rigging to be sent for replacement. The elder fellow had done some work on the propeller and other metalwork and the younger had sourced the gear needed to make the boat more safe, for a winter passage to the Outer Hebrides.

The evening before the two days of the last big push they did not go up to the pub. Both stayed in the boat close to the single electric heater, which was linked to the yard's electricity connection. They watched a DVD of the life of a great French sailor, Eric Tabarly, on a laptop. The older guy had once seen Tabarly's most famous boat near the mouth of the Loire river. She was one of the *Pen Duick* series, the one that was found drifting, on its way to a regatta of yachts built by the designer, William Fyfe of Fairlie. Tabarly was sailing single-handed. He was only doing what he'd done many times, going greater distances, on transatlantic races for example. But this time he was gone, on his never-ending journey, though his boat was towed home.

The sky was clear. There were no more snow flurries. It was a welcome break from days of driving hail but the temperature wasn't up yet. The tent had to be reassembled and an artificial environment created. They were methodical and applied the coats of primer and topcoat without short cuts. The white was applied in thin layers with rollers. It dried quite quickly when protected.

The older guy, the one with the van, departed to do his scheduled work but drove by to pick up the younger fellow after a couple of days. The red antifouling paint job was now complete and the new rigging was on its way. They both had to return to Lewis, by road, but the schedule was now secure for a February launch. This is not the usual time for taking a 26-foot boat up the west of Scotland, but John Macbeth could not afford to pay the yard dues for much longer. His lease on a flat in Stornoway was running out. Now was the time to move the boat.

John left from Stornoway, by ferry and bus, so he could be with *Dunderave* when she was launched. My housemate James and myself took the chance to travel most of the way by sea. We were given berths on a mighty vessel of steel, made famous under the name *Time and Tide*. The 67-foot ex-round-the-world Challenge yacht was bound to Oban from Stornoway for a refit. The Challenge racing fleet was a further development of Chay Blyth's adventure in *British Steel*. At that time I was crewing aboard the big Challenge yacht from time to time. Another friend who is very knacky with engines was also along for the ride.

We came down the outside of Skye, anchoring in Loch Dunvegan for the night. The visibility was so clear I was confused. I could not recognise the high land out ahead though I've often sailed up and down this route. Strange light shifts islands. It has the power to shuffle and even invert rock and earth. With a sudden change of temperature I have even seen islands tumbled together, leaving stragglers suspended above the level of water. I took a bearing to be sure I was interpreting the skyline correctly. It was indeed Barra and that had to be Mingulay beyond it. Berneray after that – the tail of the chain of the Outer Hebrides with snow along all the tops lit in the high-pressure system. We were looking at a Japanese print rather than the usual outline, softened by cloud. There was a light easterly breeze. That startling skyline was a reminder that a route is never the same.

It was probably the coldest sailing I have ever experienced. I had thermals under my layers and a two-piece padded fisherman's flotation suit over them. I was still conscious of the cold as an active thing. I wasn't the only one. There was competition to carry out any winching or trimming required. I realised I'd only brought a single pair of jeans. If they got wet, I'd be in trouble. Three of us were to jump ship on to John's *Dunderave*. Our engineering-minded pal would check everything out. Then he'd get the bus back to rejoin the lads in Oban aboard the Challenge yacht.

James stayed in Oban to do the provisioning. He'd come down on the next bus. 'Anything you're needing?' James asked. 'A pair of jeans from a charity shop,' I replied. 'I'm an in-between size. Women's size 12 will fit. No kidding. Say they're for your girlfriend.'

'Any preferences?'

'Bellbottoms,' I joked. And that's what he got me. I thought he had a smirk on him. He wouldn't take the money.

The yard had been paid by the previous owner to put her in the water and step the mast. The workers had also tuned up the new rigging. Like bloody harp strings. There was quite a bend in a mast that wasn't designed to have it. John and I set to, with spanners and a spike, slackening things. Because the job had been done by professionals we were shy about loosening the rig to the extent we thought we should, to allow for movement in a structure that had dried out for a few seasons.

She was leaking when we left the berth to run the engine and hoist sail in the bay. There was no sign of this settling down and she took in more and more. We found out afterwards that our instinct was right. It's standard procedure to apply the rig tension gradually on a wooden boat as the moistened timber expands. It looked like we would be doing a lot of pumping but the manual one was just about coping. If you think it's taking a hell of a long time to get to the sailing bit of this tale, that would be an accurate reflection of most examples of being possessed by a boat.

John's *Dunderave* was bought at a price he could afford because it was a project. It was a doable project, because the mast, sails and engine were all quite sturdy yet. And it had a recent fit of instruments with new wiring, so she should be ready to go. We had to decide if the leak was annoying or dangerous. Once we were sure that it was nothing to do with the prop shaft, rudder or the sea cocks, I suggested it was annoying. We'd looked over every inch of the hull, within and without. There was no sign of damp at our one major repair to the planking. But the decision had to be John's.

We would face some hard sailing to get her home but there were escape routes. The likely key to the passage would be working from tide to tide, navigating the narrows, east of Skye. The other possibility was heading up the Minches with Skye to starboard. But that is an exposed route in unsettled weather. I was thinking of the time when I managed a coastguard watch and a creel-boat called up nice and cool on the radio, crossing from Uig to Harris. They were hoping to get home for the New Year. A severe gale from the north was forecast. I sensed something in the tone of voice and asked the skipper to maintain communications with us. 'Please call us on channel 16 every 30 minutes.' Afterwards I found that everyone but himself had been down on their hands and knees, praying. And these were not known to be religious lads.

The old Volvo diesel was now running quite nicely. Our consultant had given us a tutorial before catching the bus back to Oban to rejoin the team on the Challenge yacht. Even if we could have persuaded him to come along, there was no space for him to sleep onboard. Three berths were spoken for and the other was packed with gear. The forecast promised a welcome change from the hail-carrying northerlies. But it looked like very fresh wind for a 26-footer, recently relaunched.

James is another tall man, dark as John is fair. He is an ace with electronic systems. He is normally spare with his words and thoughtful but is capable of some very sharp bursts of wit. He can break into a sudden laugh.

The same waypoints that were in my hand-held GPS and on the paper charts were now on the electronic chart-plotter, thanks to James. He talked us through the system. I warned everyone that there were likely to be steep overfalls when we were out abeam Seil Island and Easdale. Then we'd get a tidal push that should take us to Tobermory. But it would be a long first day.

The lumps of tidal water, white cresting, were a bit steeper than I'd reckoned but our tidal calculations were sound. We pointed the fresh white *Dunderave* out to the open sea just as the tide turned. I remembered how I had looked across to a bubbling white on the water, conspicuous against cliffs of slate, as we had punched north in *Moonspinner*. This time we were emerging from a gap in the cliffs, one not apparent from seaward. The trackline of *Dunderave* would inevitably cross over the invisible line left by my previous voyage.

The water would have been quieter if we'd waited for one more hour for the disturbance of the ebb tide to settle down. But this was my first time through the twists of the fast flowing Cuan Sound and I wanted to do this on slack water. Still, *Dunderave* proved comfortable under sail, once we were through the narrows. She had a turn of speed. James and I swapped approving nods but John was ecstatic. She was light from drying out and now had a clean, smooth bottom. The foresail had hardly any wear in it and the main was sound. We hastily improvised a system to put a reef in.

I could see that both my companions were gripped by the same sense of widening possibilities that I had felt as we emerged through the Dorus Mor in the red Stella. There were the Garvellachs, a huddle of rugged islands. 'They' say that this is the resting place of the mother of Chaluim Chille. Beyond them, to the north-west, is the jagged coastline of Mull. Another quadrant of the dominant Ben More holds its place on your distant vista. I thought back to a few trips documenting the lone boat-handlers who throw out their creels in a spirit of hope to the intense colours of the waters that suck between Erraid and Iona. Another trip, we might nudge *Dunderave* into 'Tinker's Hole', a surprise gap opening in the dark coast of the island where Robert Louis Stevenson stepped ashore with his father, the engineer. The neat quarrymen's cottages where they were billeted are still in good repair. They lie low but close to the slope where the dovetailed granite blocks, specified for the offshore lights of Dubh Artach and Skerryvore, were quarried.

But it was winter and we needed to cover some miles and get the boat into a harbour where we could warm up and stock up. We sailed well and ate well but pumped often. John kept a count of the strokes of the manual pump so we could tell if the leaking was diminishing or increasing. I would rather sail on a boat that is structurally sound and a seakindly shape but has a bloody annoying leak than a dry one that behaves strangely.

The smile only left John when we were counting the pump strokes. I had to tell them the Lady's Rock story as we passed. It took a while to work clear of Lismore. We still had plenty of tide – you could see it on the water – but the wind was funnelling down the Sound of Mull as it often does. That was a good test of the boat and the crew.

The two young men had both built up useful experience on the Lewis traditional boats. Turning a yacht through the wind is much easier than tacking a dipping lugsail boat. One tack took us a bit close to the Mull shore. The sounder didn't hit the alarm area but we were too close to a lee shore for my liking. John had found a problem on the foredeck just as we were about to tack through the wind. He did not notice my hand gesture and I had to shout a warning as I put the tiller over.

The nightmare is a man going over the side, in conditions like that. It should simply not happen. We'd rehearsed the drill for clipping on, reminding each other all the time. No one was to leave the cockpit without being secured and now we were clipped-on in the cockpit too. I knew that the most dangerous situation is when a man just holds on to the backstay to have a piss over the side. From now on we would all go down below and sit down to piss on the vintage 'heads' with its system of pumping in and out. All sea cocks to be closed after use.

If you reef down too soon you don't have the power to beat against building waves. If you don't reef enough, the tiller feels too heavy and there is turbulence everywhere, slowing you and putting more strain on. You'd be mad not to reef down in time on a boat that had just been launched after major works and with a rig that still probably had too much tension in it.

We were now abeam Lochaline. We had just put our tricolour navigation light on, shining from the top of our mast to tell other vessels that we were under sail, not motor. We were clear of the critical area for tide. With this much wind – about Beaufort 5, though it seemed more – channelled down the narrows, we could stem a little tide to reach Tobermory. John looked a bit nervous as we approached the pontoon. He had asked me if I would take her in but I knew he lacked only confidence. It's more difficult if you have to counteract gusts by putting on more revs or if strong wind is blowing from behind you. He made a neat job of it.

This had been a long day and there were some running repairs to do. We should also monitor that leak for a while. I slept well and rose early. I bought a couple of blocks and a sail-repair kit in the well-stocked chandlers. I'd noticed the beginnings of a tear where undue pressure had been put, close to a reefing point. I returned to the boat with a new black container filled with diesel. We already had a full tank but this was a back-up in case of contamination. Presents for the ship. The lads were on the pans and a kind fellow lent us his electrical adaptor so we could get some heat on to dry out some clothes. 'We don't get a lot of visitors this time of year,' he said.

The leak had got no better but no worse either. I sewed a patch on the sail at the torn reef-pennant while James plumbed in the next part of our route. The wind was swinging to a south-westerly at last. Our rest time would allow the exposed area, off Ardnamurchan Point, to settle. We hoped to be through before the new wind would induce confused, contrary seas. Previous trips leave you with a sheaf of experiences, if you can find them in your mind.

We were close to spring tides. Our batteries and electrics were behaving. We could work the evening flood to take us as far as the Sound of Sleat. Estimating our average speed at 5 knots, we should be there by midnight. We could anchor or pick up a mooring for four hours or so. If we left Armadale about 4am the following morning, we might make Stornoway that night. We would start at the time of slack water, and head on up to the Kylerhea tidal rollercoaster at the narrows between the Isle of Skye and the mainland. That should push us under the Skye bridge and right up the Inner Sound to enter the North Minch. That was our passage plan.

We had the wind dead behind us, from Tobermory to the turning point. John was understandably nervous. We had the right amount of cloth up, not overpowered. We rehearsed a slow downwind turn, making sure the mainsail sheet was controlled all the time. That way, the boom could not swing the full arc across the cockpit, with the power to destroy heads and rigging. You can take the mast down with shock-loading if you let that boom sweep out of control. We consolidated the manoeuvre in a series of downwind zigzags, to avoid the danger of an accidental 'gybe'. You simply make sure that the wind is to one side of the boat rather than dead astern. When you want to turn back towards your theoretical course line, you give good warning to everyone so the mainsail sheet (controlling rope) is taken in by crew as you turn and released again when the wind is on the other side of the boat. Anyone who has learned to sail on small dinghies will have done this until it is like an instinct.

That sequence became as smooth as our upwind tacking had the previous day. I have to admit that I put a bit of pressure on the younger men, passing on what I'd learned not so many years before. If they were to plan their own voyages in this craft they had to gain confidence. They also had to get a sense of what was safe and what was not – the right amount of sail to carry and the certainty of your angle to the wind at a given moment. I feel that some sailing instructors put too much emphasis on the finer points of sail-tuning before their students have a strong grasp of safe practice. Or at least as safe as it can be, in an old leaky boat in fierce tides in a Scottish winter.

We turned towards the wind to put a reef in before going out to the open. This was now an easier job than it had been the night before. She was going like a wee train. Just enough spray and surf for exhilaration, without anxiety. James took photo after photo of the last of the evening light illuminating the tall brickwork of Ardamurchan lighthouse. This is the most westerly British mainland point. We all gasped at the sheer drama when we looked to the north-west. Muck, Eigg and Rum all have distinctive skylines. The stone spur on Eigg and the jagged, cloud-tearing ridge on Rum are both shapes that stay with you. But the Dutchman's Cap, in the Treshnish Isles, west of Mull, is also distinct, though less dramatic.

There was a dusty stroke, which had to be the mainland, to the east and then a weaker shading to the north. That had to be the south-east tip of the Isle of Skye. Stars appeared. I can only identify a few but you can line up a prominent one on the shining wire of your stay or 'shroud' even if you don't have a name for it. This is a good alternative to straining your eyes by steering to the figure on the compass or the line on the plotter.

We found a mooring, off Armadale, with the help of a torch. Alarms were set on mobile phones. The wind would be strong by the end of the following day. We would need to catch the first of the north-going flood. That would help us get up the Minch before the seas really built up.

We lost no time in departing. Coffee was brewed as we were underway. We were rewarded. Not only did we get the full period of fair tide under us but the clouds cleared. The tide is like a river in that channel and the torque takes your bow a bit one way and then the other. We looked out for otters, but the water was as interesting as any animal. The land moves fast. Then you're looking to Kintail and the dense woods that come right to the shore. Loch Hourn at one end and Loch Long off the northern end of the Sound, cut deep into the steep-sided ground.

We were motor-sailing, putting something back into the batteries and making sure the diesel 'donkey' was behaving and warm and happy. We were able to look across to yet another iconic skyline – the five sisters of Kintail. But I was also thinking back to the transient imagery of the water we had encountered, broken by tide and skerries.

Its character was as much a part of our story as the tales behind the names of mountains.

we're free from the fog
new rock, rough from the saw
shining black basalt

diluted moon-pull
leads our vessel by the prow
through calcified fins

that rounding swell-line
over stereo seabird screech
– we read the water

spurdog waves return
from the confining shore
– grey rasping tails

The Five Sisters

The white-topped peaks turned our heads, out abeam the entrance to Loch Long.

My companions protested when I said 'The Seven Sisters'.

'I'm counting five peaks on the ridge,' said John. But I remembered why the number seven came to mind. I think I heard this first from my own mother.

The chief of the clans that hunted and farmed and fished the territory of Kintail was blessed with seven daughters. Each was as bonny as the next. A vessel from Ireland sheltered in the loch and two princes of a good family set eyes on the eldest daughters. Their father consented to the matches. The mariners could take their new brides away on one condition. The ship must return with the five other brothers of these young men. A father had to be fair to all his daughters.

That would not have been the first vessel lost on that route. Nor the last. I cannot tell you whether it perished on the passage to Ireland or on the way back. We can say that she never did arrive at Kintail again.

The five remaining daughters feared that their looks would fade by the time the princes of Ireland arrived to claim them. They became desperate and consulted a woman with the power to preserve their beauty forever. Whatever she asked, this was done.

The five sisters did keep their beauty but beyond anything truly human. It is enough to bring your heart to your mouth and it is difficult to tear your eyes from the sight of these mountain peaks, all as handsome as the other. Their looks change with the seasons but the five sisters never seem to age. They stand there, still as stone, joined in the ridge, thousands of feet up into the moving skies.

Crossing the Minch

IT WAS TIME TO TURN OUR HEADS FROM KINTAIL and look to the Crowlin islands. They were keeking out from under the Skye bridge. We'd leave them well to starboard and seek the tight but clean channel between Raasay and Rona.

This is another area where the wind just does what it wants. It shifted from our quarter to our beam. The boat heeled but the water was flat. This was a good testing ground. We needed to know that both the SCOD and the team could take the Minch in a boisterous mood.

I heard myself say, 'It seems to be localised so we won't put in the second reef yet. We can practise spilling wind on the mainsheet.'

When the boat heels far enough for the toerails to dip into water, you release the sheet rope smartly so the mainsail runs out till it flaps and the power is released. This doesn't work when the wind is behind you – in fact, you're better to pull it tight in then so it's flatter.

John was looking nervous at first as his new pride and joy leaned over, more and more. Then he looked more confident, controlling just how much he could let her go. I wonder if this is a bit like horse-riding. I imagine it's a wonderful feeling to build a rapport with an animal. If *Dunderave* was our horse she had the bit between her teeth, now.

A southerly force 7, gusting to 30 knots, was forecast. We would be cutting through the gap just north of Raasay. Now that we had punched through the squalls pawing under the spans of the bridge, it was time to prepare for our crossing. James helmed as John and I went forwards to take down the working jib and hank on the small, heavy storm jib. The rope that hauls up a sail is the halyard. Usually there is a spare one up front, perhaps used for the spinnaker when a light to moderate wind is behind you.

John lost the end of the foresail halyard and it whipped up the mast out of reach. It happens. We pulled it all down, through the block at the top. No one was going up the mast in these conditions. The sea was still flattish but the wind was now howling. We would have to trust that the back-up halyard was strong enough.

'Don't you bloody dare let that one go,' I said. I'd put some spare ropes aside to take down with me when I prepared to join the Challenge yacht in Stornoway, my transport to join this much smaller ship. When I phoned John to ask what he still needed, he had told me not to bother. He had plenty. Now I was looking at his lightweight spinnaker halyard. This was all we had, to hoist a foresail, with a near gale forecast.

But it was myself I was annoyed with. I should have rigged a stronger spare halyard before we left or when we were alongside in Tobermory. Although it was John's project, he was deferring to me as someone who now had a few similar voyages behind him. A skipper checks what his crew has done, especially when one of them is a nervous new owner with a lot on his mind. I have seen a line like that

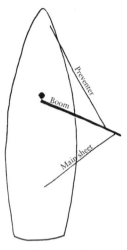

A preventer

snap and it scared me more than a gale. With the wind behind us, we could well be running on a small foresail alone if the wind reached gale force. Then we would be totally dependent on one rope that looked a bit light for the job.

Instead, we put the second deep reef in the mainsail. Then we rigged a rope from the end of the boom to a strong cleat up at the bow. This prevents that boom from swinging across the boat if there is a sudden shift of wind or the person steering loses concentration.

Dunderave took off but felt comfortable, James was helming like an old hand. The speed climbed to 6½ knots. We had plenty of cloth for the conditions. That accounts for the photo of fair John's cheesy grin as we navigated the gap. It was right there, we saw the sea eagle, maybe 50 metres off. It was perching on a rock in the narrows but took to the air as we went through. The scale of these birds is shocking. An immature golden eagle also has a whiteish tail but there's no mistaking the sedate flap and then the soaring of a barn door in the sky.

I kept a manual plot on the chart as the lads almost fought each other for their turn at the tiller of the surfing yacht. She was not taking in any more water than when we had started out. Not much less, either. We all counted the pump strokes as we took turns bailing. I passed on what I'd first learned from Kenny Morrison, steering *an Sulaire* in big seas. You put a bit of weight on the tiller to anticipate the boat's tendency to turn towards the wind. Then you allow the rudder to centralise itself, to avoid braking as the boat surges on with the wave. We were hitting 7 knots from time to time – an excellent speed for a boat of this length.

There is one more photo. It's a bit of a blur as a rain squall is kicking in. You can tell we're over the east bank out from the Shiants because of the shape of the high wave, rounding up, way above the level of our sternrails. James must have been steering by the wind on his face because his glasses are dripping. I must have taken the shot. Owner and helmsman have the 7-knot grin. *Dunderave* is in her element. So are we three. We'd be home in time for dinner but right then you can tell all three are sailing for the sake of sailing.

on a beam reach your belly takes knocks
on a broad reach you lope the swell
on the beat your bow is thrown
don't look behind you on the run
you lever the rudder to impress sea

The King of Lochlinn's Daughter

When you cut peat you sometimes come across long roots. On Lewis it's usually birch. You can see the bark of it shine vermillion, on a good day in May. The larks will be sounding, full pelt and up too high to be seen in the bright weather. Those black peats, with the remnants of branches through them, sometimes break up. But when they dry they burn very hot.

Over on the Loch Broom side of the Minch it must have been more fir than birch. You come across great roots and stumps in lochs when the water falls low. So that side of Scotland was not as bare as it looks today. The lands were covered in woodland. Some of these may have been burned so there was more precious land for grazing. But there is a story that accounts for the loss of forests from the high mainland slopes you can study from the Shiant Banks.

You may know that the Hebrides were under Norse rule till a treaty agreed in 1266. Before that there was a time of raids and skirmishes. In bare country, trees were a source of power. We needed timber for building roofs and for building boats.

And trees were not plentiful in every part of Norway. Once you go north of a certain latitude, trees get scarce there too. The King of Norway, or Lochlinn as it was known then, was envious of the forests that still existed on the miles of hills within reach of Loch Broom. He also feared the power these could give to his rivals. They could be felled to build a fleet of ships and they could be cut to heat forges.

That king had a daughter who would do anything to help her father. She wanted to show she was as brave as any son. She saw that he was worrying and asked what it was and what could she do.

The King of Lochlinn said he would be happy if he could find a way to destroy the great forest that covered the coastal lands of north-west Scotland. His daughter listened to people who knew the old ways of doing things. Then she said to her father, 'I need to take the shape of a bird. Can you find someone who can change me?'

Her father summoned a woman who knew strange arts. I have no knowledge of how it was done but the princess left the land of Lochlinn as a great white bird.

A few sweeps of these wide wings brought her into the thermals. Soon she was clear of the land. She still had all the mind of the daughter of a king but she also had the instincts of a powerful bird. It was not long before she was over the west coast of Scotland.

She made for the high wooded plains, before the mountains became rock. She glided down, here and there, just allowing her talons to glance against the new green growth on the top branches. These were set alight as soon as they were touched.

On and on she flew, with a crackling and blazing behind her. Dense smoke was hurled high into the air. There is resin in the timber from fir. Soon it was oozing as the heat ate into that good wood. When it was set alight it burned black. Soot blotted out the light from the sky. Her feathers were splattered with dark patches. These joined together till the daughter of the King of Lochlinn became an ugly, dark bird.

The people of coastal Scotland were horrified at the destruction. One man at Loch Broom, who still knew the old ways, said that the dark bird could only have the power it held if it possessed some human characteristics. These days of loneliness and burning would bring out whatever was left of that. The path of the great fire was soon heading their way. He asked everyone to gather in their animals. They were to take the lambs from the ewes, the calves from the cows, the piglets from the sows. They were to gather up all the puppies and all the kittens. Even the youngest chicks from the hens, ducklings and goslings, too.

The young of every farm animal in all these villages were gathered in a single huge pen. The mothers were put into another. When evening came, you could not speak for the bleating and moaning. There was calling and quacking. There was lowing, squealing and whinnying and screeching. Deep, sad howls. The noise filled the whole settlement and went out along the coast and far up into the air.

The great, blackened bird beat her wings till her flight took her lower and lower. She was drawn to that pathetic noise, all that suffering, so she lost her caution. A marksman was ready with his best arrows. The pick of his quiver sped to the heart of that dark thing. It fell to the ground. As the breath was leaving the great bird, her form changed. She became the lifeless shape of the daughter of the King of Lochlinn.

The witch who had put that spell on the king's daughter knew that she had fallen. She informed the king at once and a longship was sent without delay, from their allies in Orkney. It drove fast in strong wind and was soon entering Loch Broom.

Huge expanses of fine woods were left as black sticks and twigs. But the destruction had been halted. People were all too used to the fires of warfare then. They stood aside, allowing the crew of that ship to take the funeral bier aboard.

Each time the vessel reached the mouth of that sea loch they were into the teeth of a gale and had to drop back for shelter. They tried three times before they knew they would have to leave the body close to where it had fallen.

She was buried at Kildonan, at the head of the loch. That's a small green hill, just up from Little Loch Broom. The area is still green and it is blessed with tall fir, pine and larch trees.

Once we were home, the rigging was eased further for a time. The leaking healed itself, once the pressure was off. John Macbeth commissioned a neat cast-iron stove and installed it, with the help of colleagues at the college, part of the University of the Highlands and Islands. Living aboard *Dunderave* might not have helped him do his research in any less time than he might otherwise have taken. A wooden boat provides no end of distraction therapy. He stripped the mahogany interior back to bare wood and nourished it with oils and wax.

James and John honed their skills very quickly over a couple of seasons. Soon *Dunderave* became a hard boat to beat in local handicap races. Spinnaker technique became slick. John was set on sailing the SCOD to Shetland and then across the North Sea to Norway. Their department was to take part in a conference on renewable energy systems. The man who headed it had already departed in his own 30-foot wooden yacht, in an attempt to travel to the conference by sailpower. I was anxious about my own former 'students', now their own men. John converted the cockpit so it was self-draining. The job was completed the day before departure. Any waves that swept into it could now drain, out of the hull. The engine, which had proved reliable, was also protected from any water falling down from above. I lent the lads a liferaft and an electronic beacon. They departed with a fit-looking friend, to share the watch-keeping.

A postcard arrived at my home in the old sail loft by Stornoway harbour. The lads had reached the conference. The full complement from the Stornoway-based college arrived in Norway under their own sailpower, in two small wooden yachts. John was kind enough to say that my help had been a factor. Even though I had asked them to think carefully about attempting the North Sea crossing, I felt responsible. I grew worried about their return passage. It's sometimes more difficult to be cast in the role of one of the waiting ones, ashore.

Dunderave came through a full gale on the way back across the North Sea. The three aboard were exhausted. The lads sensibly ran down into Westray, Orkney. The stove could be lit and they could eat proper hot meals until they found a more favourable wind for home. They came home weary but they came home safe.

Kirsty

Craignair (sister-ship to *Kirsty*)

WORKING BOATS BUILT FOR THE SAME PURPOSE by the same yard will be sisters. I do not know if you ever really can have twin boats. I know of a set of twins who each commissioned a lobster-fishing vessel from the same yard. You can see them moored, side by side, in Tobermory harbour. The variations extend much further than the individual fishing numbers painted on their sides. For example, their wheelhouses are noticeably different, though both hulls still have a varnished finish. Each experienced skipper will have his own requirements to suit the way he works and of course his own taste. In contrast, a class of boats like the Stella or SCOD is devised with the aim of making the essential details so alike that racing between the boats is fair. Their owners' individual personalities will be brought out by their names or paint schemes.

As years pass, the members of the class will probably become more diverse. Unless the craft has racing as its only purpose (a one-design class), handicaps may have to be devised when they meet to race, to account for different sails or propellers.

I know of two yachts, of working-craft origins, built to the same plans, by the same yard, to the same drawings, within a year of each other. One of them has vestiges of peeling black paint and one is bright in fresh cream. One is propped and stayed, so her shape can still be admired by walkers of dogs, by Goat Island boatyard at the east side of Stornoway harbour. Each year, another of her planks is sprung. The tide washes through her. Her sister winters in various west coast boatyards, under cover. The shape of her hull, sloping from a shallow bow section to a deep and full keel, is identical to the one fading into the Stornoway shoreline. There is evidence of use and care all around the cream-hulled craft. There are laid decks of scrubbed timber and varnished hatches of dark hardwoods. Lacquered spars. Sails protected by matching covers of crisp canvas.

I often study the fall of her sister's planking from that high stern and note the buoyancy of her graceful quarters. She was built of the finest materials, a hull of pitch-pine and joinery and hatches of teak. That explains why she has not yet fallen apart, though planks have now parted from her timber frames, probably of oak.

Though I pass by the black boat often, viewing her from the shore or from the water, there is a great distance between her and me. I have never been invited down below deck level, though now you could enter that without breaking anything. But her sister-vessel, *Kirsty*, belongs to close friends and I have often enjoyed the hospitality of that yacht, seated on leather-covered saloon benches by a crackling wood-burning stove. It may be that my admiration of the lines of the dark sister have influenced my relationship with her light-coated sibling. I appreciate her elegance, because her full shape has been revealed by her near-naked sister.

The design they are both based on is the Loch Fyne skiff. These were built in great numbers, in different sizes, for a herring fishery that seemed as if it would last forever. All round the British Isles, open or decked craft developed into specific types to suit the range of the fishing, the waters they were likely to meet and the traditions developed in an area. The Fifie was plumb at the bow and stern, giving great directional stability, but she would be slow to turn. The Zulu also had the plumb bow but she had a steeply raked stern. That made her more manoeuvrable. The Loch Fyne skiff also had a raked stern but her keel sloped from being quite shallow forward to being very deep aft.

This had advantages. These vessels could lie in shelving harbours and they could come very close in to steep shores. They could make a lively turn but still have good grip on the water. Her rudder would still be low down so she would not lose her steering easily, even in big seas, when her bow dipped deep. Usually they carried a standing lugsail with very little area forward of a mast, which had a steep rake to lean aft. There would be a stay on each side of the mast and a forestay to the bow. Like little *Broad Bay*, as I'd once rigged her, and like Archie's *Kennary*, she would not have to dip the sail to turn

| Fifie | Zulu | Loch Fyne skiff |

Hull shapes

through the wind. She had a long sprit up front to carry a large jib, which could also be reefed to keep her in balance.

But of course, like recognisable stories, and any other thing made by any culture in the wide world, there are always variations. It was not simply that the sails of the herring drifters would be made to different heights and shapes. They could be of different types, as divergent as the shapes of their hulls. In Shetland, the Zulus would carry gaff rig rather than any kind of lugsail. That is where a spar (gaff), usually of timber, is hoisted up the mast. Another spar (boom) stretches out the foot, or lower edge of the sail. Both are fixed to the mast in that the bottom 'boom' swings on a pin and the top 'gaff' goes up and down the mast on a collar or 'jaw' that holds it close. Turned timber beads are used to reduce friction on that sliding spar.

Two halyards are required for each gaff sail. One hoists the sail and gaff up and the second (peak halyard) keeps the outer tip of that gaff up and then tensions it high, to make a recognisable shape.

This rig is elegant. It is also efficient at certain angles to the wind. Sailing yachts of different periods also used gaff rig. Enthusiasts still meet for rallies of gaff-rigged craft. They organise races and expeditions. Only a few years ago, a fleet of 'old gaffers' called in to Stornoway as part of a group circumnavigation of the United Kingdom. *Kirsty* was not among them but the fleet sailed by the shape of her black sister, exposed on the shore.

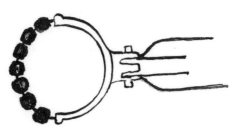

Gaff jaw

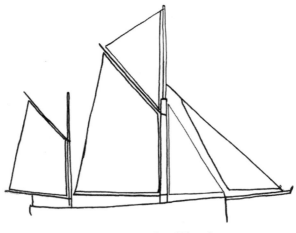

Cutter-rigged gaff ketch

The two sisters were constructed on a slip on the Isle of Bute. *Craignair*, the one that is now in decay, had a distinguished cruising history including a voyage to the Caribbean, written up for a sailing annual. *Kirsty* was built a year before *Craignair* and has also crossed the Atlantic. She is still in commission and is in good condition. She had at least one mishap, trapped against pier piles on the Isle of Wight in a storm. Her then owners loved her enough to have the extensive repairs carried out. I read of her in *Classic Boat* magazine. I met the people who remain her owners when I carried out a commission for an Tobar, the arts centre in Tobermory, Isle of Mull. An architect and an artist and their two daughters care for *Kirsty* and cruise the west coast of Scotland in this comfortable vessel.

Down the small hatch, through the decks, off-centre, close to her small steering cockpit, the companionway is steep because of that underwater shape. This also means that she has good headroom by the chart table and the galley, even though the raised cabin area is not high. Warm light enters by a deck-set prism and traditional timber skylights.

Up front, there is a saloon with these leather settees, which become bunks. There is a long, stable table. There is a substantial stove of cast iron. Then you go forwards to the forecabin with two wide bunks. Each is sided with dense timber boards with long-running grain, varnished to show warm, rich qualities. At the bow, there is capacity for a vast amount of chain so she can swing to a heavy anchor. All that weight is hauled back aboard with a manual windlass, bolted through her laid timber decks.

Of course there is some envy in admiration. We all want it both ways. As I live by a harbour, I often brew tea and coffee for sailors who call by my kitchen. I gain from their accounts of voyages to Faroes or Iceland. But if the phone keeps ringing or the emails pile up, I dream of living aboard such a boat as *Kirsty*. There is enough space to read or write or have friends to dinner in some comfort, but not enough to clutter with all the goods that seem to be filling a small townhouse. You can see her framing and her deck beams and other parts of her structure. There is no attempt to save on weight. This is a cruising yacht, built to take the colossal forces generated by a rig powerful enough to keep her moving in heavy seas. My son Sean has helped sail the gaff-rigged Shetland drifter *Swan* across the North Sea. His mother, Barbara, commissioned a sharp-shaped, gaff dayboat from a man, Mark Stockl, who is one of the few who still lives by building and repairing wooden boats. But I have only ever played with a gaff-rigged craft in sheltered waters and so did not need a second asking when my friend Andy Law asked for a hand bringing *Kirsty* up through the Hebrides to Stornoway.

My new partner in life, and often in art and sailing too, Christine Morrison, also wanted to broaden her experience of sailing different craft. It was game on for both of us.

Oban to Loch Boisdale

OUR JOURNEY HOME BEGAN IN GLASGOW. I've never sailed down the Clyde from the city centre but I have joined a yacht in Bowling Basin and made the tidal dash downriver and on to Rothesay, Isle of Bute.

Already you are in the shadows of mountains. You gain a sense of the unlimited options available to a seaworthy cruising yacht. Ireland and the Isle of Man are just down the road. The Inner and Outer Hebrides are laid out before you, the major and minor islands, the low ones and high ones. The narrow gulfs and the wider crossings, open to Atlantic swell.

Some shapes of islands are more smoothly thrown than others. All have huge variations of texture and colour, the crackles in the unreliable chemistry of their glazes.

This time we took the train to Oban. We took turns to lean our noses close to the glass. In half an hour you are rolling through the glens, straining your neck to see the tops of the rises. There are more trees at this stage. We arrived in time to do a quick tour of a supermarket. A regular motorboat shuttles you over to the boatyard on the island of Kerrera. Andy Law, owner and skipper of *Kirsty*, and his daughter Mhairi would join their ship at the end of the day. Our first task was to stock up on food for the journey. Next we could take *Kirsty* alongside to top up the diesel and water tanks.

I did a little survey of the fuelling pontoon before paddling Christine and myself out to the cream-painted yacht. Her bowsprit is fixed, and extends a long way up front. It would not be difficult to leave carnage among the long and expensive yachts berthed close by. But there was space to manoeuvre and a breeze was blowing on to the berth. We should take her in forwards, a little way out, and allow the breeze to catch her masts and assist us alongside. That's called 'ferrygliding' as you use drift or current to advantage. There is always a tendency for a vessel to kick one way or the other when you put a burst of power on the propeller. *Kirsty* kicked to starboard. She would need a warp to hold her bow in close to the pontoon when we departed. Christine nodded. She could see it and arranged a running line.

We met aboard *an Sulaire* one October when I was taking a party of artists out on a cultural experience in the Minch. The responsibilities of skippering, even as a volunteer, are immense but so are the rewards. Ten prospective Masters of Fine Art and their tutor, all explorers of Art, Space and Nature, at Edinburgh University, jumped to. They coordinated their movements to bring the open boat alive. We sailed the gap between the Tavay islands at Loch Erisort and my eyes met the brown ones of the determined and very fit woman in the bow. She was not going to give up in her efforts to swing that heavy spar, to dip it round the mast.

Christine is slim and fairly tall, with thick black hair, now with subtle hints of grey through it. She left school early to work her five-year apprenticeship to gain her trade as a hairdresser and so has never been out of work. When her father died suddenly, not long after he finally retired, she decided she could not put off her long-held desire to study art any longer. She completed her course, working across different artistic disciplines. Then she was awarded a funded place on the Masters.

In the evenings, our new team cooked and ate together. You could say that some teams bonded to a greater extent than others. Christine and I were now into the third year of our marriage. We had worked on wooden boats together and we had completed voyages together.

The motor started easily and the gear shift was very positive. *Kirsty* was soon back on her swinging buoy, just off the pontoons, stocked up and ready for the off. Andy and Mhairi would cross over from the town on the last ferry, about 10pm. It was the first day of August, so it was deep dusk when they arrived. They had grabbed some of the excellent pier food between the train and the boat ride. We sipped a dram together in the saloon, warmer still, in paraffin light.

Andy is the son of an architect and his own main sphere of interest is the designing of hospitals. He is of medium height, clean-shaven and still holding on to his thin dark hair. He plays the flute, usually more traditional Scottish and Irish tunes than classical. He enjoys well-made things but is not over-fussy in their maintenance. House, car and boat are 'lived-in'. He and his artist wife, Pat, a witty woman of ideas, make a hospitable couple. Both have a great sense of fun.

Mhairi is tall and fit and strong. She is a photographer by training. I knew her to be a sailor by intent as well as indoctrination. I had seen her sensitive, but steady, hand on a helm before. She had just completed a photo-essay of the young people who have chosen to remain on their home island of Lewis, or chosen to move there to make livings from their crafts and wits. These included Sean, now an outdoor sports instructor. She also went rock and cliff climbing with young people from the island. For her, climbing is a way of observing the structure of the landscape very closely as well as a challenge and another set of technical skills to master. She and her sister have also kept in touch with my younger son Ben through all his travels as a drummer in various bands. In common with Ben, Mhairi has a fast and inventive wit and a gift for comedy.

Christine's strength is as much due to her determination as to her general fitness or her build. You can see this when she is up on deck or when she is making large-scale prints or other artwork, demanding in stamina. She has not fully recovered from a car accident, which left her with a neck fracture and consequent stiffness in one arm. So she can no longer undertake the physically demanding work of installing major exhibitions in an Edinburgh gallery. She learned fast, as a sailor. It's possible that her sense of balance, from her experience in horse riding, helps. When a light strand of her hair escapes, she uses it as a natural tell-tale. The light wisps reveal where the wind is coming from, at that moment.

The forecast for the following day promised a good breeze for transiting the Sound of Mull but we would be likely to meet a blast from the north when we turned the corner at Ardamurchan Point. I wondered if we might take a look at sheltering in Loch Sunart. This could be a last chance to look to wind-sculpted larch and pine before we would be confronted by the apparent greys and browns of the more sparsely clad outer islands. We were all up and away before the dawn to make full use of both tide and wind. The reward was the sunrise, looking up the Firth of Lorne. None of us wanted to sleep through this departure. All of us had been this way before. This is the Law family's cruising heartland. But Mhairi was still studying the outlook that she had known from family journeys, all her life. Christine was also concentrating on the passing blocks of colour and shape.

Then the vessel settled to a routine. We were under motor still as the Sound of Mull was glass calm. Andy maintained a written log. It is usual to write more personal observations as well as factual material, which will help keep a record of how your vessel behaves in varying conditions. Often, you can sharpen the blurred edges of a remembered passage by looking back on these notes. We passed out abeam Calve Island, guarding Tobermory harbour, at about 0830. There would be plenty of wind to come, according to the new forecast, received on radio. This was a good start. We'd charge the batteries and emerge clear of the Sound of Mull without the need to tack. The north-westerly orientation of the Sound often causes a funnelling of scudding breeze, even if there is not a run of sea to go with it.

Kirsty was comfortable, with very little rolling motion, so far. Her full shape was propelled through the water with very little effort. The intention was to deliver this boat to Stornoway. A large part of my home harbour is now traversed by finger pontoons of varying sizes to secure local and visiting yachts. The few surviving trawlers and creel-fishing boats huddle in other corners when they are not working the Minch or the grounds up to the north or west.

Mhairi was to join her mother, Pat, on an arts project. *Kirsty* was to be their accommodation and mobile studio space. I had always wanted to experience the performance of a gaff-rigged boat in a stiff breeze. Today was the day.

Andy consulted on the route as he sniffed the rising breeze. We would have to motor if we aimed for the sheltered 'inside' route, the one taken by both *Moonspinner* and *Dunderave* in their voyages bound for Lewis. Today, the open-water route seemed a better option. Depending on the actual wind angle and the build-up of seas from the north, we could hope to aim well up from Barra, if we kept her moving. Perhaps the harbour at Eriskay would be an option. There is a tight entrance but there are clear leading marks.

Mhairi helmed while Andy talked me through the sequence of raising the heavy mainsail. It is synthetic cream cloth but looks and feels like canvas. We raised sail at about 0900. Christine was focused, in turn, on the heights of Mull, the variety of the Ardnamurchan peninsula and the open vistas to Coll to the east and Muck to the north. *Kirsty* wallowed as Mhairi held her into wind and sea while Andy talked me through the reefing procedure. We put the first reef in at about 0930 and the second followed about half an hour later. We should be prepared for gusts well in excess of 30 knots, to come.

Then Andy talked me through the course. He has seen this sea-area often, in many moods. As I thought, our line would be well to the south of the lonely Hysgeir lighthouse, the one 6 or 7 miles west of Rhum. There are outlying skerries, known as Mill Rocks, to the south of that. A legend on the chart says, 'breaks heavily in SE gales'. That is right beside a sounding of 18 metres, which indicates the occurrence of truly massive waves. These have rolled all the way down from the high Arctic with nothing to stop them, then they have been squeezed down the Minches between Skye and Lewis to keep on going through the Sea of the Hebrides. Most winters, winds of over 100 miles per hour velocity will be recorded around the Hebrides. The previous winter we had week after week of storm-force winds. When Hysgeir light was manned, the keepers must have seen some seas that could never be spoken of.

I thought it would be no picnic in the north-east gale we were likely to meet today. Skye can provide some form of windbreak but its steep basalt cliffs can also cause the wind speed to increase. I thought Andy's intention was a good one for this seaworthy craft as long as we were canny with the cloth. It had been a very early start – about

4am. Christine knew she needed some rest before she was fit to take a watch. She went down below decks.

The heavy displacement and deep rudder of *Kirsty* were assets as the wind increased. Our speed climbed but we held our course. I wedged my bum tight against the woodwork so I could compare a 'fix' (taken by two crossing compass bearings) with our intended line. You have to be realistic about accuracy in these conditions as the chart table and yourself are dancing to the varied beat of the ship. I expected up to 10 degrees of leeway but there was less than that when I plotted another fix an hour later. The last of the north-east-going tide might have offset some of our sideways drift. I called up the good news then went forward to check on Christine.

Seasickness is a strange thing. I thought I was immune until the time I was looking after Ben on a ferry that was slamming into heavy seas. The baby was badly sick and the nausea transferred itself to me, in the stuffy lounge. I could not take a breather out on deck because his mother was not feeling great either. I vowed then to be more sympathetic with companions who lost their will to live. I'd tried to warn Christine about the dangers of being right forwards in our bunk, where the motion is most pronounced. But she told me, once she'd laid herself down in that position, she could not move from it. It's normal to take turns on the bunks further aft, when seas are high.

All I could do was make sure she had a bucket wedged beside her and a bottle of fresh water to sip. A towel to hand. Christine was angry because she felt helpless. She could not get back up now, to do her watch. If she had remained out in the open, like Mhairi, she would probably have been OK. It was now dangerous to try moving about the ship in her disorientated state. She must stay where she could not be thrown against anything of wood or of metal.

When I got back up to the cockpit, passing out hot drinks, Mhairi said she knew not to risk going down below. Her sister, by coincidence also a Kirsty, could cook in a gale and eat like a horse while she was stirring up stews.

I had to leave Christine to her personal misery and take my place up top. We were now all clipped on with safety lines. The seas were breaking over the decks. Down below, the drips were beginning to run, some of them from the new hatches and repaired decks that had just been completed by trained shipwrights. At the tops of the waves, you could still make out the shapes. The Cuilins of Rhum to starboard and Heaval, on Barra, distant to port. Now we were in sea conditions that would have been impossible for a small open craft like *Broad Bay*. The mighty *an Sulaire* would have coped but all aboard would have been drenched to the skin. For those areas of the world blessed with viable harbours, the advent of decked craft like the Loch Fyne skiff must have greatly improved the life expectancy of fishermen.

Andy had rigged up his iPad and phone with waterproof transparent cases. Each had a chart-plotting App. So we had two means of electronic navigation. I thought they were both vulnerable in these conditions so dug in the drawer for the old hand-held GPS. The batteries were good but it would only provide a reading if it was kept up by the hatch. I looped its lanyard there and shut it down to conserve power. Now I knew we could get a position from that, too. Only 25 years ago this would have seemed like a science-fiction dream.

Though I was sorry for Christine, I was not over-anxious. Seasickness is usually only dangerous if it is prolonged for many days and the person becomes dehydrated. Chichester writes about working through it for days on end before settling into a passage. We could keep a good watch schedule with three active souls and that was also a good number for any changes of headsail or reefing the main to its third point. I realised now how well Andy knew his vessel. Like most of us, he has been tempted to go for slimmer, leaner models that might require minimal maintenance, but he knew they would not provide the homely cabin space below and they would certainly not ride on, so obediently, through building seas. Each of these powerful, high waves had its own personality.

Of course she did not point as close to the wind as a vessel rigged with triangular 'Bermudan' sails would have done, but neither did she lose power by nodding her bow and shaking off her momentum. 'You've been talking down your ship,' I said, looking at 6 knots, steady on a dial.

Both Andy and Mhairi had pride in their smiles. Andy asked me for my best estimate of a likely anchorage. We had fallen into natural roles of him as skipper and myself as main navigator. Andy led the deckwork and Mhairi did the majority of the helming. 'Loch Eynort might be possible,' I said. 'Should definitely make Loch Boisdale. Have you been into Eynort?'

Neither of us had. I went below again and consulted Martin Lawrence in the Imray-series pilot book. It was difficult to know if we would get sufficient shelter in the outer loch. The gusts were certainly force 9, now. The narrow passage to the inner sanctuary was tidal. It would be dark. It seemed a pity not to achieve that additional northing of about 5 miles but we would all be tired out. That's not the best state to be in when dealing with strange gusts across unknown anchorages.

We agreed to head into Loch Boisdale. We both knew it fairly well and there would be a good chance of a visitors' mooring, close to the hotel. We made that decision just in time. Now we could bear away from the wind and take it just aft of our beam. We began to hit the high notes, with a thrum from the surf on the fixed propeller and the sympathetic note of the heavy wire rigging. Mhairi held her well. I looked between the iPad screen, the observed cliffs and the compass. We had an excellent line in.

The waters flattened out as soon as we gained the shelter of the headland in the very last breaths of the day's light. The engine turned over first time. I pointed, Mhairi steered and Andy anchored his ship. All the blue buoys had a yacht swinging on them. The family had invested in a new generation 'Spade' anchor and the manual windlass was geared to match the heavy chain. The anchor bit the ground. There was a jolt and the chain ran out, as Andy backed off, till we saw the marker for 40 metres. Before long, Christine came to the surface. I remembered that this was her birthday. She took a glass of water and an oatcake while we had our dram.

There's a way of putting things aside
things that you'll need
or need to keep in case you do –

the falls from blocks
rove to advantage,
handy in a loose chain

like a toprope,
the endless loop that keeps you safe –
when you're climbing.

That too is not coiled
but the bights fall into each other
and they can't lock so
one pull and
the doubled lines
do fall.

There's pleasure in skill,
pleasure in seeing
how a thumb and two bent finger tops
hold the runs of rope.

It's intimate opera,
on deck or on the wall.

The Crop-haired Freckled Lass

Stories take on the hues of the land where they have embedded. We had just punched our way across from Oban to the Outer Hebrides, a route plied by countless generations of travellers.

Some stories lose their relevance if detached from the place name that fixes them in this world. Apart from these naming tales, there are others that relate to a custom or way of life, perhaps hunting or fishing. A way of doing things. And there are accounts of the inexplicable or of what was foreseen before it was seen. All these are strong strands in the stories of the west coast of Scotland. There are still others that have settled here but have been brought to us by travellers. A story told as a local yarn by, say, Angus MacLellan, from South Uist, is listed as an international folk tale with a numbered reference to its type. I might well have told my favourite one of these at anchor in Loch Boisdale till the gale gave way. But I am aware that a very similar story has rooted in North Lewis. It was also recorded from one of the travelling people who made a home for his family on our island.

This community continued to carry tunes and songs, already forgotten in the mainstreams of Scottish commerce and learning.

There was once a laird in the Uists thought himself a wise man. He wouldn't be the first and he wouldn't be the last, neither. At that time the laird had almost unlimited powers and he also acted as a magistrate. One day a tenant was brought before him. This man was accused of poaching a deer. A neighbour bore a grudge against this fellow and pointed out the place where the guts and head were buried. There was no arguing with that. In a sporting way, the laird said that he would give his tenant a chance. He would ask him three questions. The accused would have three days to answer. If he could provide satisfactory replies he would walk out a free man and if he could not, he would lose the roof over his head and the land that he leased.

'Do you understand that, man?'

'Aye, what are your questions?'

'What creature goes first on four legs, then on two and then on three?'

'Aye. And the second?'

'How high is heaven?'

'The third?'

'What am I worth, to the nearest coin?'

The poor man went home as if he was condemned. His eyes were on the ground. A very unusual thing in a man – he wouldn't say a word of what was bothering him to his wife, even though she could see well enough there was something. The couple had a daughter who was out of the ordinary. She was witty and always came in from another angle in a discussion. She had flashing eyes of green. And she wore her hair cropped like a lad. She was speckled with freckles and her father thought the world of her.

'Go and talk to your father,' said her mother. 'I'm sure he'll tell you what's on his mind.'

It wasn't long before the crop-haired freckled lass had heard her father's story and the questions that came with it. 'I don't think that should spoil our Saturday nor our Sunday,' she said. And she whispered some words in her father's ear. He cheered up at that.

On the Monday, he was at the laird's house, bright and early.

'You've had time to think?'

'I have.'

'Let us proceed then. What goes first on four legs then on two and finally three?'

'My daughter went first on hands and feet. You and I walk on two. But I've seen your own father only able to walk with a stick. So that would be the human being.'

'Aye, we'll give you that one,' said the laird. 'How high is heaven?'

'Heaven is the height of a single ladder. But it would need to be the right ladder, long enough for the job.'

The laird admitted that was also an acceptable answer. 'But what am I worth?'

'You are worth no more than twenty-nine pieces of silver.'

'That is very exact but I can assure you I happen to be worth a great deal more than that.'

'I don't think you are. Our Lord was sold for thirty and you can't be worth more than Him.'

'You didn't come up with these answers on your own.'

'No, I did not.' And the proud father told the laird that he'd had some help from his clever daughter.

'I might need to meet this daughter,' said the laird. And he did.

In fact he became a regular visitor under the roof he was going to have burned. He was under the spell of the bright eyes and sharp wit of the crop-haired freckled lass.

One evening, when she'd matched him in debate yet again, he found himself saying, 'If only you were the daughter of a laird I would have to ask you to marry me.'

'Is that right?' she said. 'And if that were to happen, no doubt you would be offering something to my father?'

'That would be the done thing.'

'So you might grant him title to a small cottage such as this one?'

'That would not be a huge thing to ask, in such circumstances.'

'So if you signed a paper to that effect then he would be the possessor of his own property?'

This was going a bit fast for the laird but he found himself signing a paper there and then. 'So now that my father is the owner of his own property he is in effect his own laird and therefore I am the daughter of one.'

'Indeed you are,' he said, 'and will you marry me?'

'No,' she said, 'I'll not marry you.'

'Why not?' he asked.

'Because you asked me on a whim and you could change your mind on a whim. You put three questions to my father. I'll only marry you if you sign another paper to the effect that if you ever ask me to leave your house, I might take three things with me?'

'And what would they be?'

'Three things of my choice at that time.'

He was so far gone now, mesmerised by her quick thinking, that he agreed. Before long they were indeed wed and it was a grand occasion. For the first time, the family of the laird and his tenants ate and drank together. There might even have been salmon and venison at the feast. It might not have been the first time the tenants had tasted such rich fare.

The estate prospered. People could talk to the laird's wife. Grievances were dealt with. Accounts were tidy and everyone was happy.

Until one day one of the tenants said, in an exchange with the laird, 'If only you had the sense of your wife, man.'

That was it. He came home in a rage. 'You've been interfering with the business of this estate. You've taken too much on yourself this time. Leave this house, now.'

'Fine,' said the crop-haired freckled lass.

First she lifted the cradle with their son and heir and put that out the door.

'What are you thinking of, woman?'

'The cradle is the first of my three things.'

Next she carried out a kist. She happened to know that it contained important papers, including the title deeds of the entire estate. This time the laird sat in his chair in a daze. But not for long. Next she lifted that with her husband still sitting on it. That went out too. He was too shocked to say or do a thing as she lifted the cradle back inside. Then she took the kist in and turned the key in the door. He was left sitting in his chair outside.

They say he first banged at the door and then he pleaded. She didn't let him back in till he promised he would show some respect to herself and to their son and everyone else who lived on the estate.

How Wide is Your Boat?

THE WIND BLEW STRONG ALL NIGHT and into the next morning. We were snug as the beamy *Kirsty* rode well to her anchor, out on a long scope. We had a breakfast of scrambled egg, toasted wholemeal bread and smoked salmon, with plenty of strong coffee. That was brewed on the boat's new system – a pressurised plunger that created the scent of an espresso. Christine was able to eat, at last. This was her birthday breakfast, postponed.

The interior did not need too much of a sort-out. Most boats would have gear strewn into unlikely places after a corkscrewing passage. The forecast promised an easing of the wind later and a shift to the west. That would be perfect for sailing on up the lee side of the Outer Hebrides. We motored out of our shelter late in the afternoon. There was still a rolling motion but the seas had settled down a great deal. We all stayed up in the open, clipped on to safety lines. We studied the Uist skylines that gave clues to concealed anchorages. You have to compare the sighted skylines with the charted information. That's when I mentioned Acarsaidh Falladh. 'Have you been into Floday Sound?' I asked. 'There's a couple of spots but the best is a bit narrow. How wide is your boat?'

'I've never been asked that question before, outside of a marina,' said Andy. Of course I thought of piloting *Kirsty* into the same pool I'd entered in Archie Tyrrel's *Kennary*. We were now on a vessel of nearly 40 feet plus a bowsprit of another 10 feet long. *Kirsty* has a draft of over 6 feet aft. But her beam was the crucial dimension. Andy agreed to take a look at the entrance and I zoomed in on his chart software so he could study it for himself. 'The electronic one does not have that much detail,' I said. 'Same with the metric chart. But I've seen it at low water.'

Mhairi was again at the helm. Christine was up front, looking out for any creel-markers in our path. Andy also went forwards as I gave the nod to Mhairi. He turned to me, looking a bit pale after catching the first sight of the entrance. He shook his head.

'No bother, there's another spot up the Sound and a good turning circle back out,' I said.

But when we were fully abeam the channel we stopped the boat in the water. 'Doesn't look so bad from this angle,' Andy said. He gave the nod. The sounder showed plenty of water then hunted around for a figure as the echo was lost in the softest mud. We chugged into the pool without incident. It was misty but not dense enough to be a problem. 'Typical west coast males,' Andy said, nodding to the group of stags, aloof up the hill. I had not noticed the separate other group, hinds this time, occupying a hollow in the lower slopes.

The anchor was dropped and we had enough swinging room to allow for a complete change of wind. Her stern would be in close to the rocky sides but it was deep in this part of the pool, right up close to the shores. It was a long time before anyone went below. The deer were not nervous. The lightest grey hairs of mist heightened rather than obscured the lines of the rising ground of Ronay. You could imagine that anything might happen, in this place.

Brine inlets
will always encroach
on primed ground –

soundings to sand
ochre contours
green bleed.

The seepage
maps its own
rise and fall.

But our charts
smudge and
fall apart

obsolete
like our dictionaries
before you can proof them.

The Sealskin

There was once a crofter in the Uists who spent every hour on
the land or at the fishing or the hunting. He was a great man for
chasing the seabirds. In the Uists, the *sgarbh* – the cormorant or
shag – was the favoured bird for the table.

The men would go out together, three or four of them. If they
went through the north ford to the west side they would land on
outlying tidal reefs. Here on the east side there were countless
inlets and bays that might yield their catch. Each man would
take a turn of watching over the boat as the others ranged far,
to find enough birds. This night it was our man's turn. He was a
bit restless at first, missing the company and missing the hunting,
but he settled to it. Midnight had passed when his eye was
caught by sudden movements. He inched his way closer, keeping
some cover, crouching down by the higher rocks. He could just
make out the shadows of a number of people on the shore.
These were not the men he knew. In fact many of them were not
men at all.

His eye fell on one of these figures. She was a little apart from
the others, lost in the pleasure of moving in a different world.
She was also beautiful. That man who had so far shown no
interest in anything but crofting and hunting could not shift his
eyes from her.

As he watched, he sensed that these folk were saying their goodbyes. Then they were lining up past a pile on a rounded rock. It looked like kelp in the half-light but then he could see that each creature was lifting something from the heap. One by one, each of the folk reclaimed a skin. The moving shape would fall low, to the rock. There would be a splash and it would be away, back in the other element.

He lost all caution and came right up to the pile of sealskins. There was one left there yet. He reached to touch it. It was soft. He had to stroke it. Once he'd touched it, he had to keep it. He could not bear to see that woman return to a world he couldn't reach. So he placed her skin safe under his coat, wrapping it with care. He stowed that coat with the rest of the gear, right in the bow of the beached boat.

Then he walked back over to the shore by the rounded stone.

'Give me back my coat.'

'What?

'My skin. I'll have it back now. Please.'

But he started talking to her. He asked her why she was left there still when all her companions had returned to the sea. First she said nothing. He waited. Then she told him that she had come a longer way than the others. It would take her longer to return. So she'd not been in a great hurry to depart with the rest. But now it was time, so once she had her skin again, she'd be off.

He was so struck by her eyes and her voice with its strange twang that he did everything to keep her talking. And he did indeed have some sort of charm about him. She was eager to get back to her own environment though and grew more impatient.

'Will you give me back my own skin now?'

'No I can't do that or I'll lose you,' he said.

He offered her some of his own clothes. She was starting to shiver. She had to accept his gansey, warm from his own body.

That was the moment when his companions came back to the boat. They could hardly believe their eyes when they found their friend standing by a beautiful woman who was now wearing some of his own clothes.

'Do you think we could find space for another one in the boat?' he asked.

Of course she did not have a lot of choice. She could not leave without her skin and he had it well hidden away. So she just stood by, helpless, as the men packed their haul of cormorants into the boat along with their own gear.

The men tried to strike up a conversation with the poor woman but she was withdrawn now, not able to say much, though they all spoke the same language. When the boat was back on its home shore, our man told the others he'd see to putting everything away. But that's not how things are done. First they'd to divide the haul of birds, share them out. After that ritual was complete, he was left with the woman he'd found.

'Don't you worry,' he said. 'I'll take you home and you'll find warmth and shelter. I won't ask you to do anything you don't want to do.'

She'd been looking for a glimpse of her skin all the time. The strong smell of humans disguised its scent. She might even have been a bit touched at how much he wanted to be with her, to be near her beauty.

Up until then, that man had shown little interest in women. He lived alone on a very good croft and put every hour of the day into cultivating the ground or taking his place on the village boat. She went with him to his home. He was true to his word. He found clothing that would do her for the time being. He lit fires in two rooms in the cottage. He made soup for her, from smoked fish that was hanging by the fire.

The next day he was out finding this and that, buying some materials. She wouldn't want for anything. But he hid her skin very carefully, behind a beam in the byre.

In time they came to be with each other at night as well as in the day. They had children together and she was a good and a happy mother. She cared for their children and took pleasure in them. So did he. She knew that he had fixed his gaze on her that night on the outlying reef and it hadn't shifted since then.

From time to time she'd look out to sea for long periods. He'd notice that and he knew that there was a deep underlying urge that would never go away. He kept changing the hiding place for the skin. Now and then he'd want to touch it again, too. He'd remind himself of that first night he'd seen her. She knew he still had her skin. She said to be sure to keep it in a dry place. She couldn't bear the thought of the damp destroying it. He promised that and he kept his promise.

The children were growing well and they never went hungry. The lads helped their father round the croft and the girls could soon bake a bannock with the best of them. At last all the cornstacks were made and that was another harvest secure. Another year passing.

Our man could then take his place in the village boat. Some days they'd gather tangle for fertilising the ground and some days they'd set a long-line for flounders.

One morning, when he was away, their youngest boy fell ill. It was nothing too serious but he might just as well have a day off school and get a chance to recover. And his mother liked his young company about her with her man away and her older children at school all day.

They could chat together very freely, the mother and her youngest. She'd give him a broken bannock to taste. The first bowl of broth was his, just to see if it was ready yet. And he'd chat away to her, not at all shy, and often get her laughing. She seemed happy enough but you didn't often hear her laugh like that.

You might have noticed this, but it's quite common for a child that looked sick enough to be kept off school to leap around like a calf in the grass only an hour or two later.

'If you're at home for the day you may as well make yourself useful,' his mother said. 'Out you go and hunt in the cornstacks for a *biorach*. There's bound to be a few left. That will make our dinner today.'

Now in Uist, like in all the islands, they're very good at using something for more than one purpose. I've heard of them putting the salted dogfish, the *biorach*, right into the heart of a coil of hay. The wind that blows through the stack will dry the fish and preserve it.

He came running in before too long, trailing the long, dried fish, carrying it by the tail.

'Take it mammy. It feels hard and scratchy. Not like that other soft thing in the cornstack.'

'What thing is that, son?'

'A beautiful thing. It's soft and it smells of the sea.'

The baking bowl dropped to the flagstone. Once she knew where her skin was kept she had to see it. It was part of her own self, after all.

Later that day, her man set foot on his croft, coming home from the sea. There was no smoke coming from the roof of their neat house. He set off at a run but he slowed for a moment when his hand was on the handle of the door.

There was a damp black patch where the fire should have been. All the knives and other sharps in the house were lined on a high shelf, out of harm's way. The children were holding together, the elder comforting the younger.

That man never did see his seal-wife again. But the children would go to that high slab of rock where a neat pile of skins had once been left. They would find the best of fish. Not the lythe and the saithe they could catch for themselves but the very best of eating fish. They might find the turbot, the gurnard, the John Dory, placed for them there. A mother providing.

We made a good passage from our anchorage to the pontoon berth in Stornoway, by way of the Sound of Shiants. Pat Law was waiting to catch the warps. It was very gusty conditions in the harbour, towards low water. There was not a lot of room to turn *Kirsty* into the wind alongside our allocated berth. It was a pleasure to see Andy and Mhairi work together on this.

Once she was secured, Andy did some practical work with the mastic gun. This reduced the deck leak. Pat and Mhairi were able to live aboard, mother and daughter, for a month or so in Stornoway, researching their joint art project. Christine did not suffer any more seasickness that trip and, so far, has been fine ever since, sailing several different vessels.

Jubilee

THE PERSONAL ALWAYS SEEMS TO ENTER an account intended to be objective. A story finds its new words in the voice of the teller. Otherwise the tale will show the signs of ageing that my own body now shows – the muscular strains, the bumps and scars. I can imagine being one of those who walk on three legs. But a story is made new every time it is told.

Now that there are almost three score years to look back on, it is time to be direct. I have been reticent in showing the love I feel for more than one boat. This is not due to sparing the feelings of the owners of the craft I've loved, sometimes their lifelong partners. It may have something to do with where I am from. The witty poet and realistic writer of magical prose Angus Peter Campbell is from South Uist. We've met to share stories more than once. 'Did you hear about the Lewisman who really loved his wife?' he asked. 'So much so, that he very nearly told her.'

Now I must speak of the constant affair in my life. I was a student when I was swept off balance. You'd think this would happen when the island boy got a taste of city life but no, it happened on my return home, one summer break. I drove to Port of Ness, close to the north tip of Lewis. I got out to watch the waves become high plumes as they hit what was left of the collapsed breakwater. Your heart goes out to the poorly dressed fishermen who turned their open boats into this turmoil to land their heavy catches of cod and ling. They were no longer there but I could hear them:

> 'The voices of the fishermen dividing the catch of the day made me lonely, for I was immediately reminded of an old poem which pitied them for their precarious lives on the sea.' *

The green and white of a dangerous breaking wave caught me and I whipped my head round to try to track it, sweeping through the flooding harbour. Then my eyes met another mass of green and black, white and rust-red. These colours were in a stationary form. But this was a living thing. She was slim and sharp in the gently rising bow. She was beamy amidships but that was carried far aft into her full stern. One side leaned against the shed of blockwork on the shoreward end of the pier so I could not walk all round her. This

---

* *The Narrow Road to the Deep North*, Matsuo Basho.

gave me a stronger focus on the essentials of her shape, the way a half-model does.

This was *sgoth Jubilee*. I had read in the *Stornoway Gazette* how the son of her builder had worked with the community of Ness to restore the last survivor of a great fleet of working craft. Most of these were brought to their short working life in a boatshed by this harbour. Scarred photos revealed the rounded sterns of the great 30-foot boats, ashore and redundant, as the markets tumbled. We lost so many of our young men in World War I. We also lost the strength and daring of crews willing to put their shoulders to the planking of these open craft. Men in high seaboots would send them down the shore on rollers to meet surf. After a night or more at sea, they would have to haul their craft back up, sliding on the huge bellies of the skate they could not sell. We lost the links to the Baltic, a main market for our herring. We lost the chain of buyers for our wind-dried cod, taken on lines, worked under sail.

By the time *Jubilee* was reclaimed by her community in the late 1970s, there were few signs of the larger class of *sgoth Niseach*. There was a scale model of one example in the boatshed and a plank or two among the dismembered oak ribs of a vessel. She had been stripped to her bones by gale after gale.

The largest class of *sgoth Niseach* would work up to 40 miles or so offshore. The handier 'three-quarter *sgoth*', like *Jubilee*, could go these distances, in favourable conditions. She is 27 feet long but very short (19 feet) in the keel. Normally she would work closer inshore, but the meeting of Minch and Atlantic currents could produce contrary eddies, turmoil and destruction, all around the coastal fringes of North Lewis. The yachtsman's pilot suggests you keep a minimum of 5 miles of water between your vessel and the Butt of Lewis. Your eyes are drawn in to the drama of it, the diving slabs of rock just beyond the white lighthouse and the thrashing cross currents.

Jubilee was commissioned in 1935. We could never admit that our men had been lost in a struggle, fuelled by industrialists and those who would cling to a dream of Empire. So the patriotic spirit remained, even in the Scottish islands, with their Gaelic and Norse warp and weft of culture. Hence her Royalist name. She was built by John Finlay Macleod. He was the man who jumped from the *Iolaire*, grounded on the Beasts of Holm, at the Approaches to Stornoway, in the first hours of 1919. He swam ashore with a light line, joined to a hawser. When that was pulled from the ship to the rocks, it was enough for a small body of survivors to reach the arms of their helpers. Over 200 perished.

The *Iolaire* was a fine ship, a gentleman's motor yacht requisitioned by the Admiralty as a troop carrier. That might explain why her wreck was sold for scrap before the bodies of all the lost were recovered. That is how the Empire repaid the widows and orphans of those who had survived the mechanised war, only to drown a matter of yards from their home island. John Finlay was awarded a medal by the Royal Humane Society but they say he never spoke of that night. He returned to his trade as a boatbuilder. *Jubilee* was only one of many like vessels, built to a keel-length agreed with the crew who commissioned her. John Finlay's son, Norman, once showed me cloth-bound notebooks with names and dates and the lengths of all those keels.

Another son, John Murdo, served his time as a shipwright on the Clyde. He survived the Normandy landings in the fight to rid Europe of the Fascists. He taught Building Science at a college in Stornoway and built several boats, with students, as a way of instilling the principles of structure. The Architectural Association School of Architecture in London also had their first-year students build boats. They devised their own method for building a coracle that could keep one person afloat. 'One up from a pair of waders' as I'd once heard the boatbuilder Topher Dawson define such a craft.

John Murdo led his assistants in stripping the layers of later life from *Jubilee*. It is dry wind that kills a vessel. That and fresh water, left to lie and cause rot. She had been kept in commission, as a creel-boat, decked, with a wheelhouse and equipped with engine and hauler. John Murdo had access to detailed drawings and technical specifications, in a Gaelic language that possessed the specific terminology for the parts of a *sgoth Niseach*. In the 1930s these were still rigged in a way that might not have changed much for a century or two.

There were difficult decisions. A museum piece, with historical authenticity, should source iron nails. Use of these would guarantee problems for those who would maintain her in the future. Had copper nails been an option for his father, John Murdo was certain he would have used them. So his renovation of the boat built by his father included the use of materials and coatings that would not have been available to a Port of Ness boatbuilder of the previous generation.

This was not to be a project to prove that a vessel could be built with basic hand tools and coated in paraffin varnish when complete. The sons could all remember helping their father, in the saw pit because mechanical means were not available. John Murdo used power tools but looked to preserve the vessel's essential character. Her individual features include a madly wide second plank down. Rather than changing the number of planks to compose the same shape, this was renewed. Like the keel, short even for a *sgoth*, this was a case of making best use of the timber available to his father at the time, building to a price. These accidental features had become part of the personality of a historic vessel.

John Murdo once told me that he thought his father had produced one of the finest shapes, in *Jubilee*, despite these limitations. The rise of the planking to that arrowhead of a bow makes her unique. It would not be so easy to gain a sense of her as a sailing vessel. One other surviving son of her original builder could lead some younger folk, to take her out. But there is often a high surf driving into this tidal harbour. Open boats risked that when their crews had no other way to make a living. Their skills were honed by the daily grind of working these demanding vessels.

The people of the Ness area are proud of their heritage but it was proving difficult to find volunteers to sail the restored *Jubilee*. You have to wait for the right conditions to launch and you have to find enough people of sufficient strength and skills, free from work or family commitments, at that moment. That might explain why she was little used after her restoration. I did have the pleasure of joining her crew once. I had completed my studies and weaved between callings as a poet and a coastguard. A colleague got the shout and two of us helped the men of Ness take *Jubilee* the short run from the Port to Skigersta, a couple of miles down the coast. It was like being requested to dance with a lady of real class but out of your league.

A chance did come, to prove my love. More than 15 years after her restoration, she lay ashore until shoots of grass sprouted between her bitumen-coated ribs. Her green-painted enamel was now matt. Flakes of paint revealed that original planks had been blue once. The new mast and yard were already soft with rot but the sail had been put aside, under cover.

In 2006, there was an interpretation project linked to a renovation of the old sail loft in Stornoway. Every element was based on recorded conversations with those who had lived or worked within this building. The vessels landing their catches or departing from the steps across the harbour were motifs in the dialogue. As the leader of this aspect of the sail loft project, I proposed renovating two vessels of historic importance. This could be an alternative to a static sculpture. Several people described with pride the *sgoth Niseach* that worked from the shores of Port of Ness and Tolsta but also came to take on provisions or bait in Stornoway. People still congregate around the harbour and discuss the comings and goings of boats.

The rebuilding of *Broad Bay* has already been described. It was also agreed that the project could celebrate the maritime culture of Lewis by contributing to a second renewal of *Jubilee*. She should be in use for training and recreation, within sight of the renovated building. That would be transformed into housing. *Falmadair*, the society established to look after *Jubilee,* was revived. The Gaelic word means 'tiller'. Volunteers scraped and burned generations of paint so we could see what was sound and what was not. She was taken by low-loader over on the ferry to Ullapool Boatbuilders. Mark Stockl replaced about two-thirds of her planking. Often the timber was sound but the degraded fibres, caused by rusting iron fastenings, made it easier to replace the whole section of plank.

We decided to use bronze screws rather than galvanised nails ('dumps') into the thick oak ribs. This was an eye to the future. The aim was to preserve this vessel by keeping her in commission. There were lessons to be learned from other community boat projects. If she was to be well used she should not be too closely associated with any one skipper. Young people had to be involved from the beginning.

Sean and Barbara crossed over on the ferry many times, with pots of primer and paint. The three of us now all lived in different houses but we could still work together. The team spirit developed as a growing community of volunteers made regular crossings from Stornoway. We would spend a day sanding and painting before catching the return ferry. Another club member came over with a measuring tape and returned again to check the tack-welded metalwork he had fabricated. I was always anxious about the possibility of internal ballast shifting. Every veteran of navigating these open boats warned me that the packing of the stone ballast was crucial.

We were able to reclaim the lead that had come from the roof of the sail loft in Stornoway. It went from the top of the building to the bottom of the boat. Mark cast ingots to the shape of the bilges. These could now be strapped in place, when installed after the relaunch. We devised a simple buoyancy system, allowing for the metalwork, anchor, outboard and crew weight. We planned to sail her home and we had to be sure she could support all that weight afloat if she were ever swamped at sea. Our chairman, a Merchant Navy skipper, won sponsorship from a company linked to International Paint. She could be any colour as long as it was the shade of red they were painting on their ships at the time.

There was a sprint finish. Mark worked through a final list of jobs, delegating more tasks to us. I fashioned a new tiller of laminated larch. The gudgeons and pintles that let the rudder swing were renewed by Calum 'Stealag', the blacksmith who made them when John Murdo Macleod brought her back to her original form in the 1970s. The ironwork was now bolted in place as the high-up was being prepared for the lift. She took very little water when placed gently back in the harbour at Ullapool. We could row her alongside a jetty and fit her ballast in place.

Her new mast, short and stout and glistening, was positioned forward of the supporting bench or 'thwart' so its length ran out over the bow. Then the tackle, which would later be hooked to the yard to lift the sail, was taken to a strong point aft. It only takes one person to hoist the mast upright while two or three others give it a heave to start it and then guide it to its housing. This is a simple operation, alongside a pier on a calm day. I could hardly imagine doing this when sailpower was demanded to take the craft clear of the shore. Driving through crashing waves to open water. It would be trickier still to lower that mast as you approached the grinding pebbles of a pounding surf-beach in a gale of wind.

A timber pin of oak was wedged in hoops of iron to hold the mast in place.

That selfsame tackle, of one double and one single block, is secured on the weather side, opposite the sail. It then supports the mast as the strains from the filled sail are distributed to the bracing structure of the *sgoth*. The simplicity of the rig means that there is less chance of snags. Remember that these working boats would carry large baskets of lines with hundreds of baited hooks placed in order around the rims.

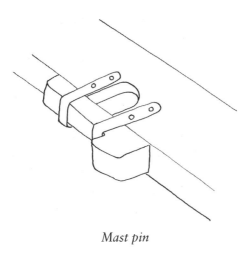

Mast pin

All went smoothly. The tan sail made for her back in the late 1970s had seen very little use. I sensed a wave of anticipation, from bow to stern. We probably weighed her down a bit more than we needed to, thinking of making her stiff, for the rolling Minch. I asked each crew member to take up a given position on the boat. You need someone strong on the halyard, someone nimble on the sheet.

You might expect disappointment when you have anticipated something for so long. I was thinking back to all the tasks we had carried out. The acts of smoothing and coating her with bright finishes. Judging a waterline, to be tentatively inscribed. We had all begun to whisper rather than banter as we worked towards this launch. But she carried us now and we were all proud as heads turned. Even the present-day fishermen looked up from the smart pace of their net-mending to watch the red *sgoth Niseach* sail by.

Sean and Barbara boarded the family yacht, a white-painted wooden sloop, to escort us down Loch Broom to the open Minch. The team on *Jubilee* represented three generations. Members of the family that once owned her were aboard. There was at least one man from a Merchant Navy background and one ex-Royal Navy. A flask of hot coffee was passed in a net on a boathook from the yacht to the *sgoth*. Both vessels were well handled in our close-quarter manoeuvres. The yacht kept us company all the way across.

Judging by the way her bow cut through the short, heavy seas at the East Shiants Bank and shed the water she'd displaced, the *sgoth Niseach* was a craft that would look after you. You would always be held to task in your duty of care to this last surviving example of a unique type of craft, built for a lost industry.

At least three of us had a hand-held GPS in a pocket but we all wanted to gain a sense of what crossing the Minch was like before electronic navigation aids could be taken on an open boat. We towed a mechanical Walker log to keep note of the sea miles covered. We sailed a compass course, corrected from a line on the chart, to allow for magnetic variation. I estimated that our short keel would slip to over 10 degrees off our intended course as we were shunted wave to wave. We were able to tighten the new sheet and beat up closer to the wind to allow for this.

I've looked back often to a photo I took during this passage. The slim white yacht is a distant ghost, through mist. The *Jubilee* crew is hunched against a rain squall. There's a couple of reefs in and she's not heeling too much. Innes Smith, the youngest aboard that day, is left on the helm, coping very well.

Then we could make out Stac Ranish. Our angle to this point suggested we were not making anything like the leeway we'd allowed for. This meant we could now ease the sheet. It was like letting her off the leash. Two of our crew moved aft to allow her bow to lift and she was away, sailing free.

Other descendants of the Ness families, linked to *Jubilee*, waved from Stornoway pier as we glided by. They had come over to town and waited just for the moment of seeing the last original *sgoth Niseach* return to the island, under sail. She was nearly home. But we would have to sail her up the sea road, to Port of Ness, where she was built, when conditions permitted.

Another Road North

THE COMMUNITY OF NESS, IN THE NORTH OF LEWIS, still send a group of hunters to the island-rock of Sula Sgeir, 40 miles north-north-east of the Butt of Lewis. The team occupies that bare island for about a fortnight. They put a temporary roof on an old stone bothy. Each day but Sunday they share out the tasks of catching, killing, gutting, plucking, singeing and salting a quota of young gannets. The *guga* is caught at a stage just before it is able to fly from the nest.

Alec John Bell, the man who made a new outboard bracket and chain plates for *Jubilee,* has been in that team. He was also to become one of our skippers. He could arrange a temporary mooring, safe as it could be, in the harbour at Port of Ness. No boats are kept there, to rise to each incoming tide, all the year round.

The gannet-hunters used to depart from this tricky harbour. They sailed in boats like *Jubilee*, completely open to the elements. These were then hauled up a steep *geo* – a rock fault that's more than a crack and less than a slope. This is another word that is a signature of Scandinavia.

These days, the team of hunters join a local trawler in Stornoway harbour and are dropped off with their mounds of provisions and gear in the bay at Sula Sgeir. It's a greyish mass, rising steep from a never-ending ocean swell. The density of gannets is similar to that on Stac an Armin, St Kilda and Sule Stack, further out north-east, towards Orkney. I've sailed close to all three and been astonished each time, trying to take in the density of these fowl in crowded skies. The nests are so thickly packed that these gannetries are like iced buns. The coating is not gannet-guano but the joined-up dots of individual fowl.

Each year, some environmental group will protest about the hunt. But this has been part of the ecological balance of Sula Sgeir since a long way back before any records were kept. The hunters are shy of publicity but in recent years they have invited a photographer and a film-maker to join them. They want to show people they trust that they have nothing to hide, in case sensational images are published and the tradition is made illegal. The men work very long hours 'on the rock'. They call their basic processing line 'the factory'.

Yet it's an honour to be invited into the team. Men go out year after year. You can see a line of simple cairns along the skyline. When one of the team reckons he may be coming close to his last year of the annual duty he puts a last stone on his own cairn, to leave his mark.

The last of the Ness vessels to take the hunters to the rock under sail was *sgoth Jubilee*. In 2010 we realised it was *Jubilee*'s 75th birthday. Our society had agreed on an attempt to recreate that voyage. I had plotted the course for Sula Sgeir more than once for larger boats than *Jubilee* and called it all off when the weather was not ideal. The writer Robert Macfarlane began a correspondence on the subject of sea roads. He had only a short period to make a voyage. He came to Lewis on the full understanding that we would be lucky to do much in the time available. He also had land routes to investigate so he could shuffle these expeditions to give us the best chance of an attempt if a weather window opened up.

We sailed *Broad Bay* – the 1912 lugsail boat you've met already – to the Shiant Islands and back. For me this was a continuation of the original boat's log. The same keel was under me on very different passages to the same archipelago.

Now we were boarding *Jubilee* at Port of Ness. She lay, out from the stone jetty, a red boat with the traditional motif of a black-and-white checkerboard on her top 'strake'. Let me introduce the crew.

Colin Myers is active for his years, an experienced racing sailor as well as a boatbuilder by trade. He can seem abrupt until you tune in to his teasing wry style. He seeks perfection and finds it difficult to take the inevitable compromises on cosmetic finishes necessary to get a vessel back in commission in a timescale.

Diyanne Ross is tall and lively and funny. She works as an artist and specialises in commissioned work in stained glass. I've seen her bold and brusque pen-and-ink drawings from other voyages we have sailed together. She has made several long trips on *an Sulaire*.

David Skelly was our youngest *sgoth* skipper, at the time. He has been taking responsibility since he was about 14 years of age but we could not call him a full skipper till he turned 16. He had sprouted in height but was still wiry and smooth in his chin. That year I'd returned a favour by helming for him in a race of Wayfarer dinghies, neck and neck with a newer and lighter boat. That one's crisp sails did not give her the victory. David's well-judged calls on when to tack gave us the tactical advantage we needed, though I'm not sure our spinnaker helped us much, in the squalls. He proved an assertive skipper who knew his craft well. He was not at all fazed by directing his two crew, both older than him.

Rob has the wiry build of a climber. I was not surprised to see his applied strength in control of the halyard nor his handiness with ropework. He is tall, clean-shaven and softly spoken. He looks at things closely. His sphere of reference is wide but he brings comparisons lightly into the conversation. He is equally willing to enter the banter. He coped with Colin's ironies, Diyanne's wild cards of logical leaps, David's jokes. The truth is that neither journey could have been accomplished without him. Both demanded full participation of everyone on board.

Alec John, our man in Ness, could not be with us nor with the *guga*-hunters this year. He was due to be a father for the second time. He would make sure the mooring was free for our return. Diyanne and I recalled how he'd brought two of the last season's birds with him, on *an Sulaire*, still soaking in salt. He boiled one at the international artists' workshop on Tanera Mor – our first call after crossing the Minch in the big *sgoth*. The smell was difficult to remove from the large airy hall. More people from the southern hemisphere could stomach it than those from the northern one. The Chinese artist liked it best.

'Texie', the Honorary Secretary of Stornoway Lifeboat, was happy to skipper *The Hebridean*, a well-equipped yacht, which was sailing from Stornoway to meet us off Port of Ness. He brought along Innes Smith as crew. That's the same young man who helmed for a time taking *Jubilee* back across the Minch from Ullapool. Like Sean, he now also held his own Yachtmaster Offshore certificate of competence. Our North Lewis craft have very different characteristics to most cruising yachts now in production, yet I believe these island vessels instil a sense of teamwork that will hold you in good stead when you work on other boats or ships.

Jubilee would be independent. We would be responsible for our own navigation and our own cooking. We had now tested the buoyancy installed during the last refit, in a controlled swamping. She was in good order. We had a liferaft and an electronic beacon aboard. Lifejackets were worn from the moment anyone stepped from the pier. None of this equipment would have been available to the Lewismen who made their livings on fleets of these vessels. And they had no sea-shepherd.

We left on the evening high tide. You want as much water as possible as there is nearly always a swell, even in calm weather. The few feet we'd need under our keel could be sucked back and fore at half tide. The weather was bright, the clear sea more green than blue and many people wished us well. 'She's not looking so bad for her years.'

We soon lost sight of any land. This was now late August. It was a very light but favourable breeze. *Jubilee* would have made fair speed in a flat sea but she was slow in the big water. The sail would shake and be noisy in the slack between the swells, then we'd gain enough power to rise and fall to the next one. The weather was dry and not really cold. We broke the peace with the outboard motor for a short time, to help us clear the tidal area. We then went for an hour under sailpower alone and I plotted our position. We were making about 2 knots, sometimes 3. That is not great sailing but it happened to be the perfect speed for arriving at first light. There was not much point in getting there sooner.

We settled to watch-keeping, chatting and brewing tea. If it had not been for the team on *The Hebridean* we would have had no idea that it all looked dramatic. Michael Skelly, father of young David, took a photograph that has become something of an icon. It shows the stretched lugsail above the Atlantic swell. But you can't see anything else. The rest of the sequence of stills shows the gradual disappearance and re-emergence of the vessel in the waves.

The navigation light on North Rona became visible. A little later we could identify the sequence that indicates the minor light on Sula Sgeir itself. A particular blue-ish quality entered the sky. It relieved the dense near-black, just before sunrise. I felt like the seabirds in the story that explains how the down was allotted to different species.

The gull, the cormorant and the eider duck waited up all night to welcome the sun's first appearance. Whoever called out first would get the down. The eider knew better than to try to keep awake all night. She let her head fall to her breast and took her rest. The cormorant's head was heavy very soon, on its long neck. Soon, it fell to her breast and she was sound asleep. Only the gull was left awake. At last she gave a big squawk, calling out a bit too soon when the blue tinge came to the night. That effort used up the gull's last strength and she too dropped asleep but her cries had woken the eider. She now called out in contented pleasure as the first of the red and yellow appeared. The sun was so charmed by the eider's gentle welcome that she was given the greatest share of the limited stock of down. And so it remains to this day.

I might have told that one on the way. If so, I was certainly not the only one who shared a story with the whole crew. I know a version of this tale from Barra but a very similar one is told on Faroes. It is not so different from an aboriginal American story of how the buzzard got its feathers. Has the story crossed the pond and shifted its focus from raptor to seabird? Some of the Lewismen recruited by the Hudson Bay Company did not come back alone. There is more than one Lewis family conscious of their Cree blood. Other migrations and returns brought Cherokee blood and culture into at least one of our villages. It's also possible that the similar legends have evolved separately, in different cultures. How can you tell?

The high outline of Sula Sgeir was now clear. As we came closer, the off-watch folk woke from where they'd settled, in the belly of our open boat. In that eerie light you could indeed see how the natural line of the rock was broken by quiet interventions. That line of cairns was just as I'd heard it described but nothing could prepare you for the sense of past lives. I could imagine the young men who had first proved themselves on this ordeal, many seasons before, admitting that this would be their last year out on the rock.

By sheer chance, we were holding off, boiling up water for more tea, when a Stornoway-based trawler, the *Heather Isle M*, came into the bay. They were not here for any fishing. Their aluminium tender was soon over the side and the outboard was running as men and gear went into the geo in shuttles. The hunters must have been wondering what the hell was going on, seeing *Jubilee* there before them. They would recognise the *sgoth* all right. She doesn't look like any other boat they might meet. We got out of their way. This was not the day for going ashore.

Instead, we circumnavigated the intimidating rock and its outlying skerries. From sea level I could not make out any turf cap that would make this rock somewhere I could call home. Not even for a fortnight. And yet everyone I know who has been a *guga*-hunter describes something that is peaceful, among all that killing. They are continuing something that was a necessary part of living in these latitudes.

Our own venture, piloting our way through a steep swell under sail and oars, allowed us to see the high rock from many angles. We were now over 40 nautical miles from the Butt of Lewis but that does not explain the sense of being somewhere strange and dangerous and far from home. There are plans of outlying islands, including Sula Sgeir, in Admiralty chart 2524. These provide enough detail to identify the breaking reefs and avoid the hidden. There was still something of a deep green shade in the bands of seas outwith the backwash. We returned safely into the bay, brewing coffee and frying bacon on a gas stove in a metal bucket. The black plastic bucket was for a different, designated purpose.

It felt awkward not making contact with the men now ashore, so we came right up to the geo to call our greeting and that was that. We'd need to be away soon. We could not expect *The Hebridean* to shepherd us for much longer. She had to make it back to Stornoway. There was a change in the weather coming and we'd need to catch the tide to get back into the drying harbour at Port of Ness.

It was a good wind direction for sailing to Orkney, another planned destination. But I knew that the seas were likely to build up to a dangerous scale before we'd reach safety. And there was a slalom of tidal forces to deal with. We had to be homeward bound.

Soon there was plenty of breeze but we had to sheet in hard to keep our course, leaving Butt of Lewis well to starboard. We had an option that the Ness navigators before us did not have on board. The outboard motor, at low revs, was enough to give us that few more degrees closer to the wind but still filling the sail. We ran it for a short time till we were back on a good line for the tight entrance at Ness. I handed the helm to David Skelly in the run down to the turning point. By now, seas were steep and our speed was up. It was a good finale but it required full concentration on the tiller-steering.

I could now keep an eye on our line of approach, taking the role of the bowman. He is the one who judges the water ahead and signals back to the stern. A gradual reduction of sail, by lowering on the halyard, works best for a big lugsail. Veterans of the offshore fishery described this being done to keep control in difficult conditions. The bowman pulls down the sail to maintain tension as the person on the halyard lowers. The person on the sheet also pulls down the back edge of the sail. Like everything aboard these vessels, this calls for close coordination and good communication, usually without words. If there is a lull in the wind, the sail can be hauled up again, bit by bit, to maintain sufficient power.

An experience like this brings you kinship with the elusive characters who worked these historic vessels, against the odds. They put up with hardship and risk. Here is the comment of one observer, a traveller's narrative:

> 'About two miles from the Butt towards the East is the fishing station known as "The Port" of Ness. It consists of an opening in the rocks a few yards wide, up from which a pavement has been laid by the laird to enable the fishermen to draw up their boats. This is all their harbour. Out of it no boat can be launched, even on the calmest day, without the men pushing them out up to their waists in water; remaining in this wet condition during the whole time at sea, which is often prolonged for two days. On returning, they are again obliged to leap into the water, to remove mast, oars, and ballast, and then, after a hard day at sea, pull their boats high and dry up the paved beach. The severity of this labour is very great, and the men are said to age rapidly under it. When at sea these men often spread raw cod livers on their bannocks, and at all times consume a great quantity of livers. This doubtless assists them to endure long exposure in wet clothes: the oil alike supplying heat to the system and lubricating the lungs so as to secure them against cold...'*

Now we had the remains of a harbour to give us some protection from the breakers. We needed only about half our sail area to

---

* from *Lewisiana or Life in the Outer Hebrides*, W Anderson Smith, first published by Daldy, Isbister and Co., London, 1875.

catch the wave we needed, then David's steering let us stay on it. We breathed in together, sensing the unstoppable lifting power. It is a tight enough entrance and you have to stay clear of the chunks of pebbled concrete that lurk close to the collapsed end of the breakwater. I looked under the scrap of sail to judge the distance and turned my head to call it to David. Then it was a matter of my commentary with a pointing finger. The bow was talking to the stern but nothing was said.

There is a huge sense of relief when you take your charge, also the love of your life, home from the ocean. There is something else about this boat. I don't believe I've heard an angry word aboard her yet.

David took her in well to Port of Ness, as our *guga*-hunter friend had done a year or two before. This is the most satisfying thing of all, for a skipper. The duty is taken over by someone you can trust. I would say it is a very similar feeling when you pass on a story to someone who tells it with sensitivity.

Port of Ness to Sula Sgeir and return

18 Aug 2010
we're steering zero
the satellites nearly agree
with Jubilee's magnetism

18 Aug 2010
stars and cloud
half a moon and a steaming light
– the looms of all of these

19 Aug 2010
detail happens
– jagged cairns along the
screaming ridge

19 Aug 2010
one circumnavigation
under cloth and oars and tea
red gurnard gasp

19 Aug 2010
it's freshened but so have we
willing her home against
a run of waves

The Two Brothers

I'd like to tell you a story about another return from Sula Sgeir. It was told to me by Alasdair Smith, a coastguard colleague at the time. He heard it from his uncle who lived in Skigersta, Ness. I've not come across a written version or sound recording anywhere so far. I felt able to flesh out this one from the outline I was told, because I now have many hours' experience at every position on *sgoth Niseach* in open water. I simply think myself back into the boat.

Up in Port of Ness, the hammers were swinging at forged iron nails, securing plank on plank of best Scottish larch. The greatline fishery was taking crews further and further offshore. The boats needed to be strong enough for that.

Tons and tons of quality deep-water fish were being landed on the northern shorelines. The boats were getting bigger, over 30 feet long. But they still had to be light enough to launch and recover from the shores so the boats were never decked. They were open to the elements. For most of the villagers, it was the first chance of earning something. So you could get enough to eat and maybe have a bit of choice in what you put to your mouth. You might even be able to gather together a few sticks of furniture. A decent set of clothes, set aside for Sundays and weddings and funerals. Some said it was a new dawn of prosperity. Others said the big offshore boats were widow-makers. Both were right.

Often, the seas would build up while the boats were out of sight of the land. There would be a longer swell further out but the seas would become steep and choppy in the shallow areas closer to the shores of North Lewis. Landfalls could be dangerous. Often the boats would have to alter course and seek refuge on a distant shore that might be safer than their home territory.

Two brothers were both very keen on getting out to sea. They both had a feel for it. When you put either one on the tiller, the boat would sail as well as it could. They worked together well enough but rivalry is a thing you don't want on a boat. One brother worked his way to the helm of one *sgoth Niseach* and his twin took command of another. You didn't choose to do that. You got asked. The crew knew who had a safe pair of hands. Who could find the fish. And a nerve of iron because 'you don't catch fish when your feet are dry'.

They both did well at the fishing and could hardly get their mother to accept the money they pressed into her hand. Neither could see how she would throw herself into the jobs around the croft, with a mad energy, whenever they were at sea.

One time the brothers took their two like vessels the 40 sea miles to Sula Sgeir. Not for ling and not for herring. The twin vessels were hauled right up the rock on their own tackle, clear of the big seas. They couldn't haul the biggest of the *sgoth Niseach* up there but they could somehow manage the mid-size boats. If they were wrecked, you were stranded.

That year there was a good haul. It looked a good day for the return. The boats were relaunched. They were soon rising with the swell and the *guga* went sliding to them, down a wooden chute. They look like hessian sacks with webbed feet. Some would say the only thing worse than the taste of them is the smell of them when they're boiling. But they are considered a great delicacy in North

Lewis. All the weight of their haul and the equipment was packed with great care. Both vessels were made ready for the passage home.

A northerly squall hit them when they left the lee of the rock. There was hail in it, under big anvil clouds. The brothers had been wise enough to reef right down, looking at the signs in the darkening sky. You wouldn't want to do anything but run on the tack you were on, keeping the wind on your quarter, not dead behind you. If you turned to face all that weather, you'd get the full weight of everything. If you lowered sail so you could hoist it the other side of the mast, you'd be powerless for a time as the big rollers came at you. The skippers had hoisted sail on different tacks. They were heading away from each other, the tracks diverging further and further with every minute.

The way I heard it, each of the brothers held up one hand, leaving one on the tiller, at the top of a wave. A greeting to be seen from the sister-vessel. Since it might be the last.

One brother and his crew were heading for the Butt of Lewis, looking for that light. The other was hoping to see Cape Wrath. These boats fairly shift in that kind of breeze. They will usually rise to the steepest of seas. But that day, conditions were about as much as anyone could take. It could be that the brother who was making for home waters was at most risk. People drop their guard when they are near a harbour they know.

His brother, looking to Cape Wrath light, was vigilant every second. He knew that skippers in the past had sailed boats like his as far as Sule Skerry and Stac Skerry to take their share of the harvest of birds. He knew to keep out, well clear of Cape Wrath, and ask his bowman to look out for flatter water. Point to it. They read it just right. The lads expected their skipper to take them down the North Minch.

Instead, he held her on the same tack, catching the east-going set, with the wind. They were now working along the north coast of the Scottish mainland. He caught a lull to sneak into long Loch

Eriboll. They had to run all down the loch to find the shore. No charts. So there they were, a *sgoth* looking for a landfall, on the north coast of Scotland.

The *sgoth* got a thump when she landed but they all came ashore safe. They needed a plank or two but there was a boatbuilder in a village not far away. It is likely that he noted the lines to see if there was anything he could learn. The boats of the north coast were also well known for their seakeeping. The skipper was able to send his words home, on the telegraph-wire. The boat that had gone off with the wind on the port side had reached safety.

Port of Ness would be boiling at the mouth. The second brother knew to keep that fierce wind on his starboard quarter all the way. He also knew that they were at most risk in the last stretch, where the seas meet tide and shallowing banks. Each one of his crew was calling for him to turn in.

He did the other thing. The skipper held her well out, to leave the lighthouse off to port. They were heading down the Atlantic coast. He kept her far enough out to find longer seas. They were huge and high but they were long and she was riding them well.

They had to surf their way down the island before the wind slackened. It cleared and they could make out the loom of The Seven Hunters a long way ahead. Then they could identify the high round top of Old Hill, not so far away. But the wind and seas were down now and they could turn in before that. The *sgoth Niseach* nosed in to East Loch Roag. They ran on till they found flat water at Breasclete, the staging post for Flannan Isles lighthouse.

They were made welcome and given shelter. There was a telegraph station. So a *Niseach* mother received word that her second son had come through that gale. The word would soon go out all over the parish. Most households would have a relation who was in one or other of these two crews. All the lads were safe. There's not that many Lewis seafaring stories end that way.

The boats would be home again to let men and boys risk their lives another day. I suppose most of the *guga* came back to Ness too. There's that much salt in them, they would not have got any worse than they were.

Port of Ness to Stromness

THERE WILL BE AN ASIDE BEFORE we begin the next voyage. It is the story of artworks that have been reclaimed so the materials can be put to use in the cause of keeping vessels seaworthy.

In 1998, I made a poem in three dimensions, with some help from two boatbuilders. Ian Richardson, a long-term resident of Stromness, took the lines that would represent the shape of a 16-foot Orcadian inshore vessel. He transferred the complex curves to wallpaper templates, full size. Topher Dawson, then working from a wind-powered workshop on the Scoraig peninsula (Little Loch Broom), sourced and cut boatskin larch to these shapes. I stored the 'strakes' in a studio, to season them to something similar to gallery conditions. Then I composed a poem and engraved it on alternate planks, leaving a blank one between each, like a line space. I had to devise a hanging system that would hold them spaced on a wall as if suspended in the air. Next, I dressed the timber, oiling each piece. I packed them so the long planks could be secured to roof rack and bumpers and taken safely, by ferries and road, to Orkney.

The work was shown at The Pier Arts Centre, Stromness, a gallery that also holds a permanent collection of the St Ives group of artists, including Barbara Hepworth and Ben Nicholson. It was part of *Green Waters*, a touring exhibition and book project, curated and edited by Alec Finlay. The exhibition went on to other venues in Scotland, England, Wales and Northern Ireland.

I had shared many conversations and a correspondence with the editor's father, Ian Hamilton Finlay, also a main contributor to *Green Waters*. Topher Dawson had steered me to *Working Boats of Britain: Their Shape and Purpose* by Eric McKee. This work was also referenced by John Murdo Macleod, who contributed drawings and analysis of *Jubilee* and a near sister-ship built by himself. In turn I passed a reference to the book on to Ian Hamilton Finlay.

It was a complete surprise to find that Ian had also made a work that referenced the plank shapes of a traditional boat. I recognised that his print had its basis in an intervention on a drawing in Eric McKee's book. The tone, intention and scale of the Finlay work are completely different to the one I made. Like many of Finlay's boat-related works, it idealises the object but also presents it in an uncommon way. In this case, the planks are shown as if painted, as the finished boat would be. The effect is of a perfect, finished structure, but dismantled. Finlay artworks can never be scuffed. They must be carefully transported and meticulously displayed. We were both expressing our admiration of the culture bound to boats but in very dissimilar ways.

A three-dimensional version of that Finlay work now hangs in the Scottish Parliament, though the source is the lines of a Northumberland coble. I realised that my own full-size poem on planks, though made first, would now appear to most as a reference to the elder artist's work.

In 2010 (*sgoth Jubilee* anniversary year) I received an invitation to show new work in the Pier Arts Centre. The building had been restored and expanded since the *Green Waters* exhibition. As it happened, the architects were Reiach and Hall (my friend and fellow sailor Andy Law is a partner of this firm though not, this time, the project architect). I began to think out an idea that would be a correspondence between the seafaring cultures of Lewis and Orkney.

I am fascinated by the way that an object designed for a function can assume a beautiful shape, as if by accident. How language, striving to be a precise, functional description, can also be beautiful.

How the texture of an object can gain interest from the marks of use or by weathering. How words are shifted and bent in usage.

I had already made the decision that there was no longer any point in displaying my engraved full-size boat planks as before. A few, from the nine, were already given away to friends. Ian Campbell, who told me the Mull snowball story, was not in good health. He told me how he had once owned an Orkney yole but given it to a younger man who he knew would bring her back into use. His son, Jonathan, devises works of physical theatre. He happened to be on Lewis with a big van. I handed him one plank, engraved with a line of text that could be a free-standing poem. I asked him to pass this on to his father.

Andy Law had just completed a studio built of larch. I gave the garboard strake (first on the keel) to the Law family. One other was set aside, because stories so often happen in threes. That one has not yet found its own home. When *Broad Bay* was being rebuilt, we were running low on larch of sufficient quality. The exhibition planks were a shade thicker than the new strakes now laid on the old keel but the builder was looking for suitable timber for gunnels and capping. Some of my former artwork was fit for that purpose. I took an industrial jigsaw to the remaining planks, to supply the timber.

Some had engraved lettering on one side. This was useful in retaining glue when several thicknesses were clamped together to form a laminate. The *Jubilee* renovation, progressing at the same time, was also tight on time and budget. You might remember that the main boatbuilder, Mark Stockl, asked me if our team could see to repairing the old rudder and making a new tiller. There was sufficient larch from the sculpture, now being recommissioned, to provide a tiller and a spare one for *Jubilee* as well as one for *Broad Bay.*

A few years later, the reclaimed larch, now a tiller, had developed its own marks from weathering and useage. I thought it would be interesting to return the former artwork to The Pier but in its altered form. The concept would have been best delivered by sailing the restored Orkney yole, *Broad Bay,* back to Orkney, as 'A Boat

Retold'*, incorporating the larch that had been previously exhibited. That was now part of the boat's fabric. Such a voyage is feasible in ideal conditions. There is a story that one of the Butt of Lewis lightkeepers was from Orkney and would sometimes sail his yole to Port of Ness after a spell of leave. But the year was getting on. I judged it foolhardy to dare these justly famous waters without a safety boat. That would have been asking too much of Texie and *The Hebridean*.

However, if the larger *Jubilee* could be sailed from Port of Ness, to be moored within sight of The Pier Arts Centre, then the concept would still be delivered. Materials, shown here before as a three-dimensional poem, would be returned in the form of a tiller, used for the passage. We were now into the month of September. I had sailed this route more than once but always in vessels with a deck over their planking. Yet, within a week of suggesting the possibility, there was the prospect of a strong crew.

This is a very long introduction to the short story of our attempt. I have to ask why I was driven to lead this adventure and why it was not difficult to find a willing team. Orkney lies a long way eastwards up from Scotland's north coast. Just as the proposed route stretches the limits of the intended geographical range of this book, I think now that I would like to make another book, exploring the issue of why so many of us are driven to push our vessel and our own experience that bit further. But, back to the underlying traditions, Alasdair Smith's family story does imply that the *sgoth Niseach* had sailed close to Cape Wrath before now. And I have heard other traditions of how fowlers from the Ness district would attempt to take a picking from Sule Stack as well as their own acknowledged territory of Sula Sgeir. Our proposed voyage would rediscover that experience.

Colin, David and Diyanne were up for the adventure. There was no safety boat this time. I thought back to our test of the buoyancy

---

A Boat Retold, a film by Sean Martin and Louise Milne, documents the restored boat's return to the Shiant Islands, with Robert Macfarlane and Ian Stephen.

system on *Jubilee*. We had simply filled her with water, in harbour, with the sail up. She carried extra ballast to simulate the weight of gear a crew would carry. We found that she would stay afloat even if fully swamped. Her stability remained, even with crew-weight to one side, until she was about two-thirds full. Then she became rapidly unstable. If we shipped some water it had to be removed before more came in. We installed a new hand pump and now carried interlocking rubber buckets for bailing. The recently serviced liferaft was still aboard and the emergency beacon to go with it.

We would carry a hand-held radio and GPS but it had proven difficult to maintain a system for showing a reliable navigation light on this type of craft. We did have numerous torches and spare batteries. Our committee gave the OK for the attempt. *Jubilee* had proved her seakeeping qualities in passages rounding Tiumpan Head en route to Port of Ness. She had punched through tidal waters such as the Sound of Harris and the Sound of Shiants and the cross currents close to the Butt of Lewis. She was quite handy under her outboard with its low-geared saildrive propellor, if we lost the breeze.

Our departure from Port of Ness could only happen within two hours either side of high water. But the key to this passage was fresh breeze. We would need sufficient power to keep up a good pace on the exposed crossing from Port of Ness to about 6 miles out from Cape Wrath. The timing of our arrival there would be vital. We would have to run with wind and tide in favour, until the current eased out in the open. Then we could afford to sail against the slighter tide for four or five hours. After that, we should pick up a push from the north-east-going current. That would help us in our approach into Hoy Sound – the turbulent waters between the high island and the natural harbour bay of Stromness, on mainland Orkney.

The time of entry into Hoy Sound is also critical. The tide can run to over 8 knots so you can't go in against it. However, if you arrive too soon, you will face the last of a weight of water that has

Port of Ness to Stromness: provisional passage plan

been shunted that way for four or five hours. It would normally settle down, an hour or two into the new east-going stream.

You can plan for such a passage, working on a likely average speed, but you can never be sure that the direction and strength of wind will be what is forecast. I am going to stick with my proposal that there is a useful comparison with the way a story comes out, renewed. That's where listeners play a part, like variable conditions.

The team would meet together and weigh up the latest forecasts. Colin is retired and so is his wife. They are both serious about their photography. Colin is also a careful and skilled craftsman in several other mediums. I once asked him to imagine and draw the shapes of the planks for a 16-foot Westray skiff. This was the type of craft I'd hoped to celebrate in my lost artwork. I could have shown Colin a slide of that work, which no longer existed, in its original physical form. But I did not. Would the shapes, composed by different boatbuilders, be nearly identical? Or would they have the subtle variations of tellings in more than one voice? One version had been 'life-size', in timber. Colin's clear and sharp print was derived from his own half-model, made to scale, then translated to lines on paper. Both studies were about the essential lines to constitute a known shape. As I'd suspected, the lines, produced by different boatbuilders, were very similar but with noticeable variations.

Colin is very calm aboard a boat. He used to trim the sails of small racing catamarans at an international level. He is fully aware of risks and wanted the experience of this voyage, for its own sake and for the photographs he might take.

Diyanne, also an artist, loves the form of the *sgoth Niseach*, the aesthetics of the object derived from practical solutions to a demanding set of requirements. We had shared several expeditions and I knew she would also contribute to the 'craic'. She had shown her competence in crewing both *Jubilee* and *an Sulaire* on previous passages we had shared. Diyanne is no Amazon but she is tall and she is strong for her slim build. She takes her rightful place aboard but does not need to act like one of the boys. This is an opportunity very seldom available to women of previous generations.

David was fast becoming a very presentable lad, his face now free of the curse of eczema. I knew he still had to be careful about what touched his skin. He is a skilled dinghy sailor and was already a competent boat handler. The lad is a great talker and good company. He was the one who should have most of his life before him. If I had thought there was a serious risk, I could never have agreed to his keen offer to crew.

We kept in touch as it looked like we might get the wind we needed. When the forecasts seemed promising, I phoned my friend Hamish Bane, who keeps a very seaworthy yacht in Stromness. He knew *Jubilee* and hoped we could bring her over so she could lie close to the Orkney yoles. He would get in touch with the Orkney Yole Association. He'd also come out and meet us in the morning. 'Just drop a text or call on VHF to confirm you've left. Yes, it's a good idea to try to arrive a couple of hours after the start of the ingoing stream.' Hamish thought the passage plan sound and the forecast as good as we were likely to get.

The waters at Port of Ness were aquamarine and turquoise. 'Could be the Greek islands,' said Colin's wife, another Barbara, as she waved us off. She took a series of photographs, documenting our sail diminishing with distance. The breeze freshened but we were able to carry the full sail for a long time. We all have photographs and I have some video footage. It shows a gradually building sea. The height of the waves, across the North Minch, was significant but these were fairly regular and comfortable, though our open boat was achieving over 6 knots out in the middle where there is insignificant tide.

Later footage shows David concentrating. The camera zooms in on his young hands on the laminated tiller. I was the only one aboard who knew the history of the individual planks of larch that contributed to our shaped lever. We were broad reaching, a comfortable point of sail for this craft. *Jubilee* was now a living thing. As David played the tiller, Colin played the sheet. They are both experts despite the differences in their ages and experience. David has the bug but he also has the gift. He has been sailing in this type of vessel since he was a young child. It shows.

Diyanne was a happy lady. There was still warmth in the sun, even with the stiff breeze. I knew the waters would grow steep soon. I also knew we should put at least two reefs in before we met turbulence. We did that. Even though *Jubilee* could take all this breeze, the waves would put more strain on. We should be considerate to our steed.

Now was the time to prepare for the test of rounding Cape Wrath, while everyone was awake and fresh.

We made our first waypoint very close to our planned time, a little ahead of it, which gave us a small margin. But once we turned on to the next course, which I hoped would be a very long one, we found that the wind direction was not quite what we'd hoped for. It was dead astern.

We eased the red halyard to allow the front of the sail (tack) to be repositioned further aft. We use a strong point just in front of the lateral bench (thwart) that supports the mast. This is joined to the other two thwarts by means of sidebenches (beamshelves) to make a bracing structure. Thus the considerable stresses generated by the rig are distributed through most of the vessel, rather than concentrated in one area.

We were able to run a bit more downwind, with this rig now, more like a Viking squaresail. The speed increased as *Jubilee* rose up on steepening seas and charged along with them. Then the tide really kicked in and we were flying. Even Colin's poker face was showing pleasure.

Four is the minimum number to work the dipping lugsail of *Jubilee*. If anyone was badly sick we would be short-handed. We might have taken a fifth person along but the interior space is not huge. We also had to think of the off-watch folk stretching out on the boards, padded by their fisherman's flotation suits. I proposed two for each watch, three hours on, three off, in daylight and two on, two off at night. David suggested overlapping our watch changeovers at night. This gives a rotation of company during the watch and also gives a little more sleep. We all agreed to this variation. The understanding is that the off-duty crew can be woken at any time when a tack or a reef is needed.

The distant shadow of the headland at Cape Wrath, now a long way astern, was replaced by the unmistakable group of four flashes with a long interval of 30 seconds. Even allowing for the capacity for waves to look twice as high at night, these were pretty big. All hands helped put in another two reefs. That was five, now. Only one more was left in reserve. We returned the tack to the forward position. The taut-wired front of the sail (luff) would provide much-needed additional support for the mast. Remember that there are no fixed wires to stay our spars. That hard-worked red rope, matt and kind on the hands, is 'sweated' when the sail is raised, until there is sufficient tension to support the whole rig. The bolted beamshelves take that strain. No knots or hitches are ever used to tie off the halyard. Instead, the friction from a simple figure-of-eight pattern is sufficient. Likewise, a skipper will always cast an eye on the sheet rope to make sure that it can be released at once. This was a very experienced team but these conditions call for extra caution.

And yet there was no sense that we had taken on too much in our 75-year-old open vessel. Orcadian and Lewis craft are so similar because they evolved to cope with challenging sea conditions. The first time I'd sailed *Jubilee* out of Port of Ness, on a bright breezy day, I had thought twice before departing. It was Norman Macleod, that son of *Jubilee*'s builder, known in Ness as *Gagan*, who said we'd be fine that day. She cut through the steep waves to break into more even water, out from the sandy beach. And she relished surfing home again. I knew then why the sail was carried low and why it needed to be so powerful.

But, out here at night, it was a matter of easing off that power. You need just enough to be in control, driving you from wave to wave. There is weight in the steering of a *sgoth*. It is a physical action. But you should not have the sense that she might go careering off, at any angle to the waves, nor round up to take one of the rollers on her beam.

At this stage there was no visible sea traffic, though this is the edge of a shipping lane. You are always on the lookout for navigation lights of white, red and green. There are different combinations and additional lights, to show the type of vessel, and so the priority of right of way. They also indicate whether you are seeing its port side or if it's head-on to you, for example. It is not as simple as power giving way to sail. If a trawler had her gear out, we should be altering, so as not to impede it.

From time to time we shone the torch on our sail. We should really have been showing a red light to port, a green to starboard and a sternlight. These can be presented in a masthead tricolour. At least we had rigged a metal radar-reflector to improve the chance of being 'seen' by larger craft.

We had been wallowing a bit as the reefs were tied in. David began to retch. I'd never seen him sick before. Diyanne looked a bit green but it was her turn on the tiller. The concentration keeps you occupied. She looked to the compass, lit by a taped-up head torch. You don't really want to be glued to peering at these numbers if there is another way. The waves were still big enough but the run of them was fairly constant. It's more difficult if seas are confused, coming at you from different directions. It was cloudy at that point and so steering a steady course was not simply a matter of holding a prominent star on a section of our rig.

Colin is not an easy man to impress. He asked Diyanne how she was holding such a steady line. Like everyone else, she had evolved her own strategy. She explained how she could see the shadow of the moon on the sail, in the absence of a visible star. The changing shape between that and a chosen part of the rig helped her keep the course.

Everyone aboard for this trip was there because they had proven experience of handling this type of craft in challenging conditions. David put on his huge one-piece suit. 'You look very like a bear,' said, but there was no response. I passed him a bottle of water and asked him to remember to take some sips. He found a resting place by the black bucket. Sometimes there is a backstory that you only discover at a later date. David had not been well for a few days. H knew he was a key player in this game. He explained to me, long afterwards, how he'd convinced himself he was well enough for the trip, after all.

Colin was quiet. He can be wordy at times but I knew he was at peace with himself tonight. I also knew he would speak up if there was anything he thought we should be doing or anything we should stop doing. I shielded the torch, interpreting the paper chart.

'Safer to zigzag downwind?' I suggested. That would give us a better margin of safety. We could not risk the stern going through the wind in these steep seas. The wind would then be on the opposite side of the boat. That would bring huge shock-loading on a mast, which would then be unstayed. By altering course a few degrees to take the wind more definitely to one side, we would greatly reduce this risk. We would also fall off our theoretical course line unless the set of tide compensated for the altered course.

To gybe this craft, we would have to turn gently through the wind as we lowered the sail, making sure it was nearly all down before the last of the turn was made. Then we would pass all that cloth and the heavy yard which supported it back clear of the mast then forwards on the other side. That should all happen as the last of the turn is completed, with the wind catching the boat's bow and mast to help her round. After that, every bit of gear would have to be shifted to the other side.

The crew did this perfectly. Squeamish or no, everyone was needed and everyone did their task. It was me, the skipper, who mucked it up. We had got very slick at the tacks and gybes, over a few seasons on the restored *Jubilee*. Diyanne was on the tack, up front, at this time, as I directed from the halyard position, just forward from the middle of the boat.

I saw that the heavy block was about to jump from its hook, in the heaving motion. Instinctively, I made a grab for it. If that heavy object swung across the boat it could be lethal. But I had let go of the traveller. 'Shit.' It was me who said it. No one shouted, no one cursed.

The fitting for the yard that would hoist up the sail was now dangling out of our reach, at the top of the mast.

I took hold of the boathook and asked for an oar. Colin groped in the 'come in handy' bag and produced some 'small stuff' of light cordage. I lashed the boathook to the oar. Then Diyanne braced me, as the short but light person and I went fishing in the sky with the unwieldy rod. We took turns at trying to catch that ring of iron. I did catch it but found that we could not pull it far enough down without dismantling the whipping. The hook lost its grip in the process.

It was then David said he thought we should proceed under engine. That could take us out of the busiest waters. We could try to recover the traveller at first light. I thought back to the first trips on *an Sulaire,* the larger *sgoth*, when she did not carry an engine of any sort. David was rightly concerned at the risk of one of us losing our footing, standing on the thwart with an arm round the wet mast. But this time, I did not think our outboard was going to help.

I looked at Colin. We had plenty of fuel but I doubted if we could make enough way in this height of sea. The prop would be out of the water more often than it was in. Colin shook his head.

'Sorry, David,' I said. Then, 'I'd rather you used the bucket, mate.' I could not bear to watch him lean over the side, to be sick. The seas feel worse when you are without power. Diyanne was concentrating on our shared task and this was keeping her own sickness at bay. At least in the open boat we were standing or seated, deep into its shell, rather than being perched on high decks.

We really did need to recover that traveller and hook the sail back on to complete our passage. There will probably be four different versions of the story of what happened next. Diyanne has told me that she thought I was playing the incident down too much. Her recollection is that I was struck by the block as I tried to catch it and she at first thought I was seriously hurt. After we'd both had a few unsuccessful attempts to recover the hook, she hit on the idea of using a belt to hold herself in to the mast. Then she, as the tallest, could hoist me, as the lightest, up to grab the boathook, above the lashing.

Our individual memories come back together at this point. Without any fuss, all the crew lifted the yard and sail to hook it back on. 'I thought the choreography was rather good, that time,' said Colin. Diyanne was chuckling. David looked relieved.

I breathed deep breaths, once the sailpower came back on. We had one more bad moment when a ship passed close. The watch officer may have been concerned, not knowing how to interpret a bright torch illuminating a sail above high waves on a September night. Her wash was all too noticeable, as it added to the general milling of interesting water.

From then on, we were cooking on driftwood. I could have done with Donald MacLean or Ursina, his able mate aboard *Sealladh*, for an extra set of hands. I decided to call up any visible vessel on our hand-held VHF once we could make out their lights. They should know we were out here and that we were doing fine. We put in our last reef at about 2am. The wind was whistling. I thought it was a steady force 5 but later we found that it was gusting to force 6, for a brief period, that night. *Jubilee* was comfortable and our speed only fell when we lost the tide for those inevitable hours. This happened when we were more or less where we'd planned to be. Our fast progress under sail made up for the time we'd lost, wallowing about.

The additional turns each side of our course line all went very smoothly. Our procedure was now to put a rope on the traveller once it was detached. No more short cuts that could cost us a lot of time in the long run. The wind eased enough for us to shake out two reefs. We had to rouse David for this and he always jumped to, working through it. He was about to join his first ship as an apprentice and I hoped that this experience would not be a setback.

But the turns were demanding for me, as navigator, now that we were sailing through dense drizzle. We could not afford to arrive at a position downtide from the middle of the entrance to Hoy Sound. So I found a place where I could squat and put the fix from the GPS on the chart. Then I laid the plastic plotting instrument (Portland plotter) on it to lay on the new course we were achieving. To do this, you wait till the person on the helm is settled and happy. You check that this is a safe angle to the wind but not too far off course. Then you ask for the average compass heading. You can check that against the GPS reading. In theory there is then an adjustment for the boat's own magnetic field (deviation).

In practice, we'd found that *Jubilee*, with no fixed engine and very little ironwork, had little effect on the compass. So we had only to allow for the 'variation' that is the difference from true to magnetic north in a given place in a given year. I had to subtract the westerly variation so our course could be transferred to the chart that is orientated to true north. You can't expect to steer or plot to within an exact degree in these conditions.

David emerged from the bilges to take a short spell at steering and it seemed to settle him. Every single member of this small but strong team was essential. Our metal radar-reflector was swaying in a very steady rhythm up front. The sky was lighter in tone but the heavy drizzle was still falling so there was no visible point of land. It did seem as if the tide was starting to help us again because the speed shown on the GPS rose steadily. My plot on the chart showed that the helming of all was steady and reliable.

Visibility was now very poor. My coastguard training had instilled the use of the single-handed dividers, a very versatile plotting tool. This is much easier than shuffling instruments with any moving parts when you are bucking along. Our fix put us right in the middle of the approach. We should be seeing the Old Man of Hoy if the drizzle relented. Instead, we saw a scrap of white sail. I remembered the text from Hamish, saying he might take *Kora*, his Rustler 36, out to have a look for us. This is a design with a proven history in challenging seas. I'd sent a reply text saying we were on our way. It was pretty close to the optimum time for entering Hoy Sound, about two hours into the ingoing tide.

Hamish turned *Kora* close to us. We had now four reefs in, out of six. He was out with his friend, a recently retired skipper with the Northern Lighthouse Board. He had a reef in his mainsail and his foresail was tightly rolled to the size of a very small jib. He told us later he had to power up the motor to get near us. He estimated we were surfing at a speed reaching 8 knots. He took a small snatch of video in which *Jubilee* looks comfortable and settled and you would not realise we were travelling so fast.

We were in luck at the turn. There is an outlying port then a starboard buoy to respect on the way in to Stromness. We were able to hold our cloth till we had cleared the ferry pier and were abeam the pontoons. It seemed a pity to start the engine now as we had not used it the whole trip since leaving Port of Ness under oars. David took one blade and Colin the other. The lad seemed fine, now. Diyanne helmed us nicely while I put out the fenders and warps for my team.

There seemed to be a bit of activity around the pontoons, close to the yoles. We snuggled into a berth to be met with a round of applause. The yole society was out in strength. We had drams before breakfast. I had a berth ashore with Hamish and his equally hospitable wife, Freda. The others occupied the comfortable *Kora*.

A day later we moored *Jubilee* within sight of a window at The Pier Arts Centre. In the exhibition, our tiller was idle against a wall. There was a hint, in a brief note, to say that the timber in its laminations had been here before.

It's your track record,
how she leans to the cloth she carries,
how her forward sections dip
and the bounce of recovery.

The swither of that, if any,
in small turbulence astern.

It's the hiss of the line of bubbles,
the one you're not often going to see
in the clutter of several waters
but you have to get the sniff of it.

The Lost Daughter

There was once a crofter-fisherman on Orkney. He had a son
to help him and his wife with the croft. They also had a young
daughter. This lass saw to it that the tatties were steaming just
when the other three were coming in from the fields.

But this day, the father, the mother and her brother came home
and there was no dinner. That was the least of their worries.
They all went down to the shore to look together. Salt was very
expensive then. Poor folk would take their pan to the shore. They
would half-fill it with seawater and top it up at home with fresh.
You'd boil everything in that.

They came across the pan, cast up on the shore, but there was
no sign of the girl. It had been a calm day so there was no reason to
think a big wave had taken her away. They searched for the rest of the
day. That evening, their neighbours joined them to make a sweeping
line, looking from the shore to the hill. In the days that followed, the
searchers covered every inch of the island. Not a sign was found.

Time moves on and they'd all to get on with their lives.
Husband, wife and brother would take turns to fall into a quiet
sadness, thinking of their lost girl.

Many years later, the father and son were at sea when a thick
fog came down. They were just not prepared. They had no idea
where they were heading. The father was keeping a good lookout
up at the bow and the son was rowing, slow and steady.

'Take her in easy now,' the father said. He'd seen the first rock
that told him they were near a shore. The fog lifted right then and
they caught sight of green land.

At first they thought it was the island of Einhallow. They both thought they couldn't have gone much further than that. But the nature of the ground was not familiar. So they were both gazing, taking it all in. The grass was that bit more green than they had ever seen it. The cattle in the fields were very dark against that, a gloss in their coats. That man and his son were real farmers so they couldn't help but look closely at these beasts. They had long thick coats, curling tight. But there was something about the way their hair was bending. Against the norm. The black in their rich coats shone so it was nearly blue.

You do get very strong light when the sun at last bursts through the haar. But then they both noticed something else. Neither of them was casting a shadow.

They could see a fine house standing by one of these perfect fields. It wasn't that grand, just well proportioned and in very good order. Even the grey stone shone.

They were both a bit shy to march up to the door but there was nothing for it. No navigator wants to admit he is lost but they had no other way of finding out where they were. As the father was about to knock, the stout door opened. Standing there, looking fit and healthy, was the young woman of the house. There was something familiar about her. She seemed to be expecting them, dusting the flour off her neat apron.

'Come on in now,' she said, 'and we'll catch up with the news. You'll meet my man and the family. The dinner's just about ready and you'll eat with us.'

Father and son were no sooner seated than a cold breeze came all through the house. They saw a tall man stoop so his head cleared the lintel above the door. He was very dark against that brightness outside so they could hardly see much of his face. He didn't say anything but nodded a greeting as the woman of the house said, 'This is the brother of my man.' Then he took his place at the table. He didn't have anything to say.

There was a second blast of cool air and another tall man was standing in the doorway. This time they noticed he had his arms folded tight around him – the way you do on a cold day. Again he nodded but he didn't have much more to say than his brother, as he took his place at the head of the table.

'This is my man.'

The father said, 'I'm right glad to meet you and see that my daughter's well looked after. This is her brother.'

The lost daughter came over to take a close look and give her brother a hug. But her man and his brother just nodded again, friendly enough. Neither of them had more than a word or two to say. 'You're welcome to eat with us.' And that was about it.

A third gust of cold air came blasting its way in. This time, a *simmins*, a tight coil of straw-rope, came rolling through the room with a young lad chasing it. The boy went running to his mother and he'd a little more to say to her. But his way of talking was strange to the father and son and they couldn't make out the words. Some of the northern islanders had a very broad way of speaking but father and son thought they knew all the tongues of Orkney.

The old man was shocked to think this must be a grandson of his own. Then he caught his own son meeting his eye. Of course there was a deep bowl of boiled tatties and another of firm white fish. Bannocks, still steaming. All piled high like they'd been expecting visitors. It's no new thing for island folk to eat fish and tatties with their fingers but the son caught his father's eye for a reason.

When the men of that house reached out their hands to the food you could see something unusual. At the base of their fingers, it was as if each was joined to the other with skin. It's not good manners to comment on an affliction so neither the father nor the son said anything at all. They ate their fill – they were hungry from the sea and just feasted their eyes on the lost daughter. The father said how she was doing right well for herself and it was wonderful to see her fine strong boy. Her mother would be desperate to see them.

'We're only here in the summers,' she said. 'And you won't find your own way back.'

'But I have to bring your mother here.'

At that she passed a knife to her father, holding it by the blade of bone. There was nothing of iron or steel in it. She said he was to make sure and keep that safe. As long as he had it in his hand, he would find a way back to this island.

They all rose from the table. 'The men will need to be back to the sea but they'll point out your way home.'

The quiet men came with them to the boat. They pointed out a headland and told them to turn to starboard once that point was on their forward thwart. Then they pushed the boat, pulled the ropes to turn her and threw them back to the man and boy. The father noted that the boat had turned against the course of the sun. That was a thing you never did, back home.

But they were clear. The fog lifted as suddenly as it had fallen. They could make out their marks and were soon beaching the boat on their home island. The son ran ahead to tell his mother the news. She came in a rush to the shore. Her husband was lifting every board in the boat. The knife of bone was not in his belt.

They never did find it again.

It might be because the boat was not turned sunwise. But there's another thing. You might know that you should never make a gift of anything sharp unless you first take a coin from the one who will hold that sharp thing. That way the friendship can never be cut. No coin had been exchanged.

In our all-too-short stay in Orkney, I was able to reconnect with Tom Muir, a local man who works at the museum in Kirkwall. He has pointed me to many Orcadian stories and many from other cultures. It was to take a later voyage and a longer stay in Orkney before I could follow up his suggested leads and record his own sonorous bass voice.

A day or two after we arrived in Stromness, members of the Orkney Yole Association circumnavigated Hoy in a day, under sail, in an 18-foot yole. This is an astonishing feat of inshore navigation, demanding expert reading of changing currents. Their skipper, Maurice Davidson, invited me along but I had to work on the exhibition. He said he was keen to join *Jubilee* for the return passage.

After the exhibition opening, I returned to Lewis by buses and ferry, leaving *Jubilee* moored at Stromness. We had to wait a long time to find a suitable wind to take her back home. I was stopped in the street in Stornoway by my friend Mary Smith. She is a singer with an international reputation and a collector of Gaelic songs and traditions of the sea. She is from the Ness district. 'Have you brought *Jubilee* home yet?' she asked. I told her we were still waiting for the right weather. 'You do realise that if you don't bring her back you might as well leave the island for good.' I could tell her that I knew that fine.

Diyanne signed up for the return. James Morrison, veteran of the *Dunderave* adventures and then chair of *Falmadair*, the society that now looks after *an Sulaire* as well as *Jubilee* and *Broad Bay*, was our other vital link. Maurice was still up for the voyage to Lewis. We restepped our mast on the boat's own tackle around midday on a date far into October.

I would say that our passage, from abeam the Old Man of Hoy to the turning point 5 miles out from Cape Wrath, was one of the finest sails I've experienced. The seas were significant but with us. Visibility good. At this speed you need a reliable team. I had one of the best. There was one bad moment, after dark fell, but it was not the fault of any of the crew. James is a safe hand on the helm. This time, he seemed to be losing the course. There was a change in the motion and cold spray was dashing aboard, over the beam. I looked at the high run of waves and our angle to the visible light on Cape Wrath. And then at the compass he was steering to.

'Forget the compass,' I said.

'I thought you said we had very little deviation?' he said.

'I did. But I bought the torch that's lighting it from a car-accessory shop.'

It lay neatly on the thwart and the directional beam was perfect but it was magnetic. Once we replaced it, we were more comfortable again, sailing close to our hull speed, with the compass behaving. Maurice turned out to be one of the best stand-up comics I've ever heard. He went into a monologue on a very personal operation, with no trace of embarrassment. His candour was as much a triumph as the circumnavigation of Hoy. And he continued to steer a perfect course, in full flight. That's some storytelling.

There was laughter with the spray. It was a wet but fast and steady passage. The wind was due to drop about the time we would turn down to the North Minch but you can't bank on that. I wedged myself in to snatch some rest. As long as the wind was just aft of our beam, it was comfortable. We had two crew up all the time, just in case there was a lapse of concentration. It was some relief when we were round the corner and wind and sea did both ease. It's difficult to sail on at a racing pitch indefinitely. We succeeded in making our waypoint while the tide was still favourable. The wind dropped as the stars grew strong.

Jubilee could probably still take more than we could, but I was happy to have an easier ride for our last leg down the Minch in a diagonal line to Stornoway. We were home safe for breakfast. After a sleep, Maurice was able to sail *Broad Bay* and experience how an Orkney-built yole had been transmuted, rebuilt and rigged as a Lewis boat.

Looking back on our expedition, we were in a proven and suitable craft but traversing a very exposed stretch of sea with an unpredictable cocktail of wind and tide. If we were to do that again in a similar craft, I would want to install a battery and fixed navigation light at the masthead first. I would also make sure we carried two VHF radio sets. You need to make contact with the ships you sight and it's all too easy to find that the battery of one has run down. I sourced a strong, spring-loaded hook for the block, to reduce the chances of it jumping free again.

Next winter, during maintenance work, we found localised rot at the stern section of *Jubilee*. This was the second plank down from the top and the damage was not extensive enough to be really dangerous. But the bad section needed to be removed and replaced before the rot spread. Boatbuilder Mark Stockl scratched his head and wondered where he could find a piece of timber wide enough and clear enough for this repair. 'I think I can help you with that,' I said.

There is a timber structure outside the restored sail loft building. One side has a plank shape for *Broad Bay* to celebrate her return to being in use. The other side also displayed the full-size section of a boatskin plank. It was the wide and curved shape of the second plank down for *Jubilee*. I'd found an exceptional piece of clear larch. This had been borrowed once before and transported to Orkney. It was installed at The Pier Arts Centre, while *Jubilee* was moored outside. After its return, it was reinstalled in the setting by Stornoway harbour. Only its outline is left now, as a less weathered shape, on the timber slats. The plank is now afloat as a part of the structure of *sgoth Jubilee*.

I am indebted to many boatbuilders, whether I met them or not, as well as to those who share stories. One last poem comes to mind now because it was built from a conversation with a man who was a boatbuilder at the time. I would also like the last words of this book to be those recorded from two different islanders. The tones of voice are very different but, to me, the unscripted words fall into place like one shaped plank meeting another.

From a conversation with Topher Dawson, boatbuilder

A vessel consists of
a buoyant body and
the salient part – a fin.
These two are united by
the method of construction:
a half-eggshell (lengthways)
and a plate on its edge.

The boat becomes narrow
below the body of it.
The full hull is
a pure shape, distorted –
cheeks sucked in
from experience.

The shape sends a vortex
from off your stern-post.
A rotating barrel of water
is left as your wake,
a line of ripples
just on one side
as the sail also leans
to one side only.

The vessel negotiates
moving water.
Her sails negotiate
moving air.

Boats are containers
to keep one thing in

and another thing out.
A waterproof vessel
has to contain
an absence of water.

Dissection proves
a boat is a structured shell
and not the solid body
you thought it was.
If the inside and outside
are exchanged,
you're sunk.

Appendix 1: Tom Muir, Orkney

My friendship with Tom Muir has continued. He made me a present of some hardwood that was too much for the power saw of the joiner who was making new windows for his house. That is now also incorporated into the structure of a vessel, presently moored in Stornoway harbour. He has been equally generous in sharing stories, both timeless and personal. His book, *The Mermaid Bride*, has now been translated into Icelandic. To give you some flavour of his strong, individual voice, here is a transcript of a family story, told as an aside during one of our recording sessions:

'Ken the fog comes in fast here. In summer. The fog just rolls in off the sea. And it just swallows up all the land in front o it. It comes in like a train. And this was dangerous for small boats at sea. Because they wouldn't be able to tell where they were going. They might end up going on a skerry or off oot into the Atlantic and lose sight o land. So this happened while my grandfaither Geordie Driver, was oot at the creels in his yole. Me mither wid be sent doon to the point o Sponess and she wid lok aroond the shore until she fun one o these shells. I think the English ca them a flat perriewinkle but my mither called them a whistling buckie – peedie shells are called buckies in Orkney. And when she fund one that wis a good whistler, she'd stand on the point at the end o the heedland and she'd blow into it and it made a good shrill whistle. As I will now demonstrate.

When her father heard that fae the sea he wid stick his fingers in his mooth and whistle in reply and she would slowly walk along the coast whistling wi her shell as she went and he would follow her at sea, until she cam tae the boat noust and then she wad stand at the noust and whistle until her faither appeared fae out o the mist in his boat.

I aways thought that it was a beautiful wee story because she was only eight years old at the time. She was the youngest in the family. So it was sending oot the youngest bairn to guide her faither in from the sea.

They were very close, my mother and her father. She didna get on that weel wi her mother but her father – she was devoted to him. She heard it was something that only her father did but I've heard since that that was done all about Orkney.'

Appendix 2: Transcript of a recording of Donald J MacLeod, Uig and Scarp Island*

'Anyway my grandfather took me to Uig under sail with the Atlantic broadside on. Eight miles, I think it is. And I spent all my holidays on Scarp, which is the finest place I've ever been in. They had a parliament. An old house at the end in ruins.

And everyone had his own stone. And in Scarp a lot of the work had to be communal work. If they went for peats to Floda if they went to ship peats from Bacersta if they went for sheep to the mainland then it had to be all communal so they had to decide what they would do but the craic was good in that Parliament. Far better than Westminster I may say and they would decide what they would do.

It was fantastic because there was boats of all... not only boats fishing but every family near enough had a boat so they'd go to Hushinish if they wanted something but there was also the little mail boat going back and fore every day for the mails. And the Scalpeachs they used the sail and the outboard. Now I was brought up in Enaclete in Uig and I was very keen on boats and knew a lot about them and I was fascinated by Bernera boats because during the war Bernera people were allowed to put their sheep up to Scaliscro and they used to come in to collect the sheep and they used to come in to fleece them up at Scaliscro.

Now our house near the shore at Enaclete, there's a little hillock above it and it was fantastic for a boy who was interested in boats. I would look down the whole length of Loch Roag. And in would come the Bernera boats, six to eight Bernera boats, one behind the other. And what fascinated me was that the Bernera boats had the sail up but they also had the outboard engine on the quarter and they used to tack across the loch and they used the helm. They didn't steer the boat with the engine. But in Scarp, one of the bad things about Scarp, was that there was no anchorage. So boats could not

---

* This account is a transcription from my recording of Donald made in Sail Loft 2, Stornoway, circa 2010. It is published here with his kind permission. He has published his own memoire in *Memories of the Island of Scarp*, The Islands Book Trust, 2010.

be left. The boats were heavy and this is one of the reasons people left. We didn't have a bay like Scalpay. You had to haul the boats. This was an awful job – these were heavy, heavy boats. They used to have these bits of wood to put under the boat. But sometimes, because dogfish weren't popular, sometimes they would put dogfish there because they were wet and slippery.

And it's second nature for Scalpeachs to be in a boat. Second nature. And the women. Just like someone going in a car here today, there was no difference at all. There was no big talk, no worry about the sea or anything else.

But I had a worry about the sea once. I don't know if I was eleven. I was on my holidays on Scarp and it was the finish of them. They decided it was time for me to come back to Uig. So my uncle Murdanie, big strong fellow home on leave from the navy, and I think it was five of them decided to go to Breanish with the boat. Under sail.

So it was great, under sail, a big sail. We got past the Island of Flodday, west of Flodday heading for Breanish. We were past it about 20 minutes and my goodness did it blow. And just in a matter of a quarter of an hour there was mountainous seas, a howling gale. The boat was going from side to side. I still remember to this day there was a huge swell but inside the swell there was about 20 waves.

The boat would go up to the top of the swell rise up to the sky, crash down and every time she crashed I thought she was just going to split open. And my uncle grabbed me because she was rolling to one side and the sea was coming in and rolling to the other side and the sea was going out. And Donald was grabbed by my uncle, who was on the tiller, sitting. And he put me between his legs and he had huge knees and he stuck them into my ribs so tight that I could hardly breathe.

This was going on. And I remember once the swell, we were in the trough of this huge swell and I looked up and all I could see of the sky was about 1 foot. And massive above us, curling white, were two huge waves. And I thought this is it. And it's the first time in my life and I can honestly say this, that I prayed to God to save me because I was sure that we would never see land. We couldn't see land where we were. We couldn't see anything else but sea. And what's amazing, these things were curling white and how was it the boat was climbing up the side of this thing and then crashing down.

Anyway that wasn't the end. Even they, decided to shorten the sail. And a man was sitting in the bow holding the rope on the sail in case the rope snapped. And I found out later the reason is that if the sail went round the mast we'd all be drowned. And he was holding on to the sail to keep the sail at the bow. So after shortening the sail and everything else they decided it had to be the oars.

So out went the big Scarp oars. As I've said a foot longer than other boats' oars and a special way of rowing with two dips in the deep swell. And they decided they couldn't head to Breanish. They'd head for Tamnavay, which was well off course. So they started rowing. The sea got a bit better. It wasn't as bad as it was. The sea got better, still bad. So we got as far as Gobh na Ardmore, the Ardmore which is near Tamnavay. We got in to the coast there, a bit of shelter. Still a swell and they rowed all the way up the coast – but they knew the coast – they rowed all the way up and where the boats used to land in Breanish was a place called Molenish. Couldn't get past Molenish. Couldn't get past Mealasta Island. Couldn't get anywhere near it with the sea. But there was a geo a bit along the coast in Breanish, past Mealasta.

And this geo must have been at least 200 feet down. And the swell still came in. So they got the boat into the geo. Didn't tie her. There was a man at the bow and the stern and they were hanging on to the seaweed. So of course the boat went up and down.

This man went ashore in this geo, on this rock. Started walking a bit. My uncle said to me, 'Follow him, don't look down, don't do anything. Hang on to the seaweed. And when he lifts his foot out of a step, you put your foot where his foot was.' And I did this and we ended up at the top of the geo. And I looked down and my little knees started shaking, banging each other and everything else. And this boat was down in the geo and it's still going up and down in the swell. So I thought – honestly my legs could hardly walk, they were just trembling – I was terrified.

We were about 2 mile, I'm sure a mile or 2 miles from Breanish. So two men were left with the boat. And the other three came with me to my grandfather's house in Breanish – Iain Mor Macaulay. Hello there, the Scalpeachs. Never a mention that there was bad sea. Hello how're you doing? We called for a cup of tea. Never mentioned about the swell or where have you landed? It was never asked or never said that we'd landed near Mealasta. And I thought, you know there was laughter and they started joking, telling jokes. And then they left.

And then the other two came and had a cup of tea. And they left for Scarp. No mention of bad seas or anything. They just went back in the boat. And poor Donald (that's me) was left and he was terrified. I didn't go to see the boat leaving but I thought I'd never see my uncle again. Because they were going back to Scarp with the sail to the same seas and they'd never make it.

Anyway, I remember that night I had bloody nightmares. Nightmares. And swell and heavy seas and goodness knows what and I was convinced that they would never reach Scarp alive. And I got up early next morning because I was so agitated. Convinced that the first thing I was going to hear was that a Scarp boat had been lost. And I spent all half the day in Breanish till the bus came to go to Enaclete. And everybody I heard I listened to. There was more people in Breanish than there was in Scarp.

When I heard a bodach or a cailleach talking I went and stood beside them sure I'd hear the news that the Scarp boat was missing. But the Scarp boat had made it to Scarp without even… they'd never even have said it in Scarp that the sea was bad.

Now, as I was on about earlier on, one thing I find peculiar now. When they went with the boats from Scarp with the sail, they had no ready-made ballast. And they searched the seashore for stones. And they didn't use the same ones. They were great big stones. And they put these down the bottom of the boat, above the keel and wedged them in.

Now thinking of it today, I remember seeing – and it was like a garden – along the keel. Just like a garden. And the puzzle to me – and there's no one can answer it – these boats round Scarp there was always a swell. Because this is the Atlantic and there's never never a flat sea. There never used to be anyway. Very seldom you'd see a flat sea. You'd always get the groundswell anyway. Why is that these stones, when the boat lurched over about 45 degrees from one side to the other, and these stones never moved. You know it's unbelievable.'

Notes on the stories

Brown Alan
Story embodied in the great lament *Alein Duinn*. There are many additional elements in the oral tradition of Scalpay and Lewis.

The Blue Men of the Stream
Legend summarised in several published sources, such as *Scottish Fairy and Folk Tales* (AL Burt, New York, 1901). My telling includes elements from another well-known international tale, *The Three Questions*.

Sons and their Fathers
This retelling is indebted to a short but clear synopsis told to me by Maggie Smith, round my kitchen table in Stornoway, November 2013. Her version is based on her recording of John M Macleod, former headmaster of Balallan school, who sadly passed away January 2014. Maggie generously shared this research with me and some elements are included.

It may be that the oral tale has continued to exist, passed by word of mouth, in different areas of Lewis. But it is also possible that Morrison's transcription of the story, placed by him as starting in August 1460 with the murders committed by Norman Macleod's sons, has preserved the details that may well have been otherwise lost. The tale is also retold, with variations and other details, in *Tales and Traditions of The Lews*, by Donald Macdonald (born 1891). This was first published in 1967 and reissued by Birlinn, Edinburgh in 2004 and 2009.

A section of the tale in a different version is included in *Western Isles Folk Tales*, Ian Stephen, The History Press, Stroud, 2014.

A powerful story of the island clearances in the Uig district was collected by Maggie Smith. A transcription can be found on: www.ceuig. co.uk/the-clearance-of-vuia-mor/.

The Girl who Dreamed the Song

Version in *Tales and Traditions of the Lews*, Donald Macdonald, Birlinn, Edinburgh, 2009. Additional elements from the telling of Maggie Smith, heard at the Tip of the Tongue Festival, Isle of Jura, 2012.

A different version by the present author is included in *Western Isles Folk Tales*.

There is a free translation and responses to the song by Donald S Murray in *Speak To Us Catriona*, The Islands Book Trust, 2007.

In the Tailor's House

Told to me by Mairi MacArthur. Based on her recording from an original source, held in the School of Scottish Studies, University of Edinburgh.

The Great Snowball

Told to me by Ian Campbell. Only last year, 2015, did I discover, thanks to a reference in Michael Crummey's novel *Sweetland*, that a tale with the same punchline is told in Northern Canada. (Ascribed to Leonard Budgell, in *Arctic Twilight: Leonard Budgell and Canada's Changing North*, Claudia Coutu Radmore, Dundurn Press, 2009.)

MacPhee's Black Dog

See note in text and online resource: www.tobarandualchais.co.uk. See also notes on variations and a retelling of the Benbecula version in *Western Isles Folk Tales*, Ian Stephen, The History Press, Stroud, 2014.

Lady's Rock

My main source is *Traditions of the Western Isles*, Donald Morrison, Stornoway Public Library, 1975. Also oral sources, Isle of Mull.

A Cow and Boat Tale

From a version in *Traditions of the Western Isles*, Donald Morrison, Stornoway Public Library, 1975. Also heard from several tellers in Uig, Skye. There, it is sometimes a horse rather than a cow.

The Waterhorse

From my mother, Johann Stephen (a daughter of the Shawbost orator and storyteller Murchadh Iain Fionlagh mac a Gobhann). Also Norman Malcolm Macdonald, Tong, Lewis.

The structure and imagery used here is strongly indebted to a version in *An Illustrated Treasury of Scottish Folk and Fairy Tales*, Theresa Breslin, Floris Books, Edinburgh, 2012.

See also *The King of Lochlin's Daughter* from JF Campbell as a source of the kind lad sharing his bannock. This is also echoed in recordings of folk tales from Gaelic-speaking parts of the Canadian Maritimes.

Black John of the Driven Snow

Transcription of the telling by Angus 'Moy' Macdonald, live at the Monachs. Angus's version, as told that day, is very close to the narrative in Angus MacKenzie's, as recorded by DA MacDonald in 1962 for the School of Scottish Studies. Both build up to the point made right at the end, but each version has its own rhythm as well as individual choices of language. The sequence of events is revealed in a slightly different order.

An Incident Remembered

Personal reminiscence of Angus 'Moy' Macdonald. Published with his kind permission.

The Tale of the Flounder

Several oral and published versions are listed in more detail in *Western Isles Folk Tales*. Main source: *Peat Fire Memories*, Kenneth MacDonald, The Tuckwell Press, East Linton, 2003.

Chaluim Cille and the Flounder

From *Carmina Gadelica*, Alexander Carmichael, Oliver and Boyd, Edinburgh, 1954.

The Five Sisters

Many sources, oral and published, including Johann Stephen. See also the Clan Maclennan version of the origin of these mountains: (www.tobarandualchais.co.uk/play/45229).

These claims to trace a line of descent back include a trusted companion of Chaluim Cille (*Colum Chille* in Irish), a man who also came to be called a saint. Monks must have been able to father children in these days or else he did a bit of living before his conversion because this one was blessed with five beautiful daughters. When the family was granted stewardship of the territory of Kintail, he named these peaks for his daughters. Thus they became the Five Sisters.

The King of Lochlinn's Daughter

Based on a recording of Ann Munro, transcribed in Bruford/MacDonald no 53 p297 and many other recordings. There are several variations on the tradition of the daughter of the King of Norway reaching the Outer Hebrides by supernatural means, including one form of the selkie story. In Lewis, the tradition of the gift of second sight is linked to allowing her spirit to return to its resting place.

The Crop-haired Freckled Lass

International tale now rooted in both South Uist and Lewis. Compare versions in *Stories from South Uist*, Angus MacLellan, translated by John Lorne Campbell, Routledge, and Kegan Paul, London 1961 (now reprinted by Birlinn, Edinburgh) p70, *The Three Questions and The Three Burdens*. Editor John Lorne Campbell notes Irish examples and another related to poaching, from Duncan MacDonald from Penerine, recorded at Lochboisdale, 1950.

See also the version recorded from Peter Stewart, a traveller settled in Barvas, Isle of Lewis (Bruford & MacDonald no 32 *The Poor Man's Clever Daughter*). There is another story within the story and variations in the questions and answers. There are several similar tales in Bruford and MacDonald. These also suggest comparison with the moral riddles in the Child ballads.

The Sealskin
The selkie story ranges far, from Ireland to Iceland, and takes two main forms, but with countless variations. One is the seal wife story, like this one, and the other is the male equivalent – the 'finman' legend, as in *The Lost Daughter*. In Faroese and Icelandic versions, the skin is kept locked in a chest and the fisherman carries the key with him whenever he goes to sea. One day he leaves it behind.

A version retold in *The People of the Sea*, David Thomson, is very similar to another Uist version included in Bruford and MacDonald. It becomes another variation of the tradition of the daughter of the king of Lochlinn coming, in a supernatural form, to northern Scotland. *The People of the Sea* has been published in many different editions, often with an introduction by Seamus Heaney.

The detail of the dried fish in the haystack is from a recording I made of a conversation in South Uist. Grateful thanks to the contributors.

The Two Brothers
Told to me by Alasdair Smith, Borve, Lewis, ascribed to his relation from Skigersta, Ness.

The Lost Daughter
Many Orcadian versions, published and oral – see *The Mermaid Bride,* Tom Muir, The Orcadian, Kirkwall, 1998. *Orkney Folk Tales*, Tom Muir, The History Press, Stroud, 2014.

The detail of the *simmins* blowing through the house usually appears three times, one with each appearance of one of the people of the sea. There are so many variants of the story that I feel able to move within them. Some do not have the detail of the *simmins* at all. There is a similar tale with the twist that the father is given the offer of taking something back home from the found island. But he chooses a golden plate rather than his own daughter.

Notes on the poems

Some of these poems were previously published, exhibited or broadcast, usually in different forms. Grateful acknowledgement to:

Buoyage, Morning Star Publications, Edinburgh, 1994
Atoms of Delight, Morning Star/Polygon, Edinburgh, 2000
Broad Bay, Morning Star/The City Arts Centre, Edinburgh, 1997
'*Freasdal*/Providence' exhibition, *an Lanntair, 1994; Providence II,* The
     Windfall Press, *Isle of Lewis,* 1994
Siud an T-eilean (contributing editor), Acair, Stornoway, 1993
Offshore/Onshore, Taigh Chearsabhagh, Lochmaddy, 2000
Adrift/Napospas vlnám, Periplum, Olomouc, 2007
Northings (Hi-Arts online arts journal), 2011
Cape Farewell *Scottish Islands Project* website, 2011
Oxford Poets 2013, annual anthology, Carcanet, Manchester
In Response to Norman MacCaig, An Talla Solais, Ullapool, 2010
Words from an Island, Skye Reading Room anthology, 2013
Green Waters, The Pier Arts Centre/Morning Star/Polygon and others,
     1998
One Clear Line, Scottish Poetry Library exhibition, 2006
Out of Doors, Poetry and Landscape, Radio Scotland, 2010
Causeways, University of Aberdeen, 2014
Transnational Literature online journal, Australia, 2014
Is a thing lost? The Pier Arts Centre, *An Lanntair, Taigh Chearsabhagh,
     an Tobar*, 2010–2011
It's About This, StAnza Artist in Residence voyage, 2004 and Survivors
     Press, Glasgow, 2004
The poem *From a Conversation with Topher Dawson...* is adapted
     from a version first published in *Green Waters*, ed. Alec Finlay

The author apologises for any possible omissions.

Acknowledgements

I made plenty of mistakes learning the craft of sailing but the boats themselves looked after me. Thus I can now retell the tales they brought me to. Thanks to my family and friends for their understanding and to all those who have shared stories, the personal as well as those that have been handed down.

Thanks also to all involved with *an Sulaire* Trust, which maintained the vessel of that name until recently, and to *Falmadair,* the North Lewis Maritime Trust, who continue to maintain *Jubilee, Broad Bay* and now also *an Sulaire.*

Pròiseact nan Ealan matched funds from The Heritage Lottery Fund's interpretation budget for *Lobht nan Seol* (The Sail Loft) renovation to contribute towards the restoration of *sgoth Jubilee.*

The voyages described could not have been made without the huge number of volunteer hours that go into the upkeep of these historic vessels. The generosity of individual boatowners and skippers made other voyages possible.

Sometimes I was able to return to the settings of the stories, on sea and land, to explore further. I am very grateful to the Cape Farewell project and to the skipper and crew of *Song of the Whale* for the chance to explore the Monachs again. Some of my descriptions, in verse, were made during the Scottish Islands 2011 project. Scientists and artists went to sea together, with a view to exploring the issue of climate change by looking closely at effects in island locations: (www.capefarewell. com/2011expedition/about/).

I would also like to acknowledge a storytelling residency from Orkney Islands Council; a Reader in Residence post (Book Trust Scotland and Western Isles Libraries); support from Creative Scotland; Peter Urpeth at Emergents, who commissioned detailed readers' reports from Tom Lowenstein; the Scottish Storytelling Centre; the Scottish Poetry Library; the School of Scottish Studies (University of Edinburgh). My agent, Jenny

Brown, held faith in this project as it developed and the understanding of my other publishers, The History Press and Saraband, is appreciated. Sara Hunt, publisher of my novel with Saraband, also helped me by her belief in this project, at an earlier stage.

Thanks to my companions on these voyages for their help, their company and for looking over these accounts for accuracy. Angus Murdo Macleod read a draft to comment from a mariner's viewpoint. Christine Morrison put an incalculable number of hours into the detailed editing of this book through several drafts.

Earlier versions of some of the stories were shared on Isles FM radio and in *Events* (Lewis and Harris).

It's just not possible to mention by name all the makers and storytellers who influenced this book. But one person has made me think about both structures and stories more than any other. Calum 'Stealag', the Stornoway blacksmith, has made parts for several of the vessels described in these pages. He draws with chalk on sheet metal and breathes fire and wit into a host of stories.

As director of *Faclan* festival, Roddy Murray invited me to introduce and interview Tim Severin and Helen Macdonald who have set an example in non-fiction writing. The same festival has brought me to the work of Henry Marsh and Gavin Francis, which has inspired me.

Working with all at Bloomsbury has proved a pleasure. The collaboration with Christine Morrison continues to be a joy. Our practice is on www.stephenmorrison.org. Her individual work can be viewed at www.christinemorrison.co.uk.